Praise for Sex, Drugs and Meditation

"Bracingly honest, funny and rewarding, this is a book you can't put down."

- **Sydney Morning Herald.**

"Stephens knows how to write a story, and she does so with honesty and good humour."

- **MindFood Magazine.**

"Perfection. Sex, Drugs and Meditation is one of the best memoirs I have read in years. Humble, witty and so very, very true. All I wanted was for this book never to end."

- **Walter Mason, The Universal Heart Book Club.**

"Truth is more compelling than fiction."

- **The Daily Telegraph.**

About the Author

Mary-Lou Stephens was born in Tasmania, studied acting at The Victorian College of the Arts and played in bands in Melbourne, Sydney and Hobart.

Eventually she got a proper job – in radio, where she was a presenter and music director, first with commercial radio and then with the ABC.

Mary-Lou has worked and played all over Australia and now lives on the Sunshine Coast with her husband and a hive of killer native bees.

Find out more at
www.maryloustephens.com.au

SEX, DRUGS & MEDITATION
a memoir

MARY-LOU STEPHENS

This edition published by Nelson Bay 2021

ISBN: 978-0-9941562-3-5

First published 2013 by Pan Macmillan Australia

Copyright © Mary-Lou Stephens 2013 and 2021

The moral right of the author has been asserted.

All rights reserved. No part of this book may be reproduced or transmitted by any person or entity in any form or by any means, electronic or mechanical, including photocopying, recording, scanning or by any information storage and retrieval system, without prior permission in writing from the copyright holder.

Cataloguing-in-Publication details available from the National Library of Australia www.trove.nla.gov.au

The names and identifying details of certain individuals have been changed to protect their privacy.

To the Hideous Mr Purvis.
Thank you for being the catalyst,
the spark that set my feet upon the path.

Before Enlightenment

We got word on the Monday. The top dogs were on their way. Something big was going to happen but we weren't told what. We were in the business of communication. We didn't like being kept in the dark. Our day was spent on the phones sluicing through contacts, searching for specks of gold. But no one was talking. They didn't know, or they'd been warned off. Either way, the next day the hammer came down.

The suits arrived in attack formation, with an arsenal of laptops, briefcases and attitude. Modern warfare in the workplace. Restructure. Redundancies. No guarantees. Reapply for the new positions. Business not personal. Collateral damage. Friendly fire. Level playing field. Good luck.

Previously I'd worked in commercial radio, where contracts get torn up and announcers sacked on the turn of a survey. But I never thought the ABC would be this ruthless. Especially as we had done nothing wrong.

Some ducked and ran, some disgraced themselves, others took

it on the chin. All of us were advised to see the corporate psychologist. By the time I got to her office she already knew the story. She'd been told about the underhand tactics, the lies and deceit, the sense of betrayal and abandonment.

She looked me in the eye and said, 'So, Mary-Lou, what makes you think you're so special?'

I was stunned. What had I expected? Sympathy perhaps, warmth definitely, but not this. I've seen countless counsellors and sat opposite many therapists. I've waited in their outer rooms, staring at my hands until my name was called. The worst was a session with a clinical hypnotherapist. The police insisted. But that was a lifetime ago. A different life. For once I was not in a psychologist's office because of my flaws or failings. I was there because I had been shafted. Big-time. I usually expect other people to fuck me over, mess with me and generally betray me. But I hadn't seen this one coming.

She leant across her desk and smiled smugly. With a counselling service provided for every contingency these days, she'd never be out of work. 'Thousands of people lose their jobs every day,' she said. 'Workplaces are being restructured all the time. I've seen clients from at least half-a-dozen different companies this year alone. So my question is not *why* should this happen to you, but why *shouldn't* this happen to you?'

I left without telling her. I refused to reveal my soul in front of her fake smile and polished spiel. I didn't tell her my job was my only reason for being. I had no husband, no children, no other calling but this. My job. A job I had dreamt into existence. A job that had saved my life. And now I felt as though it was considered worthless. Everything I had worked for meant nothing in the face of this corporate indifference. My job was my world and my world was shattered.

An older, wiser friend was more helpful. 'You've got three choices,' he said. 'Get out now and find another job, stick around and be resentful, or go with the changes. I've seen people come out of restructures with better jobs and more money, but only if they embraced the new regime.'

I chose option three. I couldn't quite come at an embrace but I jumped through hoops and acted the part. My friend was right. The rewards flowed. By playing the game I came through the restructure with a better job. I thought I was safe.

I was wrong.

A few weeks later I was waiting outside the state manager's office. A meeting was scheduled with the national manager. The suits wanted to know how I was going to implement some major changes. That's when I first saw him. Dark-haired, smooth and self-confident, wearing a black suit and very pointy shoes. He looked like a shark.

'I'm Elliot Purvis. I'll be sitting in on the meeting today. You don't mind me taking notes, do you.'

There was no point in saying no.

'Tell me,' he said. 'What have you got planned.'

He didn't ask questions, he made statements.

So I told him.

Fifteen minutes later, in front of an array of very important managers, he presented my entire plan as his own.

I felt as though I'd been punched in the stomach. When I could breathe again I directed my attention to the state manager. 'Of course you'd be aware of these points already. They were in the proposal I emailed to you last week.'

It was true. I had gone over the major points with her beforehand. I smiled coolly at the shark – he'd bitten the wrong person.

Elliot Purvis wasn't embarrassed – he didn't even flinch. He examined me as if I were a specimen preserved in formaldehyde. In that moment the energy between us shifted and I knew my newly constructed world was in deep trouble.

It's been over a year now, since that day. Over a year since Elliot Purvis became my boss. Some of his actions are subtle, but most are blatant, without a trace of guilt, remorse or regret. It seems he has no regard for consequences. I'm humiliated in front of colleagues and management. In private my work and worth are belittled. To protest or complain only brings more malevolence. I am not the only one to suffer. My colleagues and I discuss our torment but find no solution.

He confounds me. Sometimes he tells jokes and turns the warm glow of his smile on us, the next minute he will tear us and our work to bloody shreds. I am in a constant state of fear and confusion. And grief. Grief that my dream job has become the main source of my misery.

There is no prospect of rescue by management. To them he is their golden boy. He's young, ambitious and very good looking. They pat him on the back at staff parties, laugh and call him Ness. They're right, he is untouchable. We call him The Hideous Mr Purvis. The devastation he heaps upon us goes unreported. We are all too broken, made too dizzy by the destruction, to raise our heads.

I spent many years under the delusion that I could change other people. Indeed, thanks to my mother and her strong Christian beliefs, I thought it was my duty. She believed we were meant to change other people. It was for their own good. Missionaries went out into the world to tell the savages about Jesus, so the savages could be saved and go to heaven. And, although she didn't go to deepest darkest Africa or the jungles of Peru, she did see it as her mission to change everyone she met into God-fearing Jesus lovers. Therefore any child of hers, especially her daughter, should do the same. I thought I could change people, but even more so that I *should* change people. I had a mandate to instruct them in the right way to proceed at every opportunity. To give them advice whether sought after or not. To imbue them with my deep sense of righteousness and to disapprove when they, in my view, transgressed. That was the correct procedure, according to my mother's example, and my mother had taught me well.

But later I was taught something else. In my thirties, when it was time to recover from the lessons I'd been taught, from the things I'd done, I was introduced to the Serenity Prayer.

God grant me the serenity to accept the things I cannot change, courage to change the things I can and wisdom to know the difference.

When I was told what the prayer meant, I was astounded. It was a revelation to discover that I was powerless over other people, places and things. Contrary to what I'd been taught by my mother, I was not responsible for other people's actions. I was not expected to change them. Indeed I couldn't change them and I wasn't supposed to even try. The weight of expectation, duty and diligence lifted from my shoulders. It was a physical shift, a distinct lightening of my being.

Now, more than with anyone else, it is clear I cannot change Elliot Purvis. If I am to be free of this anguish I must attend to the only thing I can change. I must look within. I must change myself.

Boxing Day

The vibrant green along the highway always surprises me. There has been no rain for months. Even in other parts of Queensland I've seen gum trees dead from thirst. But here, on the coastal fringes of the south-east, where I have lived for over two years now, the dry hand of drought has left the land untouched. The back seat of my car is piled high with pillows, bags containing clothes suitable for ten days of meditating, and, because I've been warned there are no washing machines at the meditation centre, plenty of underwear. I also have my favourite one hundred per cent cotton sheets. I never go anywhere without them. I went camping once. My sheets came too. I discovered tents don't suit me. Instead I made up a bed on the back seat of the Kingswood with my sheets. My friends called it the Holden Hilton. I didn't care. Even with my feet sticking out the end I was more comfortable than in a leaky smelly lumpy tent. I've never gone camping again. Can't say I've missed it. Camping is an option at the meditation centre, clearly one I won't be taking up.

The meditation centre. The thought makes my hands grow clammy on the wheel. A series of events have brought me to this point, events that might mean nothing in isolation but intersected, almost magically, to create the journey I'm on. Synchronicity is a gift for those who are brave, or foolish, enough to catch it by the tail. Right now I'm not sure which one I am. I shift restlessly in my seat and flick the radio off. The thirty-minute drive seems much longer with a head full of doubt and questions.

I remember the lounge room of a Darlinghurst terrace house. I was in my early thirties and in Sydney. My friend Amber perched on the arm of her couch. Damaged young, she had a raft of coping mechanisms that were more inventive than most. Including the way she could talk, almost without the need to draw breath. She could fill the room, plump out the cushions, blow the dust out of the corners and make the place sparkle with her words. Trinkets for the ears. One day she got on a train, took that train to the top of the mountain and, of her own free will, entered a meditation centre. Not just any meditation centre. A silent meditation centre, where she promised to sit still in total silence for ten days. Amber. The most garrulous, fidgety girl in the inner city.

She returned less than three days later. She was far from serene. She was angry.

'What happened?' I asked.

She took a deep breath and told me. She described a prison that kept her hungry, sleep-deprived and in pain. And when, quite sensibly, she decided to leave, she discovered it was a lot harder to get out through those gates than it was to get in. The staff took it in turns to try and convince her to stay. Amber was a formidable opponent in an argument – those poor schmucks never stood a chance. As far as she was concerned she'd made a dreadful mistake and had got out of it relatively unscathed. Plus she had another marvellous story to entertain anyone who'd listen.

I listened, I always did. And something, somewhere deep inside me, stirred. I thought one day I might take a train up that same mountain.

Amber wasn't the only one to tell me about the meditation centre. In Sydney it had a certain cachet among the cool, black-clothed types who talked about spirituality with one breath and sucked in cigarette smoke with the next. They talked about being clean and sober but were addicted to cigarettes and the next spiritual high. This ten day silent meditation retreat was the best trip of them all, they told me. Painful but life-changing.

My Sydney days are long gone and Amber and I have fallen out of touch. It's been almost ten years since that conversation in Darlinghurst. I have lived in many places since then, before moving here to the Sunshine Coast. Thoughts of the meditation centre were forgotten until a friend and I met for a cup of tea.

'I have just had the most amazing experience of my life.' Pia beamed at me.

'That's nice.'

She laughed. 'I wouldn't exactly call it nice, but it was brilliant. I've been sitting on my bum in silence for ten days, meditating.'

'I've heard of that, or something like it.' Memories of Amber and the spiritual cigarette smokers came immediately to mind. 'Don't you have to sit still for hours? Isn't it really painful?'

'Other people complained a bit, after it was all over. I made myself a big couch of cushions up against the back wall. It was really quite comfortable.'

'The place you go to do this, isn't it somewhere near Sydney? The Blue Mountains?'

'There's a centre right here on the Sunshine Coast. About half an hour up the road.'

Something fluttered in my chest. The unfamiliar feeling of hope. Perhaps this could be my salvation. Amber's experience had not been great, but others had told me it had changed them forever. Some of them had even given up smoking. I discussed my work ordeal with Pia, as I did with all my friends. I was grateful to have any left.

She was sure the meditation course would help. 'It's based on Buddhist philosophy. The overcoming of suffering is a big one. You sound as though you've suffered enough. It's worth a try.'

After Pia left I rang the meditation centre to enquire about dates for the next course. I was told it started in a fortnight's time, beginning on Boxing Day and ending on the sixth of January, my birthday. I can thank my mother for the knowledge that the sixth of January is the Feast of the Epiphany in the Christian church. The manifestation of the superhuman, the realisation that Christ was the son of God. Unfortunately the course was booked out and the best they could do was put me on the waiting list. I took it as an omen. If I was meant to do the course a place would be available. I was certain it would happen. Spending the new year becoming the new me? Ending the course on my birthday, my rebirth day? Surely it was my destiny. A week later I got the call. So on this sixth of January, after ten days of silent and painful meditation, I will revel in my own epiphany. I will put all the pieces of the puzzle that is my life together and finally see the complete picture. In a sudden burst of light, accompanied by the sound of angels blowing trumpets, I will receive insight and wisdom. The Hideous Mr Purvis will cease to affect me. I will love my job and my life again.

That's the plan, but now it's time for the reality. Students are asked to arrive at the meditation centre between three and five pm for registration and I'm running a little late. I couldn't resist those Boxing Day sales. The bitumen of the highway turns into a semi-rural street and then a dirt road. A cow glares at me from behind a wooden fence. I scan for a place name, a sign to reassure me I'm not on private property but on the path to a new and happy life. The road bumps under my wheels and, with relief, I see the words *Vipassana Centre* and an arrow. I drive through the centre's gates and find a spot in the crowded car park. What's going to happen when I walk in the door? It's a silent retreat. How am I going to work out what to do? Will there be signs everywhere? Will we play charades? Am I allowed to write down questions? Will they write the answers back? I have no idea what to expect as I lug my bags towards the front door.

Inside I'm assaulted by a wall of noise. A roomful of people talking and laughing. The sound bounces off the walls in a cacophony of accents: Australian, British, German and others I can't decipher. Leaving my bags by the door I look around. At the far end of the room a young woman is sitting behind a table spread with official-looking pieces of paper. I weave through the throng and introduce myself.

'I have your details right here,' she says. 'You need to fill in this form. Then bring it back and I'll give you directions on how to find your room. Any questions?'

'Yes.' I hesitate, not wanting to appear stupid. 'How come we're allowed to talk?'

She smiles. 'Later, when everyone's settled in, we'll go to the meditation hall. You'll take the Five Precepts and agree to meditate in Noble Silence. After that there's no talking, singing, whistling or humming. Just silence. But for now you are free to talk.'

I thank her and take one of the forms. Perhaps I should do some serious humming before the gates of silence clang shut.

Ten minutes later I'm still staring at the paperwork. I've answered the easy stuff: name, address, occupation, next of kin. But I wasn't expecting questions about my drug and alcohol history. *I gave up drinking years ago,* I write virtuously. Or should I say drinking gave me up.

At the time a friend said, 'I wouldn't worry why you slept with your friend's boyfriend, so much as why you're drinking so much.'

She was being kind. Not only had I slept with my friend's boyfriend, I hadn't remembered it. I woke in his bed among splotches of vomit. I thought the sex had been a dream until I saw the used condom on the floor. Perhaps it was alcohol poisoning, maybe it was moral guilt, but ever since then even one sip of alcohol makes me nauseous and gives me a splitting headache. An instantaneous hangover without any of the fun. But I didn't give up without a fight. For months I tried every kind of alcohol before admitting defeat. That was years ago and now, only occasionally, when those first hints of summer start to warm the air and lengthen the afternoons with promise, do I muse on the delights of a crisp, cold beer. But none ever bridge the gap between mind and mouth.

The drug history is not so easily dealt with. Marijuana? Hash? Everyone experiments. But my experiments went further. LSD, ecstasy, cocaine, speed. And I am loath to mention the big one. But I'm here to change the present. I can't do that by lying about my past.

My pen hovers over the form. I take a deep breath and hold it in, pressing my lips tight. I write the word. *Heroin.* Instantly the fear erupts. Of so many secrets this is one I never let out of the bag. I keep it hidden in the dark places. But now it's out in the light, cringing and squirming. I need to lessen the blow. Quickly I add, *recreational use only, stopped many years ago.* Recreational? Strange form of recreation, throwing up and nodding off. But smack made me feel as though nothing could hurt me. Wrapped up in my warm cocoon. I felt safe, if only for a little while. I haven't spent much of my life feeling safe.

Curiosity is a powerful lure. I was in my early twenties and living in Melbourne away from the judging eyes of family back in Hobart. I wanted to try it, just to see what it was like. It made me throw up. Even after I'd emptied everything out of my stomach, I still felt sick. The merest sip of water ended up in the toilet. What was all the fuss about? I'd tried it and I didn't like it. End of story. But then I moved to a share house where the mysterious murmurings and late-night wanderings got the better of me. I had been using speed intravenously for about a year – shooting up was so much more fun than snorting. Speed was a party drug and I was running with a group of gay boys who loved to party. But I made new friends in that share house and it was a smallish step to switch over to something a lot slower. I became accustomed to the nausea, I even used it to my advantage. I'd tried to be bulimic in the past and failed, but with this, no trying was necessary. Using was a once or twice a week event at the house. The anticipation was palpable when it was time to score. Speed was a social drug and I shared it with a large group of friends. Heroin was a different beast. I kept it contained to the small group who visited the house. Hidden from my other friends. A recreational user, that's all I was. For years. But when I finally decided to stop, and stay stopped, it took at least eighteen months before I could hear the words *taste, hit, fit, smack, score or dope* without a pang of desire rising from my centre where that insatiable hole resides. It was another year before I stopped looking at spoons with suspicion, checking whether the handle had been bent backwards to allow the bowl to sit flat.

Fortunately the form is designed so that all the easy stuff is visible on the outside while the secrets stay hidden, folded out of sight. But, before I hand it back to the young woman behind the table, I have to ask. 'Who reads the forms?'

'Only the assistant teacher reads the information inside.'

And I know she's been asked this question many times by people like me, with respectable jobs and respectable lives, who are terrified that their less than respectable pasts are going to reach across time and bite them hard. And I know she knows I'm one of them.

I'm advised to hand over my valuables for safekeeping. I hesitate. When Amber wanted to leave and they tried to make her stay, she told me one of the cards they held was the fact they had her keys and wallet. She threatened to leave without them. She told them she'd walk all the way back to Darlinghurst and break into her own home if she had to. Will that be me in a day or two? If it is, I'll be copping out of more than a ten-day meditation retreat. I'll be giving up on myself and my job. The Hideous Mr Purvis will win. I hand them over.

There aren't any luxuries here. Leaving my shoes outside as requested by a sign at the door, I inspect the room I'll be sleeping in for the next eleven nights. Two beds, two small wooden bedside tables and a pedestal fan in the corner. The communal bathroom is outside along a gravel path. One of the beds has a small suitcase sitting on it and a towel hangs over the fan. My roommate has arrived already. There's no wardrobe, no chest of drawers, but I find a couple of old wire hangers on a hook behind the door and hang the clothes I can; the rest stay in my bag at the end of the bed. The door faces out onto bushland. A walking track leads up the hill for those in need of solitude and exercise, or downhill towards the dining hall for those who need company and sustenance. I choose the dining hall.

During the short walk I take in the beauty of the landscape around me. The meditation centre is on the outskirts of one of the many country towns that spread out like beads on a string, along the coast and through the hinterland. This town has one dominant feature, a small but dramatic mountain. One peak sticking out of the ground almost vertically. The sun is setting and the result is picture perfect. A few wispy clouds, wafting around the mountain, glow orange in the fading light. A small flock of kangaroos graze on the stretches of short, dry grass between the buildings. They're unfazed by the closeness of humans. Vipassana meditation is a Buddhist practice; they know we're no danger. Before I enrolled in the course I was asked to read the Introduction to the Technique and Code of Discipline, a single piece of paper printed on both sides in small type, crammed full of information and instructions. Number one on the list of precepts is to abstain from killing any living creature. The introduction also states what Vipassana is not – a rite or ritual based on blind faith – and what it is – a technique that will eradicate suffering. I hold that hope close.

At the dining hall I step around a collection of shoes, left in an untidy row near the entrance, and open the sliding door. Along one wall trestle tables are laden with herbal and black tea, milk and soy, sugar, honey and a tray of Anzac biscuits. I help myself to a cup of tea and stare at the biscuits. The old compulsion rises. I was eight years old when I realised food was more dependable than people. Up until then I'd felt safe and loved. But something shifted in my family and in my life. A change of schools left me friendless and at home I was ignored. It was if I'd become invisible to everybody around me, except when they wanted someone to pick on. I was the youngest of six children, the easiest to disregard, the easiest to taunt. It set me up for a life of desperately wanting love and attention but angry and defiant because I'd learnt I would never be given it. Chocolate became my best friend and anything with sugar in it was surrogate family. I didn't need anyone or anything else. If alcohol or drugs had been available to me at that age, I would have been an alcoholic or drug addict at eight. Instead I became an addict of a different kind, resorting to stealing from my parents to feed my habit. When I finally got sprung my parents sat me down in their bedroom for a talk.

'Are these yours?' My dad pointed at the chocolate wrappers crammed into an old school bag.

'Yes.' There was no use lying. It was clear what had happened. My older sister, who shared a bedroom with me, had been snooping in my wardrobe.

'That explains it,' said my mother. 'I wondered how you'd put on so much weight with just the food I've been feeding you.'

Then why didn't you ask? Why didn't you show some concern? Why did you ignore it? Ignore me? I'd gone from a slim happy child to an obese miserable kid in less than a year; loving parents would have wanted to know what was wrong, surely? These were the questions I asked many years later in therapists' rooms. But my mother was never there to answer. My mother had her own battles with weight. Acknowledging mine would have forced her to acknowledge her own.

'Where did you get the money from?' asked my father.

I didn't want to answer. I stared at the carpet, grey with darker flecks of charcoal.

'Well?'

My eyes flicked over to their built-in wardrobe. I knew it intimately. Every time I snuck into their room the adrenalin rush almost overpowered me. Stealthily I would open my father's wardrobe door and begin my search. Slipping my hand into the breast pocket of his suit jackets would usually yield his wallet. Brown and worn, full of neatly folded notes snug within the leather. I would steal a couple of small notes and, with clammy fingers and pounding heart, get out as quickly as I could. I never bothered with my mother's side of the wardrobe. There was nothing there I wanted. Her handbag was where she kept her money and she left it in various places. I would track it down and relieve her purse of coins and dollar notes whenever the opportunity arose.

My parents waited for an answer.

'I stole it from you.' There was nothing else I could say.

They sighed and nodded. 'Will you promise not to do it again?'

'I promise.'

But I lied.

My mind starts up its infernal chatter as I stare at the tray of biscuits. Perhaps I could have just one, or two, or even three. Tonight doesn't count – after all the meditation doesn't really start until tomorrow. I shake my head to free my mind of the all too familiar line of thinking. I don't want to spend my entire time at the meditation centre obsessing about sugar. It's ironic that it wasn't the drugs or alcohol that found me in the rooms of Twelve Step programs for years, it was my addiction to food, my first, my last, my everything.

Four tables with benches on either side take up the rest of the space; they're not as interesting as biscuits but I force myself to look around. Most of the benches are occupied by women either talking intensely to each other while chewing on, yes, biscuits or filling out their forms while chewing on the ends of their pens. The men have their own dining hall on the other side of the wall. I wonder how many biscuits they're eating. I take my cup of tea, find a spare seat outside on the verandah, where the view is better, the air fresher and there are no trays of biscuits. I introduce myself to the three women already sitting at the table, one of them barely out of her teens, and thankfully none of them eating biscuits.

'So what brings you here?' I ask the youngest as I sit down.

'My sister,' she smiles shyly and inclines her head towards the young woman sitting beside her. 'It was her idea.'

Her sister sits diagonally opposite me. The family resemblance is subtle but it's there. But while her younger sister is soft and rounded, she is angular and annoyed. 'It's the holidays,' she says. 'What else is there to do?'

'My priest told me about this place,' says the woman on my left. She has black curly hair, blue eyes with long lashes and a sprinkle of freckles on her nose. 'I'm Bernadette and, yes, I'm Catholic. But I'm okay, really I am.' She laughs and turns towards me. 'And just as well, because I think we're sharing a room.'

'Really? That's great.' And it is. I like her.

'Your priest?' asks the older sister, with a look of disdain.

'Yeah, he's been a couple of times. He told me it doesn't interfere with any belief systems or religious points of view. It's just a great way to clear your head of anything that's bugging you. I wouldn't know, though, I've never done it before.'

'Me neither,' I say and turn back to the sisters. 'Have either of you done this before?'

They shake their heads.

'That girl has.' Bernadette indicates a twenty-something woman sitting alone on a chair near the railing. Her short bleached hair is mussed up, dark roots showing. She gazes out at the tree line chewing on a thumbnail with little left of it to chew.

'She told me she's done Vipassana five times,' Bernadette whispers.

'Five times!' I'm impressed. She must be very spiritual.

'Yeah, five times and she still can't stop smoking.'

'Oh.'

'Apparently lots of people come here to give up smoking,' says Bernadette. 'It's supposed to work well on all kinds of addictions. And of course you can't smoke or drink while you're here, so it gives you a kickstart.'

'Is that why *you're* here?' I ask Bernadette with a smile. 'Did your priest send you here to give up the evil cigarettes, or perhaps the demon drink?' I'm teasing, and although I've only just met her, I know she can take it. Besides, I want to know, as do the sisters. All eyes are on Bernadette.

'Well . . .' She hesitates.

We lean towards her, poised for a juicy titbit.

She laughs. 'No.'

We take a breath and laugh with her. But I'm a little disappointed. I'm hoping we'll be friends and I like my friends to be as flawed as I am.

'I'm at a bit of a crossroads with my work,' she says. 'I just need some time out to decide what to do next. What about you?'

She looks at me and I tense. Why am I always defensive when people ask me a direct question? Scared I'll say the wrong thing, wanting to impress but also wanting to connect. I'm so desperate to be liked that I try to second-guess what I think other people want to hear. I am left in no-man's-land. I decide to do what I usually do. Dodge. Avoid. 'I gave up smoking years ago,' I say with an uneasy grin. 'Last one I smoked made me sick to my stomach. Like a cartoon kid trying a cigarette for the first time; the nausea bubbles floating above my head as I turned a sickly shade of green.' I laugh, hoping they'll laugh with me. 'I haven't had a cigarette since.'

Bernadette cocks her head. 'So why are you here?'

How can I tell her? Her work is at a bit of a crossroads. My work is being attacked by a shark. A vicious cold-eyed killing machine in black pointy shoes. Despite this, I am still in love with my job. It's a dysfunctional relationship, I know, but I can't let go. Before it came into my life I thought I had no future. My only tertiary qualification was a diploma in performing arts and, although I loved playing in bands, I'd done it for too long. At the age of thirty-five, with no skills to stand me in good stead in the corporate world, a series of dead-end jobs was all I could envisage. When I discovered radio, my life fell into place. But first I had to fall.

I lay on the floor in the tight curl of the foetal position, exhausted from crying. Too tired to drag myself off the floor and onto a chair. The floor felt good, the polished wood cool against my cheek. Bands broke up, I knew that. Sometimes I expected it, other times I had been left with nothing but resentment, but this break-up came out of the blue, leaving me skinned and gutted. I had believed in this band with a passion. I'd poured everything into it: time, money, energy, love. And for what? It was gone, destroyed in a moment. One of our key members was quitting. 'Artistic differences.' 'Leaving to pursue other interests.' The band wouldn't be the same without her, couldn't be. We were the three blondes in the front line, all singing, all playing, performing and writing cool country music before anyone had ever heard of the Dixie Chicks. It wouldn't work with one of us missing. So that was that. Now all that was left was to go through the motions. The last gigs. The dividing of assets. It was like a divorce. I've always been suspicious of so-called amicable separations and now I understood why. There's always hurt, bitterness, blame. But more than that, there's the yawning chasm that opens up. Where once was certainty, activity, direction, now there's nothing. Just a vacuum. A gaping dark pit with nothing to hold on to. Yes, the floor was a good place to be.

Eventually I struggled to my feet, put my sunglasses on and staggered outside to the sunshine of another Sydney day. The beach was waiting. I found comfort in the waves, the sun, the warmth. My breath steadied as I walked along the sand.

A familiar voice called out to me. 'Hello. How are you going?'

It was the man I called the Guitar Doctor. He'd fret dressed my guitar and fixed a few other bits and pieces. He owned an ageing, almost blind, basset hound who was always close by in his workshop. You can tell a lot about a man by the way he treats a dog, and the Guitar Doctor was always patient and affectionate.

I'd entertained a small fantasy or two about him but here he was, walking on the beach, not alone but with a woman. She was beautiful, of course, slim with long dark hair. They looked content with the world and each other. I felt another hope snap, like an old rubber band that's been stretched too many times.

I forced a smile. 'I'm fine, thanks.' Please don't ask me about the band. Please don't. Please.

'How's the band going?' he asked.

'Actually, we're breaking up.' The words were out before I could stop them, the pain too close to the surface. 'I have no idea what I'm going to do now.'

His smile faded. He looked at me more closely. I knew he could see the red blotchy telltale signs of crying. His beautiful girlfriend shifted uncomfortably and he swayed back slightly on his heels. Not even my lovely gentle Guitar Doctor could take the raw grief of someone who was, when it came down to it, just another customer.

'Sorry to hear that,' he said.

'Ah well, I guess I won't need another fret dress for a while.' I smiled, letting them off the hook.

They smiled back gratefully and walked away.

Going through the motions was hard: playing the rest of the gigs we had booked, performing with smiles instead of scowls, resisting the urge to beg for another chance. The decision was made. Best to accept it and move on. Trouble was I had nothing to move on to.

Weeks after our last performance, on a Monday morning, I awoke to the clock radio chattering out the seven o'clock news. Half asleep, I heard the Queen was sending her condolences to the people of Tasmania. I was from Tasmania, although I hadn't lived there for years. Why was Queen Elizabeth II consoling me? I rang my mother in Hobart.

'What's happened?'

'You haven't seen the news?'

'I just heard the end of the story on the radio.'

Silence.

'Mum? Are you there?'

I heard her struggle to take a breath. It was as if she had to grab hold of something deep within just to function.

'Mum?'

'Oh, darling.' She was crying. 'Something beyond words . . .' She could hardly speak.

'Mum, what is it?'

'A man, more of a boy . . . no a monster. He killed, shot, men, women . . . children.'

'Where, when?'

'Yesterday at Port Arthur. Oh God, most people when they do this kind of thing at least have the decency to shoot themselves afterwards. Why didn't he?'

I was shocked. My mother, good Christian woman that she was, was angry because this mass murderer hadn't committed suicide. To her suicide was the ultimate sin against God. But now there was a much greater sin and this boy had committed it. Thirty-five times. Even hunting down a mother and her small children.

For days the phone kept ringing. Friends and family from Tasmania. Most of them unable to express their grief and horror but still needing to connect in some way. The trauma of such a thing happening in Tasmania, our little paradise at the bottom of the world, was overwhelming. Wherever I'd lived, whatever I'd done, I always knew I could return to safe little Tassie. A sanctuary away from the madness of the rest of the world. This was the kind of atrocity that happened somewhere else. The truth was too hard to absorb.

A friend from Melbourne was staying with me. She heard the phone calls, saw my confusion and grief. She sat me down at the kitchen table and said, 'You need to go home.'

She was right. But I was an out-of-work musician. I had no money.

She pushed a thick pile of twenty dollar notes across the table towards me. 'I want you to have this.'

'But I can't . . .'

'No ifs, no buts. This is not a loan, you don't have to pay me back. Maybe one day you'll be able to do the same for me if ever I should need it. I want you to buy a ticket home.'

I arrived in time for the memorial service. My mother and I drove to Port Arthur. Like most Tasmanians, we may not have known the victims personally, but the massacre was a deep wound in us all. We went to grieve. We went to find comfort with those who felt the same pain. The leaves of the oak trees at Port Arthur were falling. Drifts of brown, scattered over the lawn. A row of bleachers surrounded a square of chairs by the water. When thirty-five white doves were released, for the thirty-five who'd been massacred, I thought my heart would break. How it kept steadily beating in my chest was beyond me. All of us were left in a kind of trance, everyone unsure of what to do next. A beautiful sound drifted towards us through the trees and as one we turned towards it. Behind a row of oaks, in the piles of brown crinkled leaves, children played, kicking the leaves high into the air. The sound was their laughter. Without words we began to move towards them and watched, silently. We began to smile. Shoulders relaxed and a low hum of conversation finally emerged. It would be all right. Life would go on. Here was the proof.

The service had been broadcast by the ABC. I found the outside broadcast van nearby. I knew Chris, one of the announcers, would be there. He'd interviewed me about my music a few times and occasionally played my songs on his program. We had formed a friendship. He was pleased to see me, even in the circumstances, and suggested we meet up for lunch while I was in town.

Later that week we ate and talked about life and death. I poured my heart out about the band breaking up. I told Chris how it had left me devastated and unsure of what to do next. Even though, compared to what had happened at Port Arthur, my troubles seemed trivial, it still hurt. I was grieving for the band, for Tasmania, and for myself.

When I'd finished he paused, looked at me and uttered one life-changing sentence. 'Mary-Lou, you want to be in radio.'

I knew he was right. It was a pure light bulb moment. I could feel the glow above my head. 'I do.' It was astounding. 'But I didn't know that until right now. How did you know?'

'Because I know radio and I know you. It's a perfect match.'

It was true. I came alive when I was being interviewed in a radio studio. I loved the sense of performance. I'd performed all my life in one form or another. Radio condensed performance down to one person, one microphone, one listener. A pure connection. I'd almost forgotten that I had presented a show on community radio in Hobart when I was in my early twenties. It was supposed to be an arts show. I interviewed musicians and bands. My natural curiosity was given a legitimate outlet. But when I left

Hobart for acting school in Melbourne I never gave radio another thought. Until now.

I stayed in Hobart for a few more days and caught up with a friend. She suggested we check out the short films being shown at the AFTRS graduate screenings. AFTRS was the most prestigious film and TV school in Australia and she was keen to see what the new young filmmakers were doing. During the intermission the dean talked about the school.

'The Australian Film, Television and Radio School . . .' he began.

And that's when I stopped listening. Radio school? It was always called the Film and TV School. I knew people who had studied there. I'd even been to the campus in Sydney, and no one ever mentioned a radio component. Until that night I'd never realised the R in AFTRS stood for radio. This was too close to be coincidence, only days after Chris had told me I should be in radio, this was a sign. Afterwards I cornered the dean. I loved what he told me about the course until he mentioned the 'c' word.

'Commercial radio?' I asked.

'Yes, the course is funded by the commercial radio body.'

It wasn't what I wanted at all. Inane giggling and advertising. I had already decided the ABC was the only place for me. I grew up in a house full of radios, all tuned to Aunty. I would have to reach my destiny another way.

Within a week of arriving back in Sydney I bumped into Simon. He and I moved in the same circle of musicians and artists.

'I've been trying to track you down,' he said. 'I'm now the program director for a new aspirant public radio station.'

'What's that?' I heard the word radio. The rest was unfamiliar.

'We don't have a full licence yet but we're working towards it.

At the moment we broadcast in two to four week blocks whenever we're given a frequency. I was hoping you'd present a show for us. Are you interested?'

'You want me to do a radio show?'

'I think you'd be great. What do you say?'

Within a week of discovering my true vocation I was being offered a gig on air. Another sign. A miracle!

I said yes.

I loved the excitement of being on air. Simon was a patient teacher. I learnt to operate the panel and after a few shows I was able to drive the beast without him having to get me out of trouble. In the meantime the ABC was shedding jobs like a Persian cat shedding fur. Budget cuts meant lay-offs. Redundancies were the order of the day. I would not be getting a job there. I would have to go commercial to fulfil my destiny. I asked Simon about AFTRS.

He surprised me. 'I went there,' he said. 'It's a great place to learn everything you need to know.'

'But you have to work in commercial radio.'

'No you don't.' He grinned. 'They tried to send me to Parkes but I refused. Instead I hung around Triple J and got a job there. It is possible, you know. Why? Are you thinking about applying?'

'I am now.'

'I can help if you like. It's quite a process.'

He was right. It was tougher than getting into acting school. I'd only had to do two auditions to get accepted into the Victorian College of the Arts, but for AFTRS I had to endure many levels of auditions in different forms and long weeks of waiting to hear if I'd made it through to the next round. I started working two jobs. If I was accepted into the course it was the only way I could save enough money to afford a year of full-time study. Luckily playing in bands had given me one useful skill. I could live on very little.

I made it to the last round. An interview at the school itself in front of a panel of radio professionals, including Lucienne, the head of the radio school. Simon had warned me there would also be a general knowledge test. He didn't tell me it would be recorded in the studio. I was doing well until the questions turned to sport. A cricket question threw me completely.

Simon's advice came to mind. 'Remember the most important thing of all, no dead air. Just keep talking.'

I ploughed on, made a joke and got to the end.

But I left none the wiser. Did I get in or not?

They would let me know.

I returned to Tasmania for Christmas still not having heard. I convinced myself I'd been unsuccessful. But I was determined to work in radio even without AFTRS. It was my destiny. I trawled the phone book for local radio stations and set out to visit every one of them. One day, after driving for forty-five minutes to visit a tiny community radio station that could offer no paying work I realised my fixation had gone far enough and, rather than humiliate myself further, turned back for home.

My mother gave me the phone message as I walked through the door. 'Lucienne called, from the radio school. She asked you to call her back.'

'Did she say anything? Give you any kind of clue?'

'No, darling, why don't you call her?'

I did, but she had left for the day. Why the hell had I wasted my time driving most of the way to a tin-pot station? I should have stayed home.

I hardly slept and was on the phone as soon as I thought Lucienne might be at work.

'Hello, Mary-Lou.' Her voice was rich and deep, sugar-coating every syllable. 'We'd like to offer you a place. Could you send us written confirmation if you're able to accept?'

I babbled, whooped and hollered, put down the phone and danced around the room with my mum. 'I'm in, I'm in, I'm in.'

'Well?' Bernadette is still looking at me. Puzzled.

A voice calls out from the dining hall, gathering us in for a meeting. It's time to get down to the business of meditation.

'I'll tell you later,' I say, knowing full well 'later' will be in ten days' time and by then my answer will be impressive in its wisdom and insight.

About sixty of us, roughly equal numbers of men and women, cram into the women's dining hall. This is the last time men and women will mingle. Segregation supposedly makes the *no sex* clause easier to stick to. Apparently there are no gay Buddhists. We're given a run-down on how the centre works and instructed on the day-to-day basics: the bells, the meals, doing handwashing in buckets. We aren't allowed to talk to or look at each other. The men can talk to the male manager and the women can talk to the female manager, but only about what they call *material concerns* – if we need an extra blanket, for example. The female manager, Lisa, is tall, slim and, thankfully, rather plain. If she was beautiful, as well as spiritual, I'd feel too intimidated to approach her. We can talk to the assistant teacher about our meditation practice but only at midday each day when she conducts interviews. The rest of the time is to be spent in silence, in word and deed. No charades, no notes, no miming.

The man doing the talking looks up from his sheet of instructions. 'If you don't think you want to be here for the ten days, now's your chance to leave.'

A ripple of nervous energy spreads through the room but no one moves. The decision is made. There is no turning back.

It's nightfall by the time we walk up the gravel path to the meditation hall; the men on their side of the compound, the women on the other. Our way is lit by the moon and small lights set at knee height along the path. The atmosphere is subdued. It's just starting to sink in, this big unknown thing we're doing. Outside the hall we wait in silence. Lisa holds a clipboard and I suspect she'll do a silent roll call each day. We've been told our names will be on a piece of paper on the floor in the place we've each been allocated. We take our shoes off at the door and file in silently. The meditation hall is large and dimly lit, with a painted concrete floor and a high roof capped by a vented cupola. A big warm cave. Deep windows on two sides of the hall are fitted with wooden louvres. The louvres are slightly ajar, allowing a light breeze to drift through. Mats are spaced evenly throughout the room and each mat has two blue cushions on it. On the low stage at the front of the hall a pile of white cushions and a rack of audio-visual controls are the only objects. I was expecting candles at least, some incense perhaps, a backdrop of some kind. But there are none. It may be plain but it's not stark. The light glows. The air is soft. Footsteps are muffled. It feels calm. So far.

After all the talk of segregation I'd imagined a wall, or at least a curtain, between the men and women. We have separate entrances, but the only thing that separates us in the hall is a thin line of white tape along the floor. The piece of paper with my name on it is right next to this line. A young man walks towards me. He's probably in his early twenties, wearing calico trousers and a loose green cotton shirt. He finds his spot and sits on the mat beside mine. If I reach out my left arm I could touch him. I don't, even though he's kind of cute.

I stand behind my mat, my two cushions and the small piece of paper with my name typed on it. Around me others fold their legs easily underneath them and patiently wait for whatever is going to happen next. It's like being back in infant school, sitting on the mat for story time. But in infant school I could sit cross-legged. Those days are gone thanks to a plastic dance floor and a bubble machine, a slippery combination. My friends thought I was joking around. Perhaps they thought I was inventing a new dance craze, *the fall-on-the-floor-in-a-screaming-heap twist*. The joke was on them when they had to carry me out of the disco. My right knee has never been the same. Not even after an operation.

Fear rises in my throat. This is the moment I've been dreading. I lower myself gingerly onto the thin foam mat, put one cushion under my bottom, the other under my right knee. That will hold it for a while. I'll have to work something else out later.

Once the shuffling and organising of cushions is over a woman in white enters through a door near the stage; shoulder-length brown hair, no make-up, in her late thirties. She walks slowly across the stage and sits cross-legged beside the rack of audiovisual equipment. This must be the assistant teacher. I wonder if her voice is as serene as her appearance. But she doesn't speak. All she does is raise her hand slightly to press a button on the equipment rack. A heavily accented Indian voice emanates from the speakers high in the corners beside the stage. This is the voice of the teacher, a teacher we will never meet. He guides us through the Moral Code. We agree to the Five Precepts: no killing, no stealing, no sex, no intoxicants, and no lying. Next we have to ask him to instruct us in some things I don't understand. The combination of the Indian accent and the strange words he uses confounds me. Everyone else chants the words as requested but I hesitate. The call and response between us and the teacher resonates painfully with the years I spent in church, not being good enough 'to pick up crumbs from under God's table' and similar lines from other prayers, muttered obediently as a child but not fully understood. Vipassana is supposed to be different. Not a rite or ritual. I squirm on my cushion but my last chance to run was back in the dining hall. I dutifully chant the words, just as I did when I was young, but they're like lemon on my lips. It's a relief when finally the vow of Noble Silence is put in place and the pressure to mumble along with everyone else is gone.

I walk down the gravel path to the communal bathroom in silence. I brush my teeth in silence. I don't look at anyone else. As far as I know no one looks at me. Those are the rules. Odd not to be able to say goodnight, or thank you, or even bless you if someone sneezes. Silently and with my head bowed, I walk back to my room, the room I'm sharing with Bernadette.

She's not there. Instead an old woman is in the other bed. An old woman with a dreadful cough. I can't ask her what she's doing here because I'm not allowed to speak. And she couldn't tell me because she's taken the oath of Noble Silence too. I'm baffled and annoyed. I was looking forward to sharing a room with the delightful Bernadette. Instead I have an old coughing woman for company. I get into bed, turn out my light and stare into the pitch dark of the country night. The sounds of the bush are close and clear: trucks on the highway shifting through the gears as they climb the hill, possums hissing at each other, the chirupping of the geckos and another unfamiliar sound. A rumbling. A rattle. A throaty kind of gurgle. It's very close. Is it just outside the window? No, closer than that. It's my roommate. She's a snorer.

Day One

The first bell of the day wakes me before dawn. I long to stay where I am; comfortable, horizontal. But the nagging drive to do everything right drags me out of bed. I have been given a gift, I must not squander it. The old woman hasn't stirred. I leave the room quietly, in the dark, and head to the communal bathroom.

The meditation centre relies on tank water. No rain has fallen for some time and none is predicted. Signs above the sinks, basins and in the cubicles ask us to save water and keep our showers short. In my diligence I hardly get wet at all. When I return, the old woman is still asleep. I'm not surprised. She coughed half the night and snored the other. The bell rings again. Four-thirty am. Time to begin the first meditation of the day, a two hour session before breakfast. Still the old woman doesn't wake. For these two hours we're allowed to meditate in our rooms. My knees ache from last night's cross-legged attempt. I won't return to the meditation hall until I have to. I build myself a nest on my bed, prop my knees up with pillows, rest my back against the wall and close my eyes. The first day has begun and it's still dark outside.

My mother was an early riser, out of necessity more than desire. With six demanding children it was the only quiet time she could wrest from her noisy days. No wonder she turned to religion. Sometimes, as a child, I would shuffle sleepily down the hallway, in what seemed the dead of night, and watch her huddled by the heater, a cup of tea by her side and a book of bible readings in her hand. Her early morning study. Bathed in the glow of the heater and the shallow light of the standard lamp, it was as if she floated on an island of peace. I would creep back to bed, not wanting to shatter that illusion. My mother wanted eight children, my father only four. Six was a compromise, I suppose – three boys, three girls – but my mother never liked to compromise. A miscarriage before I was born and another after meant she did conceive eight souls. Perhaps in her early morning prayers she whispered to the unborn two, her other babies.

The older and more uncontrollable her brood grew, the more radical my mother's religion became. Not content with the local parish church, bible study and good works, she became involved with the charismatic movement. Speaking in tongues, healing, being slain in the spirit – this became the new vocabulary of her religious life. When I was a child I told her how I'd dreamt I was on a beach with a group of people. The sea sucked back on itself, exposing miles of ocean floor. Everyone around me began praising the Lord, much like my mother did at any given opportunity. It was the end of the world and they knew it. They embraced it. They were the chosen ones. A huge rumble vibrated through the sand and on the horizon a massive wall of water headed towards us. The Lord-praisers danced and sang in happiness.

'That's all I remember,' I said to my mum.

She stopped getting breakfast ready and, for the first time in a long time, I had her full attention.

'Praise the Lord,' she said. 'You're a prophet.'

It was a vision from God and He had chosen her child. She took me to her strange meetings and told her friends I was a prophet, but when no other dreams emerged and no further prophecies eventuated, she withdrew the bright light of her attention. I was left in the dark again.

There is a myth that the youngest child is always spoilt. Not true. By the time the youngest comes along the parents have usually given up trying to control their wilful brood. Thus the youngest gets away with more than the older children did. This may seem like indulgence, it may even look like freedom, but it isn't. In my case it was something much worse. I spent most of my thirties in some kind of therapy, trying to make sense of it. One counsellor told me that growing up with a mother like mine was the same as growing up with an alcoholic parent. Never knowing what to expect, too ashamed to bring friends home, knowing that my mother was different but not knowing why. And then there was my older brother who spouted Hitler's speeches off by heart and had a Nazi flag in his bedroom. He was ten years older than me, a terrifying stranger. My next oldest brother once tried to hit my mother with a frying pan, and my oldest sister would often take to my mother with flailing hands and scratching nails.

I tried to get my mother's attention but to no avail. My closest sister in age to me was a chronic asthmatic, and between disease and disarray there was no time or space for me. But there was time for other people's babies. My mother took them in and looked after them, even though she showed no interest in looking after me. Why did she stop loving me? Why did she lose all interest in looking after me? I was only eight, I couldn't work it out. And because I couldn't work it out I thought it must have been my fault. I must have been bad. Bad girl. I sold myself out before I reached double figures. Once, in one of those many counselling sessions, the therapist told me I was the victim of gross neglect. It felt good to have it acknowledged. But what did she really know? She wasn't there.

Much more affirming was hearing it from one of my own family. I never thought they noticed. I was convinced my brothers and sisters had bought into the myth that I was spoilt and adored. I made amends to one of my sisters during my time in Twelve Step programs. Making amends to people you are close to can be tough. But Twelve Step members with years of experience say there can be unexpected gifts of grace along the way. After I'd said my piece – told her I was sorry I'd told lies about her, gossiped about her, used her camera without asking her permission when I was ten – my sister gave me just such a gift.

'We should apologise to you,' she said. 'You were neglected when you were a kid.'

I was stunned. I never thought she saw me as anything but a nuisance: a fat, pesky little sister with whom, much to her annoyance, she had been forced to share a room. But my sister had been there, growing up beside me in our sprawling dysfunctional family. She saw. She knew what went on and now she was acknowledging it, to my face, and apologising. I had been neglected. Left to fend for myself from the age of eight. My mother, obsessed with stranger's babies once she could have no more of her own and I was too old to be treated like one. My siblings, totally disinterested in my welfare and battling to survive themselves in a madhouse. I survived the only way I could. Feral and filthy. Stealing and lying. My sister told me my scalp was yellow because my hair was never washed. My teeth were furry from lack of brushing. Food was my only comfort, my only company. I became obese and my parents didn't notice, or worse, didn't care, until the fact I was stealing their money was brought to their attention. By her. Perhaps my sister had been trying to help me by showing them the bag full of chocolate wrappers. Perhaps.

All the while my mother praised the Lord, babbling in languages no one understood, and reached her arms to the heavens, ignoring what was going on at her feet. For his part my father appeared to be the epitome of patience but in reality he would avoid the awkward or confrontational in the hope it would pass by and resolve itself without him having to participate. Eventually he realised my mother's religious zeal was not a temporary situation to be disregarded until it passed, so he went to a Billy Graham Crusade at the North Hobart Football Oval and got himself saved. He was never as enthusiastic about praising the Lord or breaking into tongues at unexpected moments as my mother, but he went with her to the meetings and rallies. In our teenage years my asthmatic sister, always Dad's favourite, joined in too. She discovered, as did I, that the best chance of any attention from our parents was to play on the same team. Our older brothers and sisters had fled the nest by this stage. That left the four of us, clapping our hands and singing in tongues. My mother would be swept away in religious ecstasy and my sister, father and I went along for the ride.

Naturally I never told anyone at school that I sang in tongues with thousands of others at pep rallies. I never mentioned the bellowing preacher who put his hands on my head to slay me in the spirit. I fell down because I thought I should, and then lay on the floor, breathing in the dust and the smell of cheap carpet, feeling cheated. Why was everyone else around me feeling the rapture when all I felt was cranky?

It's a strange world to inhabit, especially when you know you really don't fit in. I tried my best but I felt like a hypocrite. I was told to pray harder. If you're miserable, pray harder. If you're in pain, pray harder. If you're sick, pray harder. If you're unhappy, it's your own fault – you're not praying hard enough. There was no room for confusion or doubt. No room for the fat teenager I had become. Everyone was perfect. Everybody was deliriously happy. Praise the Lord. When I tried to leave the Charismatic church in my late teens, my mother refused to acknowledge it.

'You're a Christian, darling, and you'll always be a Christian.' She smiled her tight little smile.

My mother owned my spirituality, or so she thought. And at the time I thought so too. It was all I had ever known.

We aren't allowed to read or write during these ten days. No distractions. So, along with my car keys and wallet, I left my journal and pen with the staff for safekeeping. But there is one piece of paper I've kept. The Introduction to the Technique and Code of Discipline. It includes the course timetable. When the next bell chimes I unfold the paper. The timetable for each day is exactly the same. Six-thirty am. Breakfast.

Walking down the path towards the dining hall I see my roommate. She may be a late riser but when it's time for breakfast she's first in line. At the entrance to the dining hall I take off my sandals, add them to the collection just outside the door, and join the queue. High stacks of plates, bowls, mugs and cutlery wobble at the end of the table. Toasters, loaves of bread and various spreads sit next to three large teapots. Lisa stands behind another table dipping a ladle into a steaming pot. Two tiny Asian girls stand next to her, both with ladles. I collect a bowl and spoon and wait in line. As I get closer I see she is dishing out hot porridge. Strange, as the day is already warm and will reach at least thirty-five degrees by this afternoon. One of the girls scoops stewed prunes and the other just stands there, holding her ladle. Backup, I guess, in case there's a ladle malfunction on the front line. Further down the table a huge tub of yoghurt, a big container of muesli and some fruit look more inviting. The slow-moving line deposits me in front of Lisa. She motions towards my bowl. While at the meditation centre, we live like monks and nuns. At meal-times, like monks with their begging bowls, we eat whatever food we're given. I'm not quite ready to be a nun. I shake my head and move on.

Once I have filled my bowl with muesli and yoghurt I search for a spot to sit. It's tricky when we're not supposed to look at anyone. The room is crowded. I could end up on someone's lap. I go outside to the verandah where there are some empty seats. Kangaroos graze on the grass in front of us. A couple of the roos have joeys. Their heads poke out of the pouches and look around with dark astounded eyes. The meditators from overseas will be loving this, it's just like an ad from Tourism Australia. Something brushes against my skin and I hear a scatter of little feet on the table. A magpie sits on the railing looking very smug, its beak covered in yoghurt. My yoghurt. Down the line of tables I see other women having the same problem, waving off overconfident magpies from breakfast bowls and plates of Vegemite toast, wordlessly shooing the winged thieves away. The older sister finishes her toast and apple and stomps off. The ground fairly vibrates with each footfall. I wonder what she's so angry about. I wonder how long she'll last. I wonder how many of us will get to the end of the ten days.

Back in my room I study the timetable yet again. GROUP MEDITATION IN THE HALL. This is the only item on the timetable written in capital letters, so these sessions must be important. Three of them every day and we have to stay in the hall for the entire hour. No sneaking out for a quick stretch under the pretence of needing a wee. The bell chimes and I join the other students, walking, like cattle at milking time, up the path to the meditation hall. Inside I stand beside my designated spot with its mat and two cushions. I've got to come up with a plan and soon. My knees aren't going to make it past this morning if I don't. Other meditators file silently around me. Some pick up extra cushions from a pile against the back wall. I follow their example. An extra cushion under my bottom and another under my left knee might help. Lisa checks everyone off her list while the male manager does the same on the other side. Finally, when we're all ready and the two Asian girls have slipped silently in to kneel behind Lisa, the assistant teacher glides through the door near the stage. She sits on her white cushions, drapes a white shawl over her shoulders and, without a word, switches on the CD. Is that all she does? I could be the assistant teacher if all it involves is pressing *play*.

On the CD the teacher chants in the strange language and then tells us to observe our breath. Not change it in any way, just observe it. As it comes in, as it goes out. Just observe. If it's shallow, let it be shallow; if it is deep, let it be deep. Just observe. Just observe. This is *anapana* meditation. Attentiveness to the incoming and out-going breath. So far so good. We're all sitting in silence, breathing. Nothing to it, really. The young woman in front of me has a very straight back. I don't think my back is as straight as hers. I'm supposed to have my eyes shut but curiosity keeps opening them.

Too soon my back hurts, my right knee hurts, my bottom hurts. The cushions that were so soft twenty minutes ago are now unyielding and hard. My left foot has gone to sleep and I'm worried that it may be permanently damaged. When I shift my foot a little, the blood starts moving and the resulting pins and needles are excruciating. I had imagined a blissful ten days of self-awakening. I never thought it would be this hard and it's only the morning of the first day. I try to keep observing my breath but the compulsion to observe my watch instead is too strong. Only five minutes have passed. I stretch my right leg without making too much noise, hoping no one will notice. The woman behind me sighs. Damn. She's judging me for moving. The familiar weight settles on my shoulders. Not good enough, never good enough. My mother was supposed to look after me. She didn't. I was neglected, rejected. Wasn't I worth looking after? Obviously not. Never good enough. Never worthy. Bad girl. The pain switches to anger in an instant. Defiance has always been my default mode. Fuck it, fuck them all. I move my left leg as well and discover not only my foot but my entire calf has gone to sleep. If I don't move it my whole left leg might become permanently numb. I could end up with palsy. I uncurl both my legs and stretch them out as much as I can in the limited space. I'm not going to risk palsy; I don't care how many times the woman behind me sighs.

When the hour is finally over the teacher starts chanting again. I have no idea what the chanting means. It's a language I've never heard before but I think I can make out a few of the words. Something about a *blonde miner*, a *naked judge* and a *dirty birdy*. My brain seeks to make sense of the nonsensical. When the chanting stops, half the people in the hall chant a short phrase three times and bow. I don't understand why and I certainly don't want to have to supplicate before anyone. The rows of women in front of me are bowing. The woman with the short bleached hair is among them. They must be the experienced meditators. After some hesitation those beside and behind me, including the two sisters, bow as well. I don't want to be conspicuous. I bow, even though it means betraying myself again.

The teacher tells us the new students can go and meditate in their rooms but the old students need to stay in the hall. Am I an old student? I'm a lot older than most of the women here, the pretty, slim, lithe young things with their wraparound yoga gear and hippie pants. But I see some of them aren't moving, so they must be old, which means I'm new and I can go. But what are the old students going to be doing when we're not here? Is there some kind of secret ritual? Do they get extra food or a treat? This is discrimination! Self-righteousness wells inside me until I realise the truth of the situation. I'd rather go back to my room and be comfortable in my meditation nest than put up with more pain here in the hall. If there are treats, they're welcome to them. I leave the meditation hall, blinking in the bright light, and crunch down the gravel path towards the comparative comfort of my room.

The bell jerks me awake. I am slumped in my meditation nest. Sleeping is forbidden during meditation time but it's the natural consequence of being woken before dawn. My roommate has disappeared. She was lying on her bed not so long ago, doing one of her snoring meditations. I check my watch. Eleven am. I check the timetable. Lunch. I suspect she's first in line.

In the dining hall Lisa serves spaghetti and the two Asian girls dish up tomato sauce and broccoli. Outside I battle the magpies and sharp-beaked butcher birds and afterwards sip lemongrass tea. The older sister has segregated herself, sitting on a chair away from the tables where the rest of us eat. She glares at the trees. Her younger sister watches her warily, then goes back to a dreamy contemplation of her food. Bernadette is at another table smiling to herself. She has a mouth that smiles easily; it would be hard work for it to frown. I wonder if any of them have been in as much pain as I have this morning. I doubt it. I watch the Asian girls cleaning up in the dining room. They move smoothly like dancers or skaters, synchronised and silent. I long to ask them questions. They look as though they've been meditating since childhood. Their every movement is considered and graceful. It's so different to how I feel: fat, clumpy, stiff and disjointed.

According to the timetable we don't begin meditating again until one pm. A walk will help keep the palsy at bay. The track leaves a faint scar among the gums and wattles, bracken and ferns. It runs parallel to a wire fence at the back of the property and encircles a small pond dotted with waterlilies. I continue up the small incline, just steep enough to get my heart pumping if I walk at a steady pace. Another student walks down the track towards me. Before we meet, she steps off the path and waits for me to pass, her head bowed. She must be an old student. She knows how to avoid the possibility of contact. I move past and hear the crackle of twigs behind me as she walks away. Signs attached to the fence ask students not to venture any further. Beyond the fence the bush is dense, less hospitable and possibly home to numerous snakes. I don't need any persuasion to stick to the path. The air pulses and hums in the midday heat. Something tickles my right arm, small and insignificant but annoying. I react before I think. My left hand slaps down. I've killed a mosquito. Usually I'd be glad. Not today. Wasn't it only last night I solemnly promised to undertake the Five Precepts? Top of the list: to abstain from killing any living creature. I look at the dead mosquito. Bad girl.

The guys at work took an office sweep. None of them believed I could last ten days without talking.

'You?' James laughed. 'You won't last a day. Hey, Colin, guess what. Mary-Lou's going on a meditation retreat for ten days . . . and she's not allowed to talk.'

'What? You not talk?' Colin guffawed, as only a man with a moustache can. 'That's impossible. I'll give you two days at the most.'

'Okay,' said James. 'I'll put ten dollars down says you'll only last a day. Colin, you wanna put your money where your mouth is? Anyone else?'

Adrian had wandered over to see what the fuss was about. 'I'm in,' he said.

Nobody thought I would last the whole ten days. Six was the highest bid and even that was scoffed at. At the time I was insulted but now it looks as though James will win the money. Not because I couldn't keep quiet but because I'm a killer.

Much as I want to avoid it, there's only one thing to do. An interview with the assistant teacher. I check my watch. Just after midday, there's still time. If nothing else, at least I'll find out what she sounds like. The interview room is tucked in beside the meditation hall. Those who want to see the assistant teacher sit on benches outside the hall and wait their turn, silently of course, not looking at each other. I don't join them. Yet. I'm nervous. Am I going to be bustled out of here when they learn what I've done? What kind of person makes a serious promise not to kill any living creature and the very next morning breaks that promise? But perhaps I was justified in killing that mosquito; it might have given me dengue fever. Surely I was just defending myself and no one can blame me for that. I don't need to see the assistant teacher. Besides, there's a queue. She probably won't have time to fit me in.

I walk nonchalantly past the waiting students, pretending I was just passing by and never intended to have an interview. But as I walk away the tension builds again. I can't believe I'm going to let this slide. I've always been a coward and this is further proof. My feet keep walking, one in front of the other, past the little wooden cottage where the assistant teacher sleeps. I never come forward when I should. I always dodge and weave. It's the fear that does it, but am I always going to be a slave to it? The gravel crunches under my feet. To my right in a cleared space between the male and female accommodation is a wooden frame. Hanging from the centre of the frame is the bell. It's about the size of a large upturned bucket but a lot heavier and a lot louder. Loud enough to be heard throughout the entire centre, penetrating into our bedrooms and into our dreams. I had a dream, a dream that I would drift through these days in bliss and enlightenment and emerge a better person. Instead I walk on in shame and defeat.

The next meditation session is an hour and a half long. Thankfully we're allowed to meditate in our rooms. Even though we're not supposed to use a mantra, my mind has found one. *I've broken the First Precept, I've fucked up, they'll kick me out, there's no hope for me.* Over and over. We're told to observe the breath, as it comes in, as it goes out. My breath is fast and hard. I want to cry. I want to scream. Observe the breath. And if that doesn't work, think of something else.

Inside the meditation centre there's a cupboard. Inside the cupboard is a big metal trunk. Inside the trunk are many cloth bags with numbers on them. Inside one of those bags is my wallet. Inside my wallet is a lotto ticket. A ticket that might win me twenty-two million dollars. I bought it on a whim yesterday, when I was still allowed to talk. What would I do with all that money? One tenth of twenty-two million is two point two million. A tithe to charity? My Christian upbringing remains ingrained. It would probably be best to set up some kind of charitable fund to get the best tax advantage. Then what? I'd like to see more of the world. I'd take my friends. We'd stick a pin in a map. No expense spared. And what about work? When I first started in my dream job I used to throw in a couple of dollars a week for the work lotto ticket. We never won, but at the time I told my workmates even if we did win, I'd keep working. They were astounded and more than a little dismissive. But I meant it – I loved the job so much I felt as though I'd already won Lotto. That's all changed. If I did win the twenty-two million I'd feel guilty, leaving them in the cruel hands of The Hideous Mr Purvis, but that won't stop me. I've suffered enough. Every time the phone rings at work my stomach twists. I always worry that it might be him.

'How dare you!' he seethed down the line a few weeks ago.

The familiar heat of fear shot through me. I didn't know what I'd done, just that he was angry.

'What's—'

'You have overstepped the line.'

My hands shook. I felt like a little kid, defenceless and confused. Once, in a previous job, I had cried from frustration and exhaustion but I had sworn I would never do it again. It was unprofessional. Men don't cry at work when things are tough or someone's yelling at them.

'You have no authority to make decisions. I'm the program director and I demand respect.' He slammed the phone down, leaving me none the wiser.

We'd all heard the I-demand-respect rant before. We'd even discussed it among ourselves. 'A person can't demand respect,' we'd mutter. 'They have to earn it.'

Elliot Purvis had no time for such theories.

My mind starts droning again. *I've broken the First Precept, I've fucked up, they'll kick me out, there's no hope for me.* My breath is hard, powering out of my nostrils. Turbocharged breath. At least now I'm observing it, all is not lost. My bottom aches. How can that be? I'm sitting on a mattress, for God's sake. Observe the breath as it goes in, as it goes out; if it is shallow, let it be shallow; if it is deep, let it be deep. Breathing in, breathing out. I killed a mosquito. *I broke the First Precept.* Here we go again.

My roommate's coughing interrupts the droning in my head. The old woman has persisted with her lying down meditation but every so often her body twitches in a fit of hawking and hacking that must be the result of at least a packet a day habit. Perhaps she's here on doctor's orders. This is her last-ditch attempt to give up smoking. Maybe she's got cancer. She does seem to be very tired. Always lying down. Except when it's time to eat. She coughs again. A phlegmy, sickening cough. A serious smoker's cough. She's here because she's desperate. She has to quit smoking or die. I admire her spirit. She's not afraid to try anything in her quest to give up the cigarettes. To beat the cancer.

When my dad was diagnosed with cancer I researched alternative therapies. I discovered a clinic in New York City that was achieving great results with a very strict macrobiotic diet. I told my dad about it. His response was not what I expected.

'Thanks, darling, but I'd rather die than eat that food.'

He always did like his tucker. But he was tall and lean and only ever had a little bit of a paunch. In my favourite photo of him he is standing in the middle distance, his comb-over blowing in the wind. It was taken on a block of land he and my mum bought on the east coast of Tasmania. They were going to build a house. My dad died before that dream could become a reality. In the photo he stands smiling proudly towards the camera, space all around him, blue sea behind him, blue sky above. That's how I imagine him now. Happy. Free.

At the next Group Sit the internal geography of the hall has changed. The old woman now sits to one side, on a low-slung plastic chair. She's loaded it with so many cushions it looks like an overstuffed armchair. If she wasn't terminally ill I'd swear she had a smug little smile on her face. It must be a grimace. Three students sit up against the back wall with their mats and cushions. I recognise their faces from the queue for interviews with the assistant teacher. So that's the trick. If I hadn't been so terrified of getting kicked out, perhaps I'd be sitting up against the back wall too.

Still not a word from the assistant teacher. She hits play and we're given more instructions by the teacher: observe our breath and the sensations in and around the nostrils. Observe if the breath enters through the left nostril, or if it enters through the right nostril. Observe if the breath leaves the left nostril or through the right nostril. The way he pronounces 'nostril' makes the word sound exotic. Nostril is not a word you hear a lot in everyday conversation.

'Good morning, how are your nostrils today?'

'Gosh, that movie was funny. I laughed so much my nostrils quivered.'

'Have you seen the new girl? The one with the exquisitely shaped nostrils?'

My right leg is at an odd angle but I'll just have to put up with it. Breath comes in, breath goes out, nose hairs tickle.

I've broken the First Precept, I've fucked up, they'll kick me out, there's no hope for me.

Don't think, just breathe.

The older sister sits behind me and to my right. She keeps swallowing. I can hear it clearly in the stillness of the hall. She must be over-salivating. Is that something people do when they're in pain? Am I swallowing? The young woman in front of me sits as motionless and straight as ever. She must be a better person than me: even-tempered, moderate in all her habits, beautiful, lovely and loved. I feel like a sack of barbed wire; spiky, sharp, unfriendly. Don't get too close. I'll rip your clothes and tear your skin. No wonder I don't have a boyfriend. I scare them away. I'll be alone for the rest of my life. Fuck my knee hurts. What am I doing here? I hate this. What the hell have I done to deserve this? Oh, that's right. I killed a mosquito. Bad girl.

I yearn to hear the teacher's chanting. It means the meditation is over and I can move without feeling guilty. We are allowed to change our postures during these Group Sits but there is a pressure to sit still. We're asked not to disturb anyone. Also there's a sense of competition. If everyone else can sit still, I can too. And I would, if only it didn't hurt so much.

When at last the chanting releases us, the assistant teacher speaks for the first time. Her voice is gentle and controlled. She doesn't say much, just tells us to take a short break, then the new students are to return to the hall. Five minutes. That's all we're given to walk down the path to the loos, wait in line, then walk back and get settled. It takes longer of course and when we return Lisa is placing cushions on the floor in front of the low stage, just below the assistant teacher. The assistant teacher calls out a list of names. Four students rise, pick their way to the front and sit. She whispers to them. They whisper back. I can't hear what they're saying. I should have my eyes closed. I'll never reach nirvana. They sit for a while then return to their places. I watch and listen as two more groups are called up and exchange whispers. When my name is called I find it hard to get up. I wonder if I can take a spare cushion with me to put under my right knee. I can't sit cross-legged without support. My knee might dislocate, as it has so many times before. I'll certainly disturb everyone then. They won't be able to pretend they're meditating alone when the ambulance arrives. I hobble up to the front and look dubiously at the lone cushion on the floor where I'm supposed to sit. Everyone's waiting. I sit, tense and stiff, keeping my knees off the floor as best as I'm able.

The assistant teacher turns to the first woman in our group.

'Have you been able to observe your breath?'

'Yes.'

'Have you been able to bring back your awareness if it wanders away?'

'Yes.'

Is that it? Not, *Are you in agony?* Or, *I know this is incredibly hard, would you like to take the rest of the day off?*

My turn. I hope she doesn't ask me a question about mosquitoes.

'Have you been able to observe your breath?'

All I can think about is my knee. The effort to keep it semi-vertical so it doesn't dislocate is my main focus. I look at her. What did she say? The woman before me answered yes.

'Yes.'

'When your mind wanders away have you been able to bring your awareness back to the breath?'

'Ah . . .'

What can I say? I can't lie. Especially not in the meditation hall. This is where I promised to abide by the precepts. No lying was one of them. No lying, no stealing, no sex, no intoxicants and there was one more. What was it? Oh, that's right. No killing. That's the one I've already broken. *I've broken the First Precept, I've fucked up, they'll kick me out, there's no hope for me.*

The assistant teacher is smiling at me. She's just asked me a straightforward question and I can't even answer without my mind wandering away.

'Sorry, what was the question?'

Her smile widens slightly.

'When your mind wanders away have you been able to bring your awareness back to your breathing?'

'Um . . . sometimes.'

Is that a lie? Not exactly. I do remember to observe my breath from time to time, just not a lot of the time.

'Keep trying,' she says. 'If you have trouble, take a few deeper, harder breaths to bring your attention back to the breath. Then continue to observe the breath as it is.'

'Thank you.'

And another chance slips by. I wanted to ask her about the pain. I wanted to ask when it goes away. I wanted to ask if we could have a little lie-down instead of having to sit all the time. There are plenty of cushions, we would all be very comfortable.

She gazes at us serenely. 'Meditate with me.'

I want to be back in my room, nestled in my little meditation nest. My knees hurt. My back hurts. My bottom hurts. And it's only Day One. What am I doing here? Spending my summer holidays in pain, in a creaking, stifling meditation hall. I should be swaying in a comfy hammock with a cool breeze and a refreshing drink of lemon, lime and bitters.

'You may return to your places,' she says, after a small eternity.

I have a standard manoeuvre for getting up from a cross-legged position with the least possible strain on my right knee. I lean to the right, slowly uncurl my right leg as I stretch it out to the left, then swing it around to the front using my still folded left leg as support. I then keep swinging the right leg around as far to the right as possible while keeping it straight. It's not until my right leg is pointing to the right that I start bending it under me so I can lever myself up with support from the left. It's quite a performance but it does the trick. Sometimes the whole rigmarole comes to a crashing halt when my kneecap gets stuck in the wrong place. Thankfully this afternoon it works. Just as well. Everyone's waiting for me. Again. They think I'm making a fuss about nothing. They're thinking, why don't I just get back to my spot, sit down, and stop making a kerfuffle? Then the next four students can have their turn at the front with the assistant teacher. If it wasn't for the Noble Silence they'd all be tut-tutting, clicking their tongues with disapproval. I go back to my spot. The other students appear to be silently meditating, eyes closed. But I know what they're thinking. I endure the rest of the session but as soon as the assistant teacher releases us I scuttle back to my room like a cockroach.

You have to be fast if you want a banana. By the time I reach the dining hall at teatime, only apples or oranges are left. The old woman has a banana. Of course. Two pieces of fruit and a cup of tea constitute a three-course dinner for new students. The old students get even less. On the table to the left of the teapots is a saucepan with a sign in front of it. *Old Students Only*. I look with curiosity at the women who help themselves to the liquid. They don't eat the fruit. They don't have a cup of tea. They fill their mugs with this special drink and sip it slowly. I wonder what's in it. Painkillers perhaps? I doubt it. These are the women of experience. They have survived Vipassana before and come back for more. One in particular catches my eye; tall, long-limbed and graceful in every way. Even her hair is graceful. She moves lightly and slowly, almost floating. I shift a chair to the side of the verandah, prop my legs up on the railing and slowly eat my fruit. I watch as she walks out across the grass. Her back is straight, her steps precise. She must have been a dancer at one stage. Normal people don't walk like that. They don't have postures like that. But she's very tall. Too tall for a dancer. I wonder how tall she thinks she is. Once during a girls' night in with friends the subject of height came up.

'I'm five foot six,' I said confidently, knowing it to be true.

'So am I,' said Tess, who I was sure was at least an inch shorter than me.

'That's incredible, I'm five foot six too,' said Karen, who clearly wasn't.

'Well that's odd,' said Robyn. 'I thought I was five foot six, but perhaps I'm taller than that.'

We were perplexed. Four women clearly of four different altitudes who, for some reason, all thought they were the same height. Perhaps at some stage during female evolution the collective unconscious decided five foot six was the perfect height and naturally we all wanted to be it.

'There's only one way to solve this,' said Tess, who was a sometime seamstress. 'I'll get my tape measure.'

Twenty minutes later we discovered the truth. None of us were five foot six. Except me. Well, actually I was more like five foot five and a half, but I maintain I was having a short day. I am, in fact, five foot six.

But I don't think the serene woman walking through the dusk at the meditation centre is five foot six. She's closer to six foot. She must be a model. A runway model.

My sisters were both models. I was the fat one. Nice face, shame about the rest. Their response to food, even at a young age, was the opposite of mine. Their Easter eggs would remain untouched for weeks, mine would be unwrapped and eaten in seconds. They picked at their food, I bolted mine down. They eschewed desserts while I licked the bowl. They loved clothes and make-up, I loved cooking and eating. They had lots of boyfriends, I had one – until he told me he was only with me to get closer to my beautiful sisters. My sisters would disappear on mysterious nights out or weekends at the beach, leaving their embarrassment of a little fat sister behind. My brothers were never interested in me. My mother was missing in action, on some spiritual plane. I would cook and eat because it made me feel less alone. Food was good company, it was always available. Even if sometimes I had to steal it. But there were times when my obsession with food was an advantage. I was thirteen, waiting in the hospital corridor for permission to see one of my sisters. She was alone in her room, all her privileges being removed, one by one, until she would eat. No letters or cards, no TV, no telephone, but still she kept losing weight. Her doctor sat down beside me and explained that now her visitor rights had been denied and I wouldn't be able to see her. He looked at the overweight confused young teenager that I was and said words I never thought I would hear: 'Don't ever go on a diet.' Even at that age I'd already suffered through several diets and none of them had worked for long. I cherished his words and felt justified in eating a whole block of chocolate later that afternoon.

When we return to the meditation hall after dinner for the third Group Sit of the day I'm surprised to see Bernadette sitting in one of the little plastic chairs. I didn't think she would give in so quickly. Suddenly I'm glad we're not sharing a room. She's abandoned me to sit in comfort while I'm left in agony. I stomp defiantly to my place and sit down, glaring at her the entire time. Maybe some of us don't want to be let off the hook. Maybe some of us actually want to do this thing properly, getting through the pain with pride, knowing we didn't chicken out at the first sign of discomfort. The assistant teacher enters, sits and presses the button. The chanting begins and so does my agony. The supposed silence commences but the rumble and gurgle of empty stomachs fills the hall. As the light outside dims even those noises are drowned out by another sound. At first it's just a soft purring but it quickly grows in strength. The melody encircles the meditation hall in glorious surround sound. On this summer evening, we are sitting in silence, many of us in pain, hoping for enlightenment or at least a glimmer of peace. But at this moment I know what I'd rather be. Fuck the karma, fuck this pain. If it means coming back as an insect, I don't care. I think the cicadas have got it right. I'd rather be singing.

When the hour is finally over we are given the reward of a short break before we are to return to the hall. I stumble down the path to the toilet, my legs struggling to function after so much constraint.

Back in the meditation hall we are presented with a surprising diversion. Television. According to the timetable it's the Teacher's Discourse. We don't get to meet him but we do get to watch him on the small screen. He is an ageing, white-haired gentleman with a kind face.

'The first day is full of great difficulties and discomforts,' he says with a twinkle in his eye.

A small murmur rustles around the hall. I'm not the only one who's spent the day in pain.

'Oh, so much pain, so much discomfort, a pain in the leg, a pain in the head, I'd better run away, this is not good for me.' He chuckles, making fun of us but in a gentle, compassionate way. I can't take offence.

He explains that this is the habit pattern of the mind and these habit patterns keep us stuck. Our aim is to be free of them. The final goal is to purify the mind, not just at the surface level but at the deepest level. We're here at the meditation centre to learn the art of living happily by finding out what causes disharmony within ourselves. We must go to the source of our misery. 'Know thyself,' as all the saints and sages of the past have said. Misery is universal, so the remedy must be universal. Everyone breathes. That is why we observe the breath and through observing it find our own truth. When the mind starts 'rolling in negativity' as the teacher says, the breath becomes slightly hard, slightly faster. The mind is connected to the breath. He tells us the breath helps us get to the depth of the problem where the negativity arises. The first step is to live in the present moment and we do that by observing the breath. He talks about craving and aversion: the misery we cause ourselves by wanting things we don't have and not wanting things we have. He explains how the mind wanders around the place, 'rolling in the past or rolling in the future', finding it hard to stay in the present. Our monkey minds, always chattering, always leaping about from limb to limb. He suggests we think of this meditation course as being an operation to purify our minds.

'You have come to your hospital,' he says. 'Don't say mental hospital.' He smiles. 'Although in some ways it is a mental hospital . . .'

I am surprised by an outburst of sound. The Noble Silence is broken by laughter. Are we allowed to laugh? The assistant teacher doesn't tell us not to, so I guess we can. I wasn't expecting this. I was expecting...actually I don't know what I was expecting. But I definitely was not expecting laughter in the meditation hall. I laugh because I'm allowed to laugh. It feels good. I've made a little mattress out of my cushions and I recline on them. Lisa comes over and asks me to straighten up. Seems even during the teacher's discourse we have to sit up straight. I was happy for a moment. I was laughing. Now I'm cranky. How much longer can this old bloke natter on? Is he going to say something funny again? Nope, he just gives us some more instructions; always meditate indoors in case a passing breeze blows away your concentration, stay for the whole ten days because this is an operation and you wouldn't leave the operating room before your surgery was complete, and even though you've probably just realised you don't get any dinner, resist the urge to go back for a second or third helping at lunchtime. Then he wishes us all the best, tells us to work hard and signs off with a little blessing, 'Be happy'. I'd be happier lying down right now. Instead we get a five minute break before we have to be back in the hall for yet another meditation. I'm tired, hungry and sore all over. I look down at my collection of cushions on the floor and wonder how I'm going to get through another nine days of this, let alone the next half hour.

Day Two

The early morning air outside is cool, the stars are abundant. I leave the old woman to her snoring and make my way to the bathroom. The promise of a new day is exciting, mystical and fresh with expectation. Anything is possible. All the hours ahead to be played out in a way never experienced before. Every day starts this way. I usually miss it by sleeping until my clock radio turns the morning into a routine: exercise, breakfast and getting ready for work.

I stand on a gravel path breathing in the stars, the trees, the peak of the mountain. New and unexplored, I could be, or become, anything. I am not shaped by daylight or habit or expectation or words. The Noble Silence is surprisingly liberating. I don't have to make small talk, explain myself, impress anyone, disappoint myself or anyone else with clumsy words. No need to struggle for something clever to say or strive to prove myself intelligent and witty. The silence is an equaliser. Ego doesn't have a chance to take root. Well, maybe. The women in the meditation hall who sit perfectly still, with straight backs and serene expressions, might think themselves better than the rest of us, the riffraff of wrigglers and shifters. I'm fat and clumsy and stupid. I can't sit still. I have a bung knee and a sore bottom. If only I could win the twenty-two million dollars I'd be okay. I could go to a health retreat and stay there until I was slim. I could afford to pay for as many massages and yoga classes as it took to be able to sit still for hours with a perfectly straight back. I'm nowhere near serene. I obsess over Anzac biscuits; I kill mosquitoes without even thinking. Plagued by doubt, fear and resentment, my mind starts up its chant: *I've broken the First Precept, I've fucked up, they'll kick me out, there's no hope for me.*

My beautiful dream-like morning is shattered. Destroyed by my own mad mind. I shuffle to the bathroom, no longer looking at the stars.

I meditate on my bed for the first two hour session of the day, sitting with my back supported by the wall while the old woman sleeps on regardless. I remember the teacher's words from last night.

'You have started making a surgical operation of the mind,' he said. 'The deep-rooted complexes are coming to the surface. The process is unpleasant but you must face the music now, and face it smilingly.'

I didn't smile last night and I'm not smiling now. Not even the tight little smile that I learnt from my mother. The smile that's more like armour than happiness. The smile that shuts other people out instead of welcoming them in. The smile that says, 'I'm good,' but looks mean. I've spent so much of my life pretending to be a good girl, I have completely forgotten who I am. The constant lying and hiding behind a tight little smile. Two lives. The external one and the real one, lurking in the shadows. I envy other people who can lie and pretend so effortlessly, just as I once envied other drug users who had no inhibitions. They didn't care if they were seen stoned and nodding off in public. I hid, knowing my pinned eyes would give me away. I was terrified of what people would think. Sometimes it was a good thing.

Once, and only once, I rang the dealer and asked him for credit.

'That's not like you,' he said. Yes, he would give me credit, but it was clear he wanted me to think about the path I was about to take.

Here was a man who spent his days selling smack, yet he was worried about me. I set off for his house anyway. Before I got there I started crying. I couldn't do it. I couldn't throw away the appearance of being okay. I couldn't bear his disappointment. Always, always, I had to be a good girl. Even when buying heroin.

It was hard work. Alcohol, drugs and food all helped take the edge off. When I was using drugs they kept my weight down. Alcohol was socially acceptable, in a country where falling down drunk is a national past-time. But when all I was using was food it showed up on my body. I couldn't hide that shame. The whole world could see it and disapprove. And that shame has been with me for a very long time.

I was put on my first diet when I was eleven. Weight Watchers with my mother at thirteen. A diet doctor at fifteen. Nothing worked. They treated the symptom, not the cause. In my early twenties when my best friend left town, I consoled myself by baking self-saucing chocolate puddings and eating them with tubs of ice cream. Every day. For a month. I can still remember the recipe off by heart. Mix 1 cup of self-raising flour, 1 cup of sugar and 2 tablespoons of cocoa. Add 1 cup of milk, 1 teaspoon of vanilla essence and 2 tablespoons of melted butter. Pour into a baking dish. Sprinkle with 1 cup of brown sugar mixed with another 2 tablespoons of cocoa and pour 2 cups of boiling water over the top. Bake for about 45 minutes, or less if you can't wait that long. It'll still taste the same.

Later, between boyfriends and bands, I lived in a lonely bedsit where the bathroom was bigger than the unfriendly kitchen. I dined exclusively on purchases from the chocolate shop on the corner. The resulting constipation had me reaching for roughage, in the form of fruit and nut chocolate.

I destroyed relationships because all I could think of was sugar. Moody and unpredictable, I was hard work for any boy or man who wanted to get close to me. Besides, I was always preoccupied with how I was going to get away from them, to binge in secret. Food was more important than anyone or anything else. I pushed them all away.

I was almost thirty by the time I got to my first Twelve Step program. It was for food addicts. I'd read about it in a magazine and wrote down the number on a piece of paper, where it stayed in the zippered compartment of my wallet for over eighteen months. Food addiction wasn't cool. Compulsive eating was pathetic. When I finally became desperate enough I dialled the number.

My first meeting was on a Sunday morning in a room in Bondi Junction. It was packed. Standing room only. I hid at the back. A woman sat behind a table and read from a folder. Her words frightened me. She talked about God. God? I hadn't expected Him to be involved. I wanted to fix my addiction to sugar and she was talking about God. Realisation hit and I suddenly found it hard to breathe. Clearly the whole sordid farce was a plot by my mother. She knew one day I would reject her religion so she had devised a way to force me to believe in God. She gave me this addiction. She knew eventually I would have to come to this room. And when I did I would discover my last hope depended on believing in God. It was a set-up. My all-powerful mother had won.

I stayed to the end of the meeting only because I was too polite to leave. As soon as I could, I scuttled for the door. I was stopped before I could make the front steps. I smiled grimly, expecting the usual rant, but instead was handed a pamphlet for newcomers and left to my own devices. I rushed outside into the sunshine. I needed time to think. The shock still resonated through my body. I drove to my favourite place. The cemetery. Those lucky corpses. The drugs hadn't killed me but perhaps I could eat myself to death. Under the Moreton Bay figs I took out the pamphlet and began to read. The words jumped off the page. They described my life; the bingeing, the pain, the lying, the terror of not being able to stop. But the Twelve Steps stopped me cold. There was that word again. God. Did I have to become a Christian to find relief? I kept reading. *You don't have to believe. You only need to 'act as if' you believe.*

Really? I didn't have to pave my way into recovery with good works and Christian thoughts? I could just act as if I believed in God and that was enough? Could it be that simple? Was I allowed to act as if and not be thought of as a hypocrite? So many questions. I had to go back to find out the answers.

At the meeting the following week, I got beyond the word God and I listened. I heard people share their stories. It was as if they were telling mine. All the things I had done. The dark secrets. The shame. I was not alone. These people understood. I was home. I worked those Twelve Steps and I worked them hard, over and over. The word God no longer bothered me. Perversely, because I did not have to believe, I became free to believe that a power greater than myself could help me. After about six months I started going to Alcoholics Anonymous as well, because I was told that's where the strong recovery was. I also went to Narcotics Anonymous, even though I was clean, because my sponsor wanted me to deal with residual issues. I went to Al Anon for adult children of alcoholics because my counsellor told me it would help me with my dysfunctional upbringing. I did everything that was suggested. I was a prime target for those jokes about a Twelve Step group for those addicted to Twelve Step groups, but I was so desperate to get it right, to do it perfectly, so I could, at last, feel good about myself. Almost every evening, and sometimes at lunchtime as well, I was at some kind of Twelve Step meeting.

In the food addicts fellowship all the good girls like me were on food plans. We never called them diets. But they were. Every morsel weighed and measured. And definitely no sugar. After I'd lost weight I thought I'd be free. But instead other issues demanded my attention. As a newly slim woman my wardrobe changed from floaty and voluminous to slinky and revealing. I flirted with men and women indiscriminately, delighting in reeling them in with no intention of ever following through. The power was intoxicating. It was great playing in bands and looking good. I could tease from my safe position up on stage. That was part of the job, wasn't it? When a man told me I was confusing sexuality with personality I had no idea what he meant, but my sponsor did. She told me I had left substance related addictions behind only to be engulfed by the world of process addictions. I'd never heard the term before. She explained they were behaviours that can become as addictive as any drug, like gambling or shopping, or in my case flirting and teasing. Hooking people in, she called it. Of course there were Twelve Step programs for process addictions as well and my sponsor pointed me in the direction of Sex and Love Addicts Anonymous. I quickly learnt to avoid the mixed meetings. They were filled with men looking for a quick and easy fuck. The women-only meetings were attended by women like me. We just wanted to be loved, no matter what it took, or took away. I met women like myself who thought they were bad, unworthy of love. We sold ourselves out to get something that even slightly resembled love. I made my closest friends in those rooms. This is where the real truth was told.

I wasn't so much of a sex addict – my Christian upbringing had put paid to that. But I could understand other women, rutting for attention. My first sexual experience was delicious. I was six and he was five, playing doctors and nurses in the cubby house. We loved to put sand and leaves in the crack between each other's buttocks. It felt so good. It was fun and it was innocent until my oldest sister saw what we were doing and told my parents. In a moment this harmless pleasure became dirty and sinful.

When I was eleven I had a boyfriend – yes, me, a boyfriend! He was more sexually advanced than me. After school at his house, both his parents at work, we would play the dog biscuit game. It was his idea. We'd take turns to drop heart-shaped dog biscuits down our underwear and the other one had to fish them out. It was warm and moist and strange territory indeed in his underpants. I didn't like it and I knew it was wrong, but at least it meant I had a boyfriend.

In my teenage years male attention was sparse. When I was fifteen I resorted to giving a red-haired boy a hand job at a party.

I'd have gone all the way, too, if we'd been allowed to go upstairs. I was sick of being the only girl who wasn't getting love bites on a regular basis. If I thought it meant he'd like me, I was wrong. He avoided me from that night on.

I was eighteen when I lost my virginity. It was taken from me. I thought I deserved it. Bad girl.

In Twelve Step programs good girls did service, so I did lots of it: treasurer, secretary, retreat committees. I sponsored newcomers and helped them through the steps. I gave out my phone number to all who asked for it. My phone would ring day and night with members needing a friendly ear. I'd been a member of Twelve Step groups for about five years when a split threatened to destroy the food addicts fellowship. I was asked to serve on the First Tradition committee. Along with the Twelve Steps there are the Twelve Traditions, designed by the founders of Alcoholics Anonymous to keep things running smoothly and resolve any disputes. The First Tradition is: *Our common welfare should come first. Personal recovery depends on AA unity.* The aim of the First Tradition committee was to find a way of keeping the fellowship together. The breakaway group wanted to change the rules, to put certain imperatives around food in place, whereas up until now each member had been free to find a food plan that worked for them. It was heartbreaking work and in the end useless. The split eventuated, in a storm of resentment and bitterness. I found myself infected with those same defects of character, convinced that Twelve Step programs were full of hypocrites. Just like the church. Yes, I was home. And I didn't like it any better the second time round. After years of being clean, sober and sugar-free, I expected something magnificent. Especially after all that service, wasn't that supposed to count for something? But life had dealt me the same old shit.

I remember that first bite of sugar. It was a morning tea at the radio school. I had a piece of cake, then another and another. It tasted great. I'd been abstinent from sugar for the best part of two years but by the time Easter rolled around I was the Bunny's best friend. I stopped going to meetings. Didn't need them. My life was on track. I was one of the chosen few at AFTRS. I'd be leaving Sydney before the end of the year. Didn't know where I'd be going but there wasn't much point maintaining my Twelve Step life in Sydney when I'd be somewhere else soon. Besides, the Twelve Step programs were full of sick people. People who caused rifts and splits, hurt and resentment. I wasn't sick. I was well and happy and on my way to a new life.

Radio school was fun, stimulating and hard work. The school's policy was to cram all the knowledge we needed into less than a year, with the aim of finding us jobs before the Christmas slow-down. There were no holidays and we often worked weekends. We learnt everything: announcing, programming, copywriting, producing, news and sport. The school encouraged us to discover where our talents lay and in which direction we would like to go.

When I told Lucienne my aim was to be the music director for ABC Local Radio Australia-wide, she laughed. 'You'd be bored senseless.'

'Why?' As far as I was concerned it was my ultimate job. A long way off but worth aspiring to.

'You'd be programming for talk radio on the AM band. Even the best music sounds like mud on AM. You'll create music logs for announcers who'll ignore them and play what they want, if indeed they play any music at all.'

Her opinion surprised me but I wasn't deterred.

Towards the end of the year the job offers started coming in.

Two students landed work before we even graduated. The rest of us wondered when it would be our turn. We thumbed through the latest issue of *Jocks' Journal*, where the jobs were advertised. One caught my eye. It was at 2TM in Tamworth, a large town less than six hours' drive from Sydney and famous for one thing. Country music.

When I was younger, I never, ever, thought I'd play country music. I was way too cool. I'd been in indie pop bands, R & B, blues, jazz and funk bands. They were cool. Country music was not cool. But in my mid-twenties, living in Melbourne and dabbling in smack, I watched a video of *Sweet Dreams*, the biopic of Patsy Cline's life, and I was undone. The melody, the range, the arrangements, there was nothing hokey about it. I hunted out her music and listened to it endlessly. Even made myself a country skirt with horses on it. I was hooked.

Two years and one band later I made it to the Tamworth Country Music Festival. Every summer it draws performers and punters from all over Australia and the world. I walked around in a happy daze. There was music everywhere: in every club, pub, park and cafe, in the library, in the street. There were even buskers in the toilets. I was playing in an acoustic trio, Mary-Lou's Lucky Stars, and soaked it all up. I'd been back every year ever since with different bands and line-ups, with CDs and posters, with excitement and delight.

I reread the ad for 2TM. I already knew the town and some people there. But the station wanted someone with experience. I put it aside.

A few days later, Lucienne called me into her office. 'Are you going to apply for the Tamworth job?'

'They want an announcer who's been working in radio for five years. I hardly think I qualify.'

'I think you should apply anyway. For the experience of applying if nothing else.'

I did and was amazed when the station called and asked me to drive up for an interview. The manager sat behind his imposing desk and played bad cop. The program director leant forward on his chair. Eager and happy. Like a puppy. After fifteen minutes I began to think the interview might be more than just practice.

'We've taken students straight from AFTRS before with great success,' said the manager, reclining back in his chair.

The puppy wagged his tail and turned to him. 'So can we give her the job?'

Had I heard right? Were they going to offer me the position?

The manager shook his head. 'Proper channels. Other applicants to consider. Procedures, et cetera.'

I had researched the station. I knew they had no women on air and neither did their FM station. They needed me, if only to voice commercials. More than that, the program director was keen to offer me the job. Perhaps Lucienne had known all along. Maybe they had asked her to recommend a female student who'd be willing to relocate to Tamworth. Blokes were easy. Young men, no ties. They were good radio fodder in an industry where moving often is a necessity.

I smiled at them both. 'I guess it depends on whether you need a female voice on air or not.'

As soon as the words came out of my mouth I regretted them. The puppy's face fell. The manager turned a mottled shade of purple.

'We do,' he spluttered. 'But we're not allowed to say. Equal employment opportunities and all that.'

I took a breath, relieved. The job was mine.

I had left a country band, or been abandoned by one to be honest, and landed a job in the Country Music Capital of Australia. The irony was delightful.

After two hours of meditating in my room followed by a long-awaited breakfast of yoghurt and muesli, I enter the meditation hall for the first Group Sit of Day Two. I'm determined to attempt something I've dubbed 'The Straddle'. The straight-backed girl who inspired this determination is already meditating, pert and still, in front of me, while the stragglers and wrigglers avoid the inevitable. I've noticed she alternates between sitting cross-legged and The Straddle so I'm hopeful it will help. I arrange my cushions into a column in the middle of my mat as I have seen her do. I mount the column, like a British matron from a 1940s comedy getting ready for the hunt. The cushions immediately compress under my weight until I'm almost kneeling on my heels. My right knee screams its complaint. The Straddle is a spectacular failure. I disentangle myself from the column of cushions and pretend I never attempted it in the first place.

Once the meditation is under way, and we're observing our breath and the sensations in the area below the nostrils and above the upper lip, I realise I have a problem. I am sitting off-centre, facing slightly to the right. The panic rises, but I can't rearrange myself yet again, not so soon after the meditation has started. People will think I'm a complete idiot. Perhaps it's a slight case of obsessive compulsion, like the time I had to switch every light on and off three times to prevent certain disaster, but I can't concentrate on my breath or the sensations unless I'm perfectly aligned. Already my breath is loud, fast, jagged. My face is a mask. A grimace. A tear crawls down my right cheek. Of course. Everything leans to the right, turns to the right, is skewed to the right.

I hear somebody move. Someone else has changed their position. Oh thank you, thank you, thank you for moving. You moved first. Now I won't bear the brunt of the disapproval. I put my hands down on the mat on either side of my legs. I turn my body slowly, making as little noise as possible, until I'm centred, exactly straight. I sigh, relax, and breathe. Breathing in, breathing out, observing, aware of sensations, aware of the breath.

I've broken the First Precept, I've fucked up, they'll kick me out, there's no hope for me.

Bugger.

My mantra of hopelessness persists through another two hours of meditation. It is unwelcome company while I eat my lunch of vegetable curry, dhal and rice. It doesn't even leave when I eschew the carrot cake. If I want it gone I must talk with the assistant teacher. The dining hall is at the bottom of the hill, the meditation hall and an interview with the assistant teacher are at the top. In between is the bathroom, where I stop to delay, if only for a moment, what must be done. But it takes more than a moment. About thirty women are doing the course. There are only four toilets. The queue ends in the undercover area in front of the bathroom that also serves as the laundry. I stand in line beside buckets full of soaking clothes. When it's time to do my laundry,

I'll have to queue for a bucket as well. I'm glad I brought a lot of underwear. We stand in silence and hold the door open for each other without acknowledgement. We wait our turn. To the right of the bathroom are two separate buildings, each with four bedrooms. My room is in the low-set building made of rendered besser block. The other is a small weatherboard house with verandahs and a clock on the front wall reminding us how slow the time goes here. Tents are pitched in the space between the buildings, more than I remember seeing yesterday. To the left, on the other side of the centre, are the male dining hall, bathroom and dorms. Judiciously planted trees and shrubs screen the opposite sex from prying eyes. How strange, though, that when I'm in the meditation hall I could just stretch out my left hand and touch one of those forbidden creatures, gently stroke the fuzz on his arm, feel the warmth of his skin. My thoughts, race to where they shouldn't.

When I finally reach the meditation hall, three women are already sitting on the wooden bench, waiting to see the assistant teacher. How many men wait on a similar bench on the male side of the hall, I wonder? The kangaroos are a welcome distraction to help while away the time. A couple of mothers with joeys in their pouches graze on the lawn behind the assistant teacher's cottage. One of the joeys sticks its head out of the pouch and nibbles the grass. Clearly unimpressed, it retreats inside to its mother's teat. A couple of younger roos who have learnt to like the taste of grass move slowly with their heads down, eating constantly. A large male follows them closely. I'm fascinated by what appears to be a reverse tail between his legs. With a shock I realise what it is. I've never seen a kangaroo with an erection before. It is startling: long, thin, pointy and curved. Clearly this kangaroo is not interested in keeping the Third Precept.

Lisa, who is organising the order of interviews, beckons me at last. As I walk towards the door my mind tries to hold me back. *It's not too late, I could walk away. I don't need to confess my sins. It's understandable, I reacted instinctively.* But isn't that why I'm here? To stop reacting. To stop those quick bursts of anger, the slow burn of resentment, the snap judgements, the fierce defences. I open the door. The assistant teacher sits opposite on a chair. Calm, composed and ready to take my confession. In front of her on the floor is a cushion. I sit down. Carefully.

'Hello,' she says.

I know I'm allowed to talk to her but I've taken a vow of Noble Silence. 'Hi,' is all I can manage. Even speaking that one word feels wrong.

The assistant teacher finally breaks the silence. 'How can I help you?'

Even now I want to avoid this, to dodge and weave as I have for most of my life. Twelve Step programs are full of mottos, sayings and acronyms. They have a good one for fear. Fuck Everything And Run or Face Everything And Recover. Between them, my parents exemplified these two opposing approaches to life. Ignore it and it will go away was my father's philosophy. Confront it and you will triumph was my mother's. Whose daughter will I be today?

'Well . . . I'm just wondering about . . . the pain.' And so I am my father's daughter. Do not confront anyone or anything and most importantly do not confront yourself. Avoid at all costs.

'The pain.' She smiles.

'Yes. It's rather hard to deal with. I'm having trouble with my knees. My right knee in particular.' I begin to relax. I've deflected the fear by focusing on something else. It's an old trick I learnt when there were no drugs, alcohol or chocolate around.

'Just keep observing your breath,' she says. If you feel pain anywhere else, keep going back to observing your breath and observing the sensations in and around your nostrils.'

'Okay, I'll give it a go.' I go through my getting up routine to ensure my knee doesn't lock in the wrong position. Halfway up I hesitate. It's not too late. But what can I say? She'll know I didn't want to admit to killing a mosquito and that will be twice as bad.

'Is there something else?' she asks.

She knows, she knows, she knows. 'No,' I answer. 'Just find it a bit hard to get up sometimes.'

I leave the room, walking in slow motion, heavy and thick. She asked me straight out, 'Is there something else?' and I said, 'No.' I lied. I lied, and it's too late to take the lie back. It's out there. Along with the killing. I came to confess a sin and I've left not absolved of one but guilty of two.

I cannot stand myself or the whining in my head. *I've broken two precepts, they'll kick me out, I've fucked up, there's no hope for me.* I had my chance and I blew it. Like I always do. I am exhausted by this crap. Tired beyond measure. I want to sleep, to snore through the afternoon meditation like my roommate. But I refuse to lie down. I've done enough wrong already. Instead, when the bell rings for the next meditation session, I sit, straight-backed in my room and let my mind wander. I can't control it anyway.

If I won that twenty-two million dollars I'd buy a house right on the beach. A huge deck where I could watch the ocean and the sky. An outside bathroom with a deep bath, big enough for two but no more. I tried a ménage à trois once thinking I was adventurous and sophisticated. I wasn't.

What else would I have in my dream home? I grew up in a house with a huge stone fireplace dominating the lounge room. I loved lighting the fires: the first flame licking through the paper, the kindling catching alight, the flames growing, the logs starting to burn, the pops and cracks as the wood heated up and ignited. Even though this is Queensland, it still gets cold a couple of nights a year. I could watch an open fire for hours – it's entertainment and company. I wouldn't need a man. Be nice to share it with someone, though. In the kitchen I'd love a gas oven. Gas obeys immediately. When you turn it on it's hot and when you want it off it's gone. That's what I'd like in a man. A gasman. If I won twenty-two million I could have whatever I wanted: a piano, a conservatory, a beautiful garden and a gardening teacher with grey hair and old-fashioned manners who could teach me how to grow lemons and lettuce, crepe myrtles and plumbago, lavender and roses. Lovely. But not like my roommate. I don't want a gardening teacher who snores. I'd welcome visitors. But I'd have a guest wing, because privacy and space are important. A meditation room, with an enormous chair for meditating in. Custom built for me and my poor knees, filled with the softest goose down.

If I won all that money would I keep my little house? It would make a good investment property. My lovely little home. I hope nothing happens to it while I'm away. I didn't ask anyone to check on it or collect the mail. I don't like asking for favours. I stand on my own two feet. I hope I didn't leave anything on that I shouldn't have. I can't have left the iron on because I never iron anything. It's a waste of time. I do own an iron but it's old and there seems to be sand in it. I bought it second-hand, no use wasting money on a new one. Perhaps I left the stove on and it's glowing red-hot, setting the cupboards next to it on fire. Or maybe termites have found a way into the woodwork and will have eaten the entire house by the time I get back, munching through the frame, windowsills and doorjambs leaving nothing but dust. I'll have nowhere to live and no insurance either. No one insures against termites.

My lovely home. It took so much courage to buy it. I'd never had a mortgage, I hate being in debt, but I thought my job was secure at the time. Everything was progressing well until my solicitor put the brakes on.

'Pull out of this contract now.'

My heart stopped, my tongue stuck in my mouth. 'Why?' I managed to squeak.

'There's something wrong with the insurance. It's been in the wrong name for years. It isn't valid. Someone could have injured themselves, perhaps even five years ago, and you'd know nothing about it until they come after you for damages. They'd be within their rights if it's within the statute of limitations. If you buy this place you could be sued and lose everything. I've seen this kind of situation before.'

'Can't I fix it?'

'I can't stop you but I certainly won't help you. I want nothing to do with it and I'll put it on record that I advised you against proceeding. If it were me I wouldn't buy it. Pull out of the contract now, while you still can.'

I didn't. I persevered. With every fear I'd ever known buzzing through my body, I dealt with the insurance company, put the situation to rights, and now I own a little piece of paradise, which is probably right at this moment being consumed by fire or termites or both.

I've got to make sure my home is okay. I could make a phone

call, if phone calls were allowed. I could ask a friend to drive past. But I haven't left a set of keys with anyone and it's hard to tell if termites have eaten you out of house and home just by looking. I've heard stories of people vacuuming up against a skirting board and it disintegrating, just a thin layer of paint left holding it together. I might get home and find my house is held up by paint. I'll open the front door and be left standing with a doorknob in my hand and a pile of rubble round my feet.

There's only one thing for it. I have to leave. I've spent my life looking for a place where I felt safe. I walked through fire to make it mine and now I'm stuck in this stupid meditation centre unable to talk, forbidden from making a phone call, and incapable of protecting what's precious to me. My home. It's burning. It's being eaten. I have to get out of here. Right now.

Tears stream down my face. My nose is blocked. My body is a solid slab of tension. My knees are throbbing. My back has razors and nails slammed into it. I can't stand this. I have to go home. I keep breathing. I can't breathe through my nose but I keep breathing. One breath followed by another, followed by another. I will talk to the assistant teacher after this meditation. I won't wait for them to throw me out. I will leave of my own volition. I will go home. Home to the second-hand armchair I had reupholstered in blue. Home to the tea set that belonged to my grandmother. Home to the lemon tree I planted in the backyard, which is yet to bear fruit. I will put out the flames. I will stop the termites. I will spend the rest of my summer holiday protecting my little house. Then I will return to work, to The Hideous Mr Purvis. I will offer up my job to him. I will say, 'Take it, smash it, break it, do whatever you want with it. I have no hope left. I cannot change.'

Day Three

The rubbish is everywhere. On the verandah, in boxes, piled up around scraps of furniture. Strewn around the yard, decayed and shredded. The front door, half open, exposes the extent of it. I know the whole house will be like this: crammed full of discarded papers, files, photos and mementos. The detritus of a life. Clutter, like mud that sticks to shoes, getting thicker and heavier with every step. I stand, shoulders slumped, exhausted already. But this is my house. If I refuse to acknowledge the state it's in I will be stuck. Suffocated. Buried in the junk.

I'm woken from the dream by the first bell of the day. I lie on my back and stare into the dark. The teacher describes our minds as restless, agitated, destructive. More like wild animals creating havoc than monkeys playing in the trees. A wise person tames and trains the wild animal, he says, and uses its enormous strength for good. I long to be free of my brutal, catastrophic mind. I crave the peace and serenity I see in other people but never in myself. The teacher says we must fight our own battles. Work out our own salvation. Only I can rid myself of what he calls defilements of the mind: anger, fear, hatred, resentment. I have made this mess. Only I can clean it up. And only then will I find what I continually search for. A place where I belong.

After breakfast I stand in a queue waiting for one of the three shower cubicles to become available. All I hear is the running of water, the occasional flushing of a toilet. Strange to be in a bathroom full of women with no talking, no laughter, no gossip. At last I stand under a small trickle of cool water. There's no hot water left but it doesn't matter. The air is already warm. Another scorcher on the way. I pick up my toothbrush and discover I've left my toothpaste in my room. Fortunately someone has left theirs in the shower caddy along with their soap and shampoo. Halfway through brushing my teeth I'm struck by a thought. Is this stealing?

This is not my toothpaste. It belongs to someone else. I didn't ask them. They didn't give their permission. Toothpaste will not go back in a tube, especially when it's been used. I am stuck with the consequences of my actions. A toothpaste thief.

Stealing is in my nature. Money and food when I was a child, and in high school, shoplifting. It wasn't until I lived in Melbourne that my skills developed to a level that wouldn't see me waiting in a department store office while security rang my parents. There were two girls in my year at acting school who often wore clothes, perfume and baubles way beyond the reach of their student allowances. They dazzled me. I wanted to be like them – brave, confident and assured – much more than I wanted the beautiful and expensive items they stole. They taught me a few basic tricks, little knowing what they had unleashed.

Stealing became another addiction, the buzz and the adrenalin overruled any rational thought. I managed to talk myself to freedom from the clutches of security in a high-end designer clothing emporium in the city. Three of them worked on me but I didn't break. Deny, deny, deny. I walked out scot-free wearing a pair of stolen five hundred dollar trousers. My thievery went beyond clothes and perfumes; I stole major electrical appliances. The video of *Sweet Dreams* that had changed my musical life was played in the VHS player I'd stolen. I chose an appliance store in a suburb far from where I lived; it had boxes of VHS players piled up in the middle of the shop floor with a demonstration model on the top. I manoeuvred one of the boxes out of the pile and got it to the floor. I walked around the shop several times and when it was clear I picked up the box and walked out. No alarms, no hand clamping down on my arm as I left the store. A tram came by and I got on it, cool as the proverbial. Inside I was a mess of adrenalin, terror and gut-cramping fear. I expected the store owner to come running after the tram at any moment. Stealing did dreadful things to my endocrine system but I was hooked.

I stole for friends, I stole for my boyfriend so he'd love me, and I stole because I could. But after the thousands of dollars' worth of goods I'd lifted and got away with, I was arrested for stealing a ten dollar roll of film. Not only that, I was arrested in my boyfriend's small home town. We were on holiday, staying with his parents, and I didn't have any film for the camera. I couldn't talk my way out of that one. The evidence was in my bag. I was shunted off to the police station, where my genuine tears had an effect on the police officer. He was unused to seeing any remorse from felons in that hard-bitten working-class town. He even pleaded my case in court. I was given a good behaviour bond and no conviction. Meanwhile my boyfriend and I had to lie to his parents. It was such a small town, I'm sure someone told them, but they never mentioned it.

I thought the arrest would put an end to my shoplifting but the addiction was too strong. Eventually, though, the stress and nervous tension became overwhelming. A car door would slam in the street and I'd jump in terror. I became convinced people were following me, chasing me down the street, even if I hadn't stolen anything. Paranoia has never served me well, but in this instance at least it finally put an end to my shoplifting. But it didn't put an end to my stealing.

In Twelve Step programs they say resentment is the number one killer. When I was living in Sydney I resented having to work. I wanted to spend all my time making music and touring the country with my new band. So I stole from the source of my resentment. My job. But my job happened to be in a charity shop. I stole not only clothes, which I then sold at a second-hand shop down the road, but money straight out of the till. I wouldn't ring up some of the purchases and at the end of the day I would slip a twenty into my pocket with no one being any the wiser. That was until I got to the rooms of the Twelve Step programs. Working the steps would set me free, I was told, but working the steps would also have consequences. Steps Eight and Nine are about making amends. You make a list of all the people you have harmed, become willing to make amends, and then go and do it. But I had stolen from a charity. If I was to make amends, to tell them what I'd done, I would be charged. This time I wouldn't be let off with a warning, as I was when I was caught shoplifting. Stealing from a charity was no ten dollar roll of film. This kind of theft was sure to see me in prison. What had this Twelve Step program got me into?

My food addict sponsor recommended I talk to one of the AA

old-timers. They were more used to this type of situation. When I told the old-timer my story I had the sense he'd heard it all before. He didn't bat an eyelash.

'The Ninth Step says we are to make direct amends to the people we have harmed,' he said. 'Except when to do so would injure them or others.'

'It won't injure them.'

'But it will injure you.'

'What do you mean?'

'You are included in the *others* in the ninth step.'

'I am?' I was relieved but also disappointed. Wasn't that just a free pass for anyone working the steps?

'There is no point in causing harm to yourself if there is another way of making amends. You still need to make amends.'

'Right.' No free pass after all.

'Is there another way you could make amends?'

'I could repay the money. I could return all the clothes and goods I've taken without paying. I could slip extra money into the till quite easily. It's not as if we ever do a stocktake.'

'I suggest you take an honest look at how much money you've stolen and include the money you've made from selling the clothes. If you can return all that money, you will have made your amends.'

It was so simple. So clean. The financial hardship I went through repaying the money was nothing compared to the lightness I felt within myself. I also returned all the goods and clothes I hadn't paid for, slipped them in the back door as donations. My flat was a lot barer and my wardrobe much depleted, but the joy and freedom were immeasurable. I kept discovering things I had stolen during my shoplifting days and gave them to charity as well.

I didn't want anything in my life that had been tainted by my addiction to stealing. I was free and clear. Until today.

Today I stole someone's toothpaste. I've broken yet another of the precepts. The whining starts up again in my mind. *I've broken three precepts, they'll kick me out, I've fucked up, there is no hope for me.*

It will take a lot of effort to clean out my house if I keep shovelling the junk back in.

Usually food makes me feel better. It quashes the feelings of inadequacy and guilt. But not even a lunch of pasta bake and beetroot salad can alleviate the pain of self-condemnation. I trudge up the path to wait on the wooden bench outside the meditation hall for an interview with the assistant teacher. Third time lucky I'm hoping. I'm grateful that the hall is shaded by wide eaves. Even the kangaroos are too hot to move. They loll in the shade of the gums and stretch out in the cool dirt under the assistant teacher's' cottage. A few determined students walk the worn, dusty path through the scrub and along the wire fence. I would prefer to be having a siesta but the dream is still vivid. It's time to come clean. When it's my turn I enter the interview room and sit down in front of the assistant teacher.

'Hi.' Why hadn't I prepared a speech? My time sitting on the bench would have been better spent rehearsing instead of obsessing.

'How can I help?'

'Well, the thing is . . . it's kind of . . . I didn't mean to . . .' Sometimes I credit myself on my eloquence. Not today.

She waits.

I might get kicked out. I might have to face the humiliation of being marched back to my room, ordered to pack up my stuff and escorted to the gate. But my house needs cleaning. 'I killed a mosquito,' I say, and immediately lurch to my own defence. 'I didn't mean to, I did it instinctively, before I really knew I'd done it. Something was biting me and I slapped it without looking. I've broken the First Precept. Does that mean I have to leave?'

There is the slightest pause, but it stretches out in the heat like the kangaroos outside.

'No,' the assistant teacher says. 'Just try to be more careful next time. Don't react, think about what you are doing. You've learnt a lesson and are mindful of it. Now let it go, and try not to kill anything else.' She smiles.

'All right.' One down, two to go. 'Well, then. This morning I used someone else's toothpaste. They'd left it in the shower. But I didn't ask them, I just used it. Is that stealing? Have I broken another precept?'

Her smile remains in place. 'If you need toothpaste, you can buy some from our supplies. Lisa can help you.'

'I have toothpaste – I just didn't have it with me. But isn't what I did stealing?'

She shakes her head gently. 'Use your own toothpaste next time.'

Yes, of course, she's right. I'll use my own toothpaste. 'What if I forget my toothpaste again?'

'Just use your toothbrush and water in the interim.' Her smile is slightly strained.

'Oh yes, okay.'

The air grows still. The humidity is oppressive. I look at my hands. 'What about lying?'

She's surprised. 'Have you been talking to the other students? The Noble Silence is for your benefit, to help you with your meditation practice. You'll gain greater benefit if you observe Noble Silence.'

'No, I haven't been talking to other students. I lied to you.'

'To me?'

'Twice. I wanted to tell you about the mosquito yesterday but instead I told you I had nothing more to say. And in the meditation hall, when I told you I could bring my awareness back to my breath if my mind wanders away. I can't. My mind is all over the place. I can barely observe my breath or the sensations for a second before I'm off thinking about something else.'

Her smile is back. 'That's normal. It takes practice, and that's why you are here, to practise. Make the best use of the time you have here. Observe your breath. Breathe a little harder if you have to, to get your concentration back.'

'So you're not going to kick me out?'

'No. I think it's important you stay and keep practising. There is a lot of work to be done.'

'I'm allowed to stay?'

'Yes.'

The heaviness lifts from my shoulders. I have cleaned house. I walked through the fear. I feel liberated, free enough to ask for one more thing. 'It's about the pain . . .'

Her face settles back into its set serene appearance, but she says nothing.

'I have bad knees. I've even had an operation on the right one. I'm afraid it's going to dislocate every time I sit cross-legged.'

'Have you tried using a meditation stool?'

'No, I didn't know they were an option. I don't have one.'

'Ask Lisa to get you one from the storeroom. We have quite a few.'

'Thank you.' A meditation stool could help.

She smiles again and the interview is over. I am released back into the heat of the day. As I walk along the gravel path back to my room I remember a story the teacher told during the discourse.

A young man had been studying with the Buddha for quite some time. He listened to all the teachings and hung around the monastery but he never did any work. One day he asked the Buddha why there were so many students, nuns and monks who spent a lot of time with the Buddha and yet were not enlightened. He wanted to know why the Buddha didn't just say a magic word, or lay hands on them or mutter an incantation and grant them instant enlightenment. He wanted to know why such a great man, a fully enlightened person like the Buddha, wouldn't want them all to be enlightened too.

The Buddha smiled and asked the young man, 'Where do you live, where's your home?'

The young man told him.

'So you would have walked between here and there many times.'

'Oh yes, many times.'

'And when someone asks how to get to your home town, you could tell them, could you not?'

'Yes, naturally.'

'Do you ever hide any of the details of the journey from them?'

'No, of course not. I'd love them to visit my home, it's a lovely part of the country.'

'What do you tell them?'

'Well, it's quite easy, you go to the crossroads and take a left. Travel down that road for about ten miles until you get to the fork in the road. Take the right and keep walking for another six hours or so. You'd probably want to take a rest, there's an inn at the junction. The next day, keep walking up the hill. Over the other side is a river. Stay on the western side of the river and travel north until you get to the waterfall. Just above the waterfall, you'll find my town.'

'And do all those people who you give such clear directions to reach your home town?'

'No, how could they? Some are just curious or think they might want to visit one day. Only those who walk the path actually get there.'

'Exactly,' said the Buddha. 'Many people come to me saying they want enlightenment. I tell them how to achieve it. I don't hide anything from them and they nod their heads and say, *Oh, what a lovely path, what a lovely destination, but it really is too much work.* How can such people ever reach the final goal? All must walk the path themselves. All must do the work. I can only tell them the path I have walked myself. Anyone who takes but one step on the path is one step closer to the final goal, but you have to walk on the path yourself.'

I am on the path. I may have taken only one, imperfect, stumbling step, but I am on the path.

The meditation stool does not prove to be the salvation I had hoped for. It's little more than an angled slat of wood nailed to two smaller pieces of wood. At the next Group Sit I try using it in the approved fashion: in a kneeling position, legs tucked under, sitting on the slat with a cushion under my bottom. It takes the strain off my aching back but puts more pressure on my knees and, unpleasantly, the tops of my feet.

Within ten minutes the pain in my right knee is unbearable. I can't breathe, let alone observe my breath. I lean forward and take my weight over onto my left knee. I'm able to slip my right leg out from under the stool. I stretch my leg out in the small space between the women meditating in front of me. I can't leave it there, so I bend it and place my right foot flat on the floor. I look as though I'm proposing on bended knee. Ridiculous. But for once I don't care what people think. All I care about is lessening the pain. Now I have to figure out what to do with my hands. If I let them dangle my wrists hurt and the blood pools in my fingers. If I rest them on my thighs my wrists are bent and the circulation is restricted, resulting in pins and needles. I clasp them in my lap and hope for the best.

We're packed into the hall. A seething, sweating mass of bodies. All of us battling with the pain and heat. The rustling of leaves outside, the gentle padding of the kangaroos, the creaking of the hall itself as it expands under the relentless sun should be the only sounds we can hear – but they are not. I've identified several types of meditators. There are the sighers. I don't know if they're breathing hard deliberately, as we've been told to do by the teacher if we get distracted, but occasionally they'll take a deep breath through their nose and then exhale quite dramatically. There are the burpers. Their tummies rumble and squeak. The air rises and finally there is a small explosion. Some burpers muffle it by keeping their mouths closed. Others open their mouths and let the burps fly free. And then there are the swallowers. These are the most aggravating of all. The sound of a swallow in a silent meditation hall is nauseating. The trouble with swallowers is they keep doing it. They are never content with just one. I want to smack them in the throat.

The farters are lighthearted in comparison, little ripples and humorous pops. My dad was an enthusiastic farter. He always left the room to do it. It made us kids laugh. Did he really think we couldn't hear those long, loud and tuneful bottom burps in the next room? For all his faults, he was a gentle man. His desire to avoid confrontation played to my advantage when, at the age of thirteen, I decided I didn't like him. I refused to talk to him and left the room whenever he came in. Why? I was thirteen. When I was doing Step Nine with my mum, making amends for all the pain I'd caused her, being thirteen was on the list.

I expected her to say, 'Don't be silly, dear, you were just being a typical teenager.'

Instead she paused and said, 'Thank you, dear, it was a difficult year. We never knew what to do. We had to walk on eggshells the whole time.'

That's when I realised how truly horrible I had been. But my father never once complained. One of the many counsellors I went to tried to convince me my father had molested me when I was little. She insisted I didn't remember it. Repressed memories were all the rage that year. I never went back to that counsellor again.

My eclectic musical taste is due to the treasures I found in my father's record collection. As a child I would explore his shelves of neatly catalogued vinyl, dipping into Fats Waller, Old English lute songs, Broadway tunes and Bob Marley and the Wailers. His only indulgences were a good sound system and his World Record Club membership.

He had always suffered from asthma. Always had his puffer close by in case of an attack of the wheezes. A bad bout saw him in hospital when I was a kid. It was confusing and awkward to see my dad all tucked up in bed when he was the one who usually tucked me in. It was even harder to see him become more and more childlike in his final years. I wouldn't recognise his voice on the phone, it was so small. And when I'd come home to visit he was more helpless each time. His skin so thin and puffy from the cortisone, he could hardly move without bleeding. I was living in Melbourne when he died. Cancer had weakened him but it was the asthma that killed him. He was only sixty-one. The phone rang early on my mother's birthday. I thought it strange that she was ringing me and not the other way round. Even though I knew something was askew, and whatever it was it was not going to be good, I sang her 'Happy Birthday'.

'Thank you, darling,' her voice was soft and gentle. 'But that's not why I'm calling.'

'I didn't think so.'

'Your father . . .' She stumbled just for a moment and I knew. I knew his struggle, his brave face, his pain, his helplessness, his frustration and his sadness were over. I also knew his funny laugh, his quirks, his gentleness and generosity were gone too.

'I'm coming down,' I said.

'Oh, darling, there's no rush. Just get here when you can.'

'I'm flying down today, I'll be there this afternoon.'

'That would be wonderful.' Her voice was small and tired. The only man she'd ever loved was dead.

Through the hard years of their marriage, the mean times and the shaky periods, my mother was steadfast. She hadn't minded looking after him when the cancer bit. He chose to go with radiation rather than hormone therapy because the hormones would make him impotent. I marvelled at them, still at it, after all those years. He recovered well enough for them to take their dream trip to Europe and the Holy Land and to visit my brother in Turkey. Afterwards his health declined again. My parents moved to a smaller place, our family home and garden being beyond his strength. Slowly, slowly the life ebbed out of him.

I wrote a song. I called it 'Strange Homecoming'. It took me two years to finish it. Grief has its own timetable.

Never see your face again, never see your smile,
Never have the chance to just sit and stay a while, stay a while.
A phone call in the morning, too early to be good news,
'Oh, Jesus, there's no easy way to say this, no easy way to say it.
But I make her say it anyway, and I know the words that she will choose,
Forty years of marriage and six children,
Now to be the bearer of bad news, bad news.
Strange kind of homecoming 'cos it's not home without you there,
Keep thinking that I'll see you, out in the garden, or sitting in your favourite chair.
My brother's eyes are red, my sister's eyes are blue,
We're all thinking the same thing, what's our mother going to do, what's she gonna do?
She spent her days looking after him, so like a child he was again,
Now her days are like a strange and lonely river,
That she must learn to navigate and then,
Those sleepless nights, that never end.
Two years later and I'm still crying in the mornings,
Someone said it never goes away.

The man who loved me since before I can remember,
And he died while I was away,
No chance to say,
It's okay.

It was another year before I could sing 'Strange Homecoming' without sobbing. Of all the songs I ever wrote and recorded this was the one that garnered record company interest. But I wouldn't sign their contract. Not for that song, not under their conditions. I would not give them total control and sign away my power of veto. I thought they'd rewrite the contract. They didn't. Instead they told me I was too difficult to work with. I caught the train home from their office. Graffiti on an overpass read *God provides*. I didn't think so. Not when I'd just blown the only recording contract I'd ever been offered.

When the chanting starts at the end of the meditation, even while the teacher is going on about *dirty birdies* and *naked judges*, I start disentangling my left leg from the meditation stool. I perch on the stool, trying to find a spot on my bottom that doesn't hurt. I fail. I long to stand and stretch. Ease the tension of half-kneeling in pain for the past hour. Finally the chant is over and the other students bow. I decide not to. The path to my hometown does not include bowing.

Apart from the sighers, burpers, swallowers and farters in the hall there are also the sniffers and the occasional sobber. Someone is crying behind me now. The sob gets caught up in her throat and she almost breaks the Noble Silence. I sneak a glance at her. She blows her nose, trying to hide behind her long dark hair. She stands and walks quickly towards the door. A muslin curtain covers the inside of the doorway to stop too much sunlight glaring into the meditation hall. The door is already open when she reaches it, the light muted by the curtain. She reaches up to pull the curtain aside. The sun creates an aura around her body. She looks like a sad dark-haired angel returning to heaven. I wish her well. I like her because she's not a serene, straight-backed perfect meditator. She's messy around the edges like me, and like me, she's not having a good time.

Day Four

At breakfast the anticipation is palpable. Today everything will change. A restless excitement infects everyone. Even the kangaroos suddenly take off in long loping bounds towards the scrub and out of sight. Over the past three days, while doing the *anapana* meditation, we have been preparing for what is about to happen. We've been practising morality within the bounds of the precepts and mastering our minds within the bounds of our breath. I hope the other students have done better than me. The teacher says we have been developing our wisdom, firstly through what he calls 'received wisdom' – the theory he's been teaching us, then by intellectual wisdom – examining what we've been taught t to decide whether it is logical and beneficial. At the next meditation we will enter the secret realm of the Vipassana world, the field of experiential wisdom. This is the only wisdom that can liberate. After that I will become enlightened and peaceful. I will shine as a loving beacon to all and they will find rest in my presence. Today, after I learn the Vipassana technique, the pain will leave my body and I will meditate as serenely as the straight-backed woman in front of me. She is an old student, she already knows this technique. That's her secret and soon I will know it too.

In the meditation hall we settle slowly like sediment in a glass. Finally, when the shuffling becomes sporadic rather than constant, the assistant teacher clicks the switch on the CD player and the teacher's voice fills the hall.

'Concentrate on a spot at the top of the head, the top of the head.' His voice is almost a song. 'Be aware of all the sensations in that spot, a spot no bigger than a fingertip. What sensations do you feel? Might be heat, might be cold, might be tingling, a tickling sensation, might be a sensation like ants crawling, ants crawling.'

His voice is like a chant, filling the room with tingles, tickles and ants. The top of my head is very obedient: it's hot, cold, tingling, throbbing and crawling. What's going to happen next? Will a portal open in my head? Will white light stream from the skies and enter my brain, granting me instant illumination, grace and happiness?

The teacher continues. 'Slowly begin to work your way down, work your way down, slowly until your attention takes in the entire scalp area, the entire scalp area.'

Perhaps my whole head will dissolve. Perhaps the tightness of anxiety, resentment, fear and disappointment will dissolve with it, in a mass of tingling bubbles, and I will float away to become one with all.

By the time we've moved through the forehead, eyebrows,

eyes, cheeks, nose, chin, neck and we're on to the arms, I get the general idea. The disappointment is crushing. Vipassana is no more than a basic relaxation technique I've done hundreds of times in every acting class I've ever attended. Except it's not relaxing. I'm hot and my buttocks throb with pain. By the time we get to the toes, I'm ready to throw up and throw in the towel. The bile of resentment rises in my throat. I swallow it down as noisily as any of the swallowers around me who've been annoying me for days. I've done this technique before, it's nothing new. It didn't lead to enlightenment. It just led to the rest of an acting class.

Acting school and I didn't really suit each other. I only went because I got in. It all started in infant school with the nativity play. I was cast as Mary and the buck-toothed boy I had a crush on was Joseph. He completely froze on stage and I had to feed him his lines. I still thought he was wonderful. In my lonely primary school years I was in a couple of plays, but in high school we had a brilliant drama teacher who, of course, I was a little bit in love with. He noticed me. He gave me good roles. I starred alongside students who were older than me and got great reviews in the school paper. The only place I really felt at home in high school was in those theatrical productions.

By the time I got to the Victorian College of the Arts in Melbourne I had spent more hours on stage playing in bands than I had acting. But the little bit of amateur and professional acting I had done left me convinced I could do better. Yes, I could act but I wasn't very good. So I auditioned, and to my great surprise, got in. Later the teachers at the VCA admitted they didn't know what to do with me. And as for me, I longed to be back playing in bands. I stayed for the required three years because they never kicked me out, even when I submitted a cassette of four of my songs as my thesis piece. And I would have been labelled ungrateful if I quit. We were told constantly how special we were, so many others had auditioned and not been accepted. If I left of my own volition it would have been like spitting in their faces. So I stayed.

It's not only the bogus relaxation technique that reminds me of acting school exercises. It's also the emphasis in Vipassana of being in the moment. Our mad monkey minds go all over the place, swinging from tree to tree, chattering away, dwelling on the past, worrying about the future, making us miserable, causing our suffering. The teacher says living in the present moment is the answer to our suffering. At acting school the teachers said it was the key to a great performance. *Be in the moment, be in the moment.* That's all I heard day after day for three years. It almost sent me mad. Literally.

Late one night, after a long day of struggling to *be in the moment,* I walked alone to the tram stop. I was busily being aware of everything around me: the way the streetlights turned everything a strange shade of yellow, the sound of my boots on the footpath, the whoosh of the cars on St Kilda Road, the brush of my scarf against my cheek. Two people waiting at the tram stop began talking to each other.

'She doesn't get it, she doesn't realise what she has to do,' said the first one.

The second one agreed. 'All she has to do is open her eyes to what's going on around her.'

I'd never seen them before, I didn't know them, but I knew they were talking about me. This was a test. I had to open my eyes, I had to pay attention. They wore overcoats and scarves and stood in the shadow of the streetlight. I couldn't see their faces but I knew they wanted me to listen. The tram braked in front of us with the sound of metal on metal. They stepped to one side and let me on first. Was this another test? The light inside the tram was harsh. I paid my fare and walked through the almost empty carriage to a seat halfway down. The other two spoke to the driver, angled away from me so even in the light I couldn't make out their faces. But I could hear their words.

'Will this tram take us where we want to go?' one of them asked.

'All the way, but you have to pay attention, otherwise you'll end up at the depot,' answered the driver. 'This is my last run tonight.'

This was a message, just for me. But what did it mean?

An old lady sitting at the front of the tram leant forward in her seat towards them. 'We've all got to keep our eyes open these days, don't we, and our ears,' she cackled.

Oh my God. She was in on it too. Everyone on the tram had a message for me. Everyone was there for the express purpose of guiding me. I had to keep my eyes and ears open. I had to pay attention. For too long I'd missed the clues. I'd been blind, insensitive, ignorant. All the people on the tram had been put there for my benefit. I mustn't screw this up.

The tram moved off, and as it did I had the sensation of a tunnel opening in front of me. A strange energy tingled through my skin. My chest tightened. I held my breath. It was as if I were being sucked into a vortex. The two at the front of the tram turned and walked towards me. They were surrounded by light but still I couldn't see their faces. Everything would be made clear in a moment. In a second they would be right in front of me. The pull of the tunnel became greater. Light bent around me. Everything outside the tram was a dark blur. The energy dragged me forward with a power I'd never felt before. I realised this was it, this was the moment. I had to make a decision. If I went into this tunnel of light it would take me to a reality different to any other I'd known. But not only that, a reality different to any that my friends and family knew. If I went into this tunnel, all those who knew me would never know me again. They would think me mad. I would be existing on a different level of consciousness, a level they wouldn't understand. A feeling of intense grief gripped me. The thought of being separated from them filled me with sadness. A tear rolled onto my cheek. The sensation shocked me back into my body. The tunnel of light disappeared. The two people from the tram stop walked straight past me and the tram kept trundling along its track. In less than a second the extraordinary became ordinary again. I got off at my stop and went home to the life I knew. Not a powerful tunnel of shining light, but a share house in suburban Melbourne.

A few months later one of my housemates wrote a note and left it on my bed. *Someone should drop an anvil on your head.* So much for being in the moment. Apparently I never noticed what was going on around me, including bills that needed paying and dirty dishes in the sink.

Finally the agony and disappointment is over and we are released into the full heat of the day. Vipassana had revealed itself to be nothing more than bog ordinary. This technique is never going to help me with The Hideous Mr Purvis. It is never going to help me soar above his behaviour. What am I supposed to do next time he undermines or belittles me? Think about a fingertip-sized bit of the top of my head? Useless nonsense. I can't understand why anyone would come here and subject themselves to ten days of torture just to learn this.

I limp down the gravel path towards the toilets and stand in a silent line with the rest of the female students. Are they as disappointed as I am? What gets me is the old students already knew what they were in for and yet they have come back for more of the same. It makes no sense at all. I have hardly pulled my trousers up before the bell rings out again. What am I supposed to do now? I'm almost halfway through the course. I have invested heavily in this. Once again it reminds me of acting school. I haven't been kicked out and I would appear ungrateful now if I left. Perhaps there is more to come. Perhaps that was not the entire technique. Perhaps something else will be revealed. I walk back up the path.

Outside the meditation hall, as I'm taking off my sandals, I notice a new sign on the board beside the door. I read it greedily. I have reading deprivation. Reading is regarded as a distraction but I don't care, it's a delicious one and I miss it. I've read the Introduction to the Technique and Code of Discipline on average three times a day and I read the course timetable every two hours at least. I've read all the signs around the centre many times. There are many of them, due to the Noble Silence, I expect. Every day on the noticeboard outside the dining hall a new word is explained. Recently the definition of *samadhi* was given: concentration, control of one's mind, the second of the three trainings by which the Noble Eightfold Path is practised. I need a lot more *samadhi* to control my untamed mind. I stare at the new sign and read it over and over. The sign asks students not to use strong perfumes or scents because it can disturb fellow meditators. I wonder if it is directed specifically at me and my protection from psychic vampires.

I'm always going to naturopaths and alternative healers, looking for a cure for being me. I've been offered all kinds of advice, but one naturopath told me something so bizarre, it knocked everything else out of the picture. Apparently I had a hole in my aura at the nape of my neck and unless I did something about it I was easy pickings for psychic vampires. She advised me to rub sandalwood oil on the spot every day, otherwise it was mental and emotional curtains for me. I was so taken aback I didn't even question it. To this day, every morning after moisturising and before deodorising, I rub sandalwood oil on that little bump at the base of my neck, and so far so good. No psychic vampires. But what if I were to go without my protection from them? Is it safe here? I know the kind of evil thoughts that rampage through my monkey mind and a lot of them are murderous. Surely a little bit of smelly psychic protection won't do any harm? With the hot days, no rain, brief showers, a shortage of buckets for doing laundry and the ban on sensory camouflage, I worry that other kinds of scents may become more disturbing. I already smell bad even to myself. Sweat and pain are a potent mix.

Later that afternoon I meditate in my room while the old woman snuffles in her sleep. Early in the course the teacher had mentioned such snuffling.

'A warning,' he said. 'Take rest when you are very tired during meditation in your room, but for no longer than five minutes. But you might think you can keep observing your breath while lying down. Five minutes becomes ten and then fifteen. Very soon you are doing a snoring meditation. Someone else in your dormitory thinks, *what a good idea,* and they start a snoring meditation also. Soon it becomes a snoring dormitory, and then a snoring meditation centre. Ah no.' He shook his head with a smile. 'No snoring meditations. Your job is to remain alert, awakened. Five minutes rest only.'

Clearly the old woman had slept through that particular instruction.

The fan buzzes ineffectively in the corner. I try to go through my body *piece by piece, part by part*, as the teacher instructed. All it does is make me itchy. I need to stretch my legs and go to the toilet. It's hot outside. Hot and dusty. More tents have sprung up on the dry grass behind the accommodation blocks. Every day new meditators arrive, filling up the hall and the dining room. The queues for everything get longer. As I walk past the laundry trough and the rows of buckets full of soaking laundry I see something extraordinary. An empty bucket. I walk steadily back to my room, trying not to break into a run. Running is not allowed. But what if I get back there with my dirty underwear and smelly shirts only to discover that someone has got to the bucket before me? My pace quickens. I grab my plastic bag of dirty washing and return to the toilet block. The bucket is still there, invitingly empty. I fill it with cold water and a small amount of soap powder, sloshing it around until it lathers. I submerge my underwear and a couple of shirts in the cool water. I sniffed the crotch of a pair of trousers this morning, thinking perhaps I could wear them one more time. I was wrong. In they go. Doing handwashing has never been so satisfying.

Footsteps crunch on the gravel path and I turn to see Lisa

walking towards me. Pushing my clothes into the soapy water once more, I lift the bucket out of the trough and put it on the ground next to all the other buckets full of soaking clothes. I'll come back at teatime to rinse them out, when everyone else is eating their two pieces of fruit or sipping their *Old Students Only* drink. That way I'll avoid the queue for the laundry tub.

Lisa approaches. 'You are not supposed to do your washing during meditation times,' she says, her voice low.

I know this. There are signs in and outside the bathroom saying exactly that. I've read them many times. My excitement at finding an empty bucket got the better of me.

'I'm sorry. There are never any buckets and I wanted to grab this one while I had the opportunity.' The words feel awkward in my mouth and I realise I'm whispering.

'No washing during meditation hours,' she repeats. 'If you can't find a bucket, come and see me.'

'Oh. Okay.' I feel like I'm eight years old again. Bad girl. 'Sorry,' I say and wipe my wet hands on my trousers.

I creep back to my room like a whipped dog. My roommate is still snoring. I don't understand. How can she be so carefree about flouting the meditation rules, yet the one time I do something wrong I get sprung? The old woman stirs in her sleep and rolls over, away from the wall to face me. I find it difficult to meditate. I know she's asleep but when I close my eyes I can't help feeling she's spying on me. A room to myself would be heaven. I grew up without any privacy, always sharing rooms, always being interrupted, not even being able to go to the toilet without someone banging on the door. Such is life in a big family.

If I won that twenty-two million dollars I'd have to take care of my family first. Three brothers and two sisters all waiting with expectation and envy. I'd have to give them enough to make them feel satisfied. Would a million each do it? Probably not, but it would be a start. My mum would be fine. She wouldn't expect anything. 'Don't worry about me, darling,' she'd say. 'I have everything I need.' And she'd mean it. Living alone in her tiny flat with a view of the church roof. The church where she's been a faithful member for most of her life. She's mellowed in later life. The rampant Christianity has been replaced with a quiet, steady faith. More open to other religions and ways of being, possibly because she's more secure in hers. I feel a tear squeeze under my eyelashes. Why am I crying? I love my mum but I always feel as though I'm not quite what she hoped for. Hope is supposed to be a good thing, the thing with feathers that perches in your soul and never stops singing. But the weight of hope is heavy, the leaden thud of disappointment a constant echo.

I was her last child and so she pinned her last hopes on me. I could never deliver on that expectation and spent the rest of my life with an ache so deep it was like a cold shadow I couldn't recognise, let alone name. 'My baby,' she called me, but couldn't even see me when I became a wild, dirty child. Stealing and secretive. Maybe it was because I really wasn't a prophet after all. Maybe it was because I cut myself off from the happy-clappy Christians and called them hypocrites. But everything I did felt like a disappointment.

The excitement of being at acting school was quashed by my perception of my parents' expectation that I become a doctor or a lawyer. All that money spent on a private school education just to end up on the stage. I took my parents to task. Dad said, 'Darling, we just want you to be happy.' My mother stayed quiet.

I knew my first major relationship was a huge disappointment to her. A bearded bass player eleven years older than me. I fell in love with his bass playing and stayed for the sex. He was the first man to treat me with gentleness. He taught me to enjoy sex and with him I felt safe enough to do so. It was a revelation. But still he couldn't believe I'd chosen him. My mother couldn't believe it either. She was appalled that I was sleeping with him and told me she'd always regard that relationship as my first marriage. When she finally got to meet him she was even more appalled.

'Really, darling,' she said. 'Did you have to choose someone who looks so much like your father!'

I was incredulous. Yes, they both had big noses and straggly teeth, and they were both balding. But apart from that they looked completely different.

The air of disapproval followed into my next major relationship. Another musician who clearly wasn't good enough. I didn't dare tell her I was living with him. Luckily by that stage I was in Melbourne and secrets were easier to hide.

But through all the years of rebellion I did try to gain her approval in an overt and physical way. My sisters may have chosen the thin life and all that entailed, but I chose to be loyal to my mother. *See how much I love and admire you, Mum. I love you so much I want to be just like you. My sisters don't really love you. They want to be thin. But look, here's the proof of how much I love you. See. I'm fat, just like you.*

Just before the bell is due to be struck for the next Group Sit through the open window of my room I hear the sounds of the other women getting ready: footsteps crunching on the gravel path outside, the screen door to the bathroom opening and closing, taps being turned on and off. Going to the toilet without having to queue is a priority. The old woman keeps snoring. She'll leave her move as late as possible. I stretch and give my bottom a bit of a massage, knowing there's a lot worse to come.

Lisa waits beside the pile of shoes outside the meditation hall. She ticks my name on her list as I slip off my sandals and pull the curtain aside. The area by the windows is now two rows deep with newly arrived meditators and there are more mats and cushions set up near the aisle, making it trickier to negotiate the path to my spot. As I tiptoe past the others in my row I look for the dark hair of the crying girl. Gone. Perhaps she too was disappointed by the unveiling of this so-called special meditation technique. She realised it would never set her free so she set herself free instead. Her spot has been claimed by a mousy brown head with a sprinkling of grey, a compact body and the shawl of an experienced meditator. The old students have special shawls, usually white, that are light and soft. I wonder where they buy them from and if you're only allowed to have one once you've proved your meditation prowess, kind of like a black belt in karate. I'm wearing a Hawaiian shirt, for God's sake, and a pair of crinkly cotton elastic-waisted pants I bought from an op shop.

The meditation begins. The teacher instructs us again on how to meditate Vipassana style. Once again the disappointment thumps me in the guts. The pain builds in my buttocks, my left knee, my right foot, my hands and my back. I'm not supposed to focus on them. Instead I start at the top of the head and work down to my toes, then start at the top of the head again. If the pain gets too much, go back to the breath, just observe the breath. Through the body, part by part, piece by piece, over and over, in the heat, with the burpers, sighers and swallowers. But no crying girl. She has gone. I miss her even though I never met her. 'Be happy, be happy,' the teacher says at the end of each evening's discourse. I wish her happiness wherever she is.

I keep breathing and observing sensations. As the heat and pain build within my body the strangest thing happens. Energy courses along the routes I've been mapping with my mind, from the top of my head to the tips of my toes. I feel as though I'm sitting under a gushing tap. It's extraordinary and overpowering. The force almost knocks me sideways. I've never felt the power of the energy in my body like this before. It pours through my skin, wave after wave starting in my scalp, running through my arms, body and legs, down through my toes. A constant stream of sensations that I have access to for the very first time. Perhaps this is it, the mystery of Vipassana.

After the meditation the new students are called to the front for a quick check-in with the assistant teacher. I can hardly wait to tell her about my breakthrough. She'll be so impressed. I know I am. Patiently I wait my turn with my right knee propped up on an extra cushion.

At last she turns to me. 'Mary-Lou, are you able to feel sensations throughout the body?'

'Yes, it's amazing,' I whisper excitedly.

'Good. Keep practising. Continuity of practice is the secret to success.' She turns to the student beside me.

Is that all? *Good?* And then a quote from the teacher? He's always saying continuity of practice is the secret to success. Well, I think I've grasped that concept and I want to tell her more.

'It's like a tap.' I whisper a bit louder to get her attention. 'Like a tap.'

She turns back to me.

'Like a tap, flowing incredibly fast through my body.'

She nods and smiles. She turns again to the next student.

I'm astounded. I thought she'd be as excited as I am. I thought she'd at least say, *Wow!* Or praise me for being such a great student. But what do I get? Nothing. I bet the other students don't have a tap flowing through them.

When she's finished talking with the last of the non-tap-experiencing students she says, 'Meditate with me,' and closes her eyes.

I bet she doesn't feel as though she's sitting under a powerful energy tap. Maybe that's why she pretended to be unimpressed. She's not so serene. She's hiding it well but she's seething with jealousy, I know it.

Here in the subtropics, twilight is short. The night slams down hard even in summer. But the break for teatime is early, like everything at the meditation centre, and it's only just after five pm. There's plenty of light left in which to rinse my clothes and hang them out. As others eat their fruit or sip their mysterious drink, I hold my hand under the tap as it fills my rule-breaking bucket of laundry. The water is cool in the last heat of the day. It trickles over my hand. I relish the sensation but it's nothing compared to the experience I had in the meditation hall. Perhaps there's something to this technique after all.

I squeeze as much water out of my clothes as I can, wringing the cloth into tight corkscrews. I was taught how to do this by the most unlikely of people. In my early days of playing in bands I was living in yet another share house in Hobart. This one was a terrace not far from the water. I had a bedroom with doors that opened onto the upstairs verandah. It had a great feel to it, peaceful and funky. I loved it, even though there was no washing machine. I washed all my clothes by hand. At least I didn't have to wait for a bucket. One washing day I had hung my clothes out to dry when my housemate's girlfriend came out into the backyard.

'No, no, no,' she said. 'This won't do at all.'

She was an odd girl. Kind of groovy but in an offbeat way. She had strong and definite opinions on everything and voiced them at every opportunity. And if the opportunity wasn't there, she voiced them anyway. I was a little afraid of her.

She unpegged one of my dripping shirts. 'Let me show you how it's done.'

She proceeded to wring out the shirt until there was not a drop of water left. I was impressed, I didn't know she possessed such skill. Her sister went on to become a very well-known fashion designer, so clearly they both knew a lot about clothes.

'Now you try,' she said. I didn't dare say no.

Under her tutelage I wrung those clothes to within an inch of their lives. The result was no drips, whereas before there had been puddles.

'Much better,' she said, spun on the heel of her black ankle-length boots and went inside to discuss politics with her equally opinionated boyfriend.

As I peg out my well-wrung clothes I'm grateful to her. She was an enigma to me, I never quite felt at ease in her presence. But she took the time to teach me a simple, practical skill. It's a wonderment, the gifts we're given along the way, the lessons we learn, if we're willing to be taught. Even that strange naturopath with her cure for the hole in my aura. I freeze in mid peg. The breath catches in my throat. I thought the sandalwood was working but that was only because I didn't know what a psychic vampire was. I realise with a shock that it doesn't matter what I dab on the nape of my neck. Elliot Purvis, a psychic vampire of the worst order, has penetrated my sandalwood defence, no problem at all.

Day Five

I wake in the early hours and check my watch. Just after two. It's the cold that has woken me. My one hundred per cent cotton sheet is not enough to keep the cool night air at bay. Quietly I rummage around in the bag at the end of my bed and find the warm rug I was instructed to bring, even though at the time I couldn't figure out why. Who needs a rug in the middle of a Queensland summer? Now I know. Inland the nights are still cool. The rug is not very big but it's better than nothing. Perhaps after the morning meditation I'll ask Lisa for a blanket. I haven't wanted to ask for anything. I don't want to appear weak and needy, like those sitting on the little plastic chairs or up against the back wall. I prefer to be self-reliant, that way you can never be let down. Besides, I haven't wanted to bother Lisa. She has enough on her plate with all the female students to look after, as well as serving the food. And yesterday, when I went to the toilet during the morning meditation, she was there scrubbing the bathroom floor.

I nestle down under my small rug. If what the teacher said in the discourse is true, about everything being made out of bubbles, then a blanket isn't going to do much good. Bubbles won't keep me warm. He was talking about impermanence and how we're made out of subatomic particles that constantly arise and pass away. Like a river. We see a river and think it is the same from moment to moment. It looks like the same river but the water that flows by us is constantly changing. And we are the same, a constantly changing mass of bubbles, arising and passing. I certainly don't feel as though I'm made out of bubbles. Even lying down my back aches. Most of the time I feel like a slab of wood: solid, dull, dense.

As usual, by the time the bell rings for breakfast after the first two-hour meditation session, the old woman is long gone. She's probably guzzling tea and toast by now. I unfold my legs, rub my knees and stretch my back. Outside the trees are grey and bleached as the heat of another blinding day builds in intensity. Even though I'm hungry I opt to have a shower before breakfast to avoid the queues. Crunching over the gravel path I glance over at the dining hall. Already many of the women sit on the verandah with their food, the magpies watching and waiting for their chance.

I'm not the only one who'd rather go hungry than stand in line. Two of the shower cubicles are already occupied, but my favourite is free. It's designed to fit a wheelchair so it's bigger than the others and an extra window lets in more light. I look down at my dusty feet. My toenails need cutting. Will I cut them now? In a place where all I do is meditate silently, with occasional breaks for food and rest, cutting my toenails rates as quite a distraction. I decide to keep it as a treat for later on, something to look forward to.

After my shower, clean and smug, I kick off my sandals and slide open the door to the dining hall. Inside a few stragglers nibble on toast or chew slices of apple. I help myself to muesli and yoghurt, pour a cup of tepid tea and move out to the verandah. Pulling my chair up to the railing, I rest my feet on a spare chair and gaze out across the grounds. The graceful woman is doing a round of the walking track. She floats through the scrub as if she's in a commercial for shampoo or fabric softener. In the evenings she drinks the mysterious old students' drink, so she must get even hungrier than me, yet I've never seen her race to the dining hall when the bell rings for breakfast. Tall and slim, perhaps she is used to going hungry. I wonder what it would be like to be so beautiful. When I was younger a man told me I would never know who my true friends were. When I asked him why, he told me it was because I was beautiful and people would use me to be close to that beauty. Even then I recognised a bad line when I heard it. He never got into my pants. But I have fallen for a bigger line. I equate beauty with goodness and moral superiority. Beautiful people are beyond the rules that govern the rest of us. They live on another plane. I have been caught in the sticky net of this myth. My oldest sister was beautiful, her face on billboards and magazines. She terrorised me when I was young, frightened me in the dark. Told me I was too old to play with dolls when I was seven and scorned me for trying to sunbake with her and my other sister when I was eleven. 'You're too fat to sunbake,' she said. But she was beautiful and idolised by many. Her beauty took her around the world, gave her access to more money than I could imagine. She always looked good, therefore she must be good. I always looked bad. Bad girl.

The teacher told a story about beauty. A man had a beautiful wife, oh so beautiful. She thought she was pretty hot too. She had long, shiny hair, such beautiful hair. But one night the man found one of her hairs in his food.

'Oh, dirty hair, disgusting hair,' he said. 'What is this hair doing in my food? Now I must throw my dinner out.'

She also had beautiful fingernails, long and painted red. But one night he found a piece of her fingernail in his soup.

'Oh, what is this in my soup? Disgusting fingernail.'

And she had beautiful teeth, white shiny teeth. What a beautiful smile, what wonderful teeth, like pearls. But if a tooth fell out? 'Disgusting tooth. I will not keep this tooth, it is no precious jewel. No. I will throw this out.'

The teacher talked about the illusion of physical beauty: superficial, apparent reality, not the truth. Attachment to something so ephemeral will only cause misery. He is right, of course. But my attachment remains.

I rub the back of my neck and ease the tension in my shoulders. I'm going to need a good massage when this is all over. Some of the women have chosen to sit or sprawl on the grass beside the dining hall, braving the copious amounts of kangaroo poo. The dried pellets are everywhere, making stretching out on the ground more of an obstacle course than a relaxing experience. Every break time there is a race for the few wooden benches scattered through the grounds. Grey with age, they offer no comfort, not even a back support for our aching bodies. But still they are highly sought after. These benches provide a seat away from the kangaroo dung and the ticks we have been warned about, lurking in the grass and the scrub. The older sister stumps over to the walking track, her face an angry mask. Up the hill slightly to my left the queue is forming outside the bathroom. Students with their wash bags wait for a shower. I look for Bernadette but I don't see her.

Today is going to be a scorcher. I'm sweating already. The birds wait for my attention to waver and their chance to steal a beakful of my breakfast. They won't be so lucky today. I realise how hungry I am and tuck in. In between bites I notice a woman sitting on the grass, braving the dung and the ticks. She leans back on her elbows and stretches her legs out in front of her. Her shawl slips from her shoulders and I see the outline of her body. Her rather large body. Either she's been drinking too much beer or she's very pregnant. I'm amazed I haven't noticed her before. I know I'm not supposed to be looking at anyone, but I am surprised I haven't caught a glimpse of her bountiful belly.

Babies, children. My mother had so many, it's hardly seemed necessary for me to have any. I've assumed one day I'll meet my perfect man and he'll already have kids from a previous marriage. Because his biological imperative will already have been met, he won't want or expect me to reproduce his genes. But Mr Perfect hasn't made an appearance yet and I'm about to turn forty-two.

A boyfriend once said to me, 'I can hear your biological clock ticking.'

'Well, your hearing must be better than mine,' I replied. 'Because I don't hear a thing.'

They don't last long, the boyfriends. I need too much space and permission to be vague about commitment. It's not satisfying for them in the long run, I know, but I can't change it. I think it's freedom. It is, isn't it? Freedom means being alone, independent, being able to do whatever, whenever. No one relying on me. No one looking me in the eye with a question that demands answering. Kids do a lot of that, as well as boyfriends. I have decided children aren't for me. I'd never be able to give them all the attention I wanted when I was young and never got. I'm too scared I'll pass on my predisposition to addiction. Why would I want to bring a child into the world who'd be as miserable as I was, and still am?

Strange how life has a way of giving you what you thought you didn't want but turns out to be the best thing you could have hoped for. Or as a friend of mine said, 'How do you make God laugh? Tell Her your plans.'

My sister adopted a baby girl but her partner died not long after. Distraught and terrified, she put her daughter up for adoption again. It broke her heart but she thought it was for the best. She wasn't coping, her nerves had betrayed her, and her daughter needed a stable home. We spent hours going over the pros and cons while my sister knotted herself deeper into fear and confusion. It became clear to me that she didn't want to give her daughter up.

'What if I help take care of her?' I asked. 'Would you keep her?' It was the simplest of questions but it changed my life.

My sister's response was immediate and heartfelt. 'Yes.'

I knew nothing about babies or children. In the past I had kept friends with children at arm's length. I didn't want anything interrupting my social plans. Now I searched out these very same friends and their generosity astounded me. Nappies, car seats, feeding and fever advice, childcare, toys. My home was transformed and so was my heart. This small being. So precious, such a miracle. And in the future, if regret at not having children of my own might ever have become an issue, it has been nipped in the bud. My sister does most of the caring but I help share the load and in return I have the gift of a child in my life. This child astounds me and amazes me. I am blessed. She loves me and I adore her with a ferocity that sometimes scares me. No harm will come to her, I'll make sure of it. I demand it. I wonder now how she is. I miss her and I worry. When I'm not obsessing about winning Lotto or my house burning down, or The Hideous Mr Purvis, I worry about my young, defenceless niece. I imagine scenarios where she is drowning, or run over by a car, kidnapped or worse. The screaming in my head drives me to distraction. And that is what it is. A distraction. In a place where there are none, I make them up. I cannot stand being still in my own mind. It seems I am incapable of it.

Later that afternoon, when the bell is still resonating from calling us to the Group Sit, some students are already in the meditation hall, settled and breathing. I hesitate outside the door, wanting to leave it for just a little while longer. Luckily there's yet another new notice on the board outside the hall. *Please leave all water bottles outside the meditation hall.* I read it four times just for the pure pleasure of reading.

Does this mean hot water bottles? I've seen some of the students, including the older sister, filling up hot water bottles from a kettle in the bathroom and been puzzled by it. The heat of the days is intense, why would you want a hot water bottle? Period pain perhaps? Or other pain? I should try one on my back. Or perhaps the signs refer to drinking water? I keep mine beside me at all times, drinking frequently to replace the sweat that trickles and sticks in the humidity. Among the silent shoes at my feet is a collection of bottles, so I guess that must be it. My faithful friend will have to stay outside. Slowly I take off my shoes and leave them with the rest. Lisa stands at the door with her clipboard. She knows what I'm up to. Delaying sitting for as long as possible.

There are others who are tardier than me. They hover just outside the shade of the hall, stretching and waiting until the last possible moment. I long to join them but Lisa has already ticked my name off her list. Reluctantly I place my water bottle next to my shoes and walk through the door into the cooler gloom of the hall.

'Start again, start again,' says the teacher on the CD. 'Start with a calm and quiet mind.'

How I long for one of those.

'A peaceful and equanimous mind.'

Equanimous? What kind of word is that? I've never heard of it. He's made it up. Equanimity, yes, but equanimous? That's what we're supposed to be. Through the pain. Equanimous. Stupid word. I don't want to be a word I don't even believe exists. As soon as I get out of here I'm going to look it up in a dictionary. Then I'll read the whole dictionary just because I can. I hope the tap turns on again today. I long to feel those powerful sensations flowing through my body. Anything but the pain. The straight-backed girl in front of me confounds me. She never moves. Her posture is always perfect. I slump and I sway. The swaying is ridiculous. I don't know what happens but I find myself swinging from side to side and have to open my eyes to make it stop. My body doesn't know how to handle this amount of sitting, this amount of pain, this amount of attention. I normally try to avoid thinking about my body but here I have to focus on it, part by part, piece by piece, endlessly. My right leg is bent in front of me, propped up on a leaning tower of cushions. I should have sued that disco with its plastic floor and bubble machine. Clearly they had never heard of occupational health and safety. I was so naive. I even went back to work after a few days with a knee three times its normal size. I was waitressing, for God's sake. Waitressing with a limp. On my feet for those eight-hour shifts. Damaging my poor knee even more. I didn't know any different, I was too young. It was my first job. I didn't know about medical certificates, sick leave or litigation. Or maybe it was the drugs.

I finished school in Hobart not knowing what I wanted to do with my life. My parents agreed a gap year would be a good thing and that I could spend it in Sydney. My asthmatic sister was living there in a family-owned apartment close to Kings Cross. I moved into the sunroom, big enough for a single bed and not much more. A friend of my father's had written a letter of introduction to take to the manager of a large hotel in the city. I was given a job even though I had no experience. I got up early every morning to feed plates of pancakes with eggs, bacon and maple syrup to hungry American tourists. I made friends with one of my fellow waitresses. Melanie wasn't much older than me but she had years of experience in areas unknown to me until then. She introduced me to a world I'd never encountered in my small-town private-school existence. Her boyfriend was a drug dealer and so were all his friends. From the Middle East, they had grown up with bombs, bullets and shrapnel wounds. The only reason they got to grow up at all was because they were survivors, hardened and cunning by the time they were ten years old. After a short time living in Australia they came to believe that Australians were weak and vain, mouthing platitudes and pretending to be strong but in truth nothing but soft-bellied mewling infants. They despised us, mocked us, regarded our laws and lawmakers as powerless and made a killing in the drug market in more ways than one.

I liked Melanie, she had a smile and warmth that was compelling. Even though I was out of my depth with her boyfriend and his compatriots, I found myself spending more and more time with them because of my friendship with her. The men didn't mind having me around. I was young, white and a virgin. Quite a prize. They gave me drugs and let me play along. I couldn't really take it seriously. It all seemed like a movie. I guess the drugs helped in that regard. A month or so after I damaged my knee I received my first ever tax return. It was enough to toss in my job. I didn't need much money. My sister and I lived rent free in the family-owned apartment, I got drugs for nothing and I was hardly eating. My sister was studying dance in the city and we never saw each other much at the best of times. Our lives were lived at opposite ends of the day. I hung out in the back street hotel the dealers and their girls lived in, sleeping through the days and drifting through the nights. Our preferred nightclub was a twenty-four hour disco under the Coca Cola sign at the entrance to the Cross. It was there Mahmoud, one of the dealers, smashed a man's face with a baseball bat. I was tripping and watched with wide black eyes as blood flew through the air in sharp triangles of red. The girls in the gang were given a bodyguard, an Australian bikie whose brain was fried from too much acid. He was strong but ineffective. All he gave us was the illusion of safety. We were only allowed to be seen on one side of Kings Cross. The other side was owned and operated by a rival gang. We carried knives, kept to the shadows and were given an endless supply of hashish and LSD. They must have kept the harder stuff away from me on purpose. When one of the girls, Sarah, fell asleep on my shoulder in a taxi, I thought she was tired. It wasn't until much later I was told she was a junkie, nodding off in her smack cocoon.

That night we went back to her parents' place. A mansion in Bellevue Hill. They spent all their time overseas. She and her boyfriend disappeared into a bedroom and I found a spare room to crash in. During the night her boyfriend came in, got into my bed and pinned me to the mattress. His eyes were glazed but his intention was clear. I tried to stop him, I hit and kicked and bit. I fumbled for an aerosol can on the bedside table and sprayed it in his eyes. He hit me hard across the face. The force of it shocked me but I refused to give up. He tried to push his erection into me but I squirmed and bucked, anything to stop the horror of what was happening. Perhaps it was the drugs he was on, perhaps it was because I was a virgin and my vagina was too tight. He managed to penetrate part of the way but clearly the effort was too great. He gave up, pushed me aside and walked out. I stumbled to the door and pushed a chair up under the handle, like I'd seen in the movies. I was stuck. I didn't even know the address of the house. I couldn't call a taxi and I was too scared to leave the room in case he came after me again. I huddled in a corner, shaking and sore, and waited for morning.

When the other girls arrived the next day I felt safe enough to leave the room. Sarah and her boyfriend were still asleep. I couldn't stop crying, I'd already thrown up, and my face was bruised. I told them what had happened.

'Every girl expects to get raped at least once in her life,' Mandy said.

'Yeah, that's right,' said Harla. 'And Sarah will get pissed off if she finds out her boyfriend tried to fuck you. Don't say anything and just forget about it.'

So I did. I shut up. I popped the free pills and LSD, smoked the free hash and kept out of Sarah and her boyfriend's way. I did talk about it, though. Years later in those psychologists' and counsellors' rooms. And from time to time with my boyfriends, when the terror of that night made it impossible to have them touch me.

Violence and rape weren't enough to dissolve the sticky fascination I had with this alien way of life. But murder was. Michael was a dealer but he had a warmth about him none of the others did. More than once I saw him being kind to Mandy's kid, a two-year-old boy who was often left unchanged and hungry. But Michael was found soaking in his own blood in the foyer of that back street hotel. Knifed over a heroin deal. Living in a gangster film suddenly no longer appealed. Reality hit me like a sledgehammer. It was time to go back to the safety of my small town.

I retreated to my parents' house, stayed in my room, staring at the walls and crying. Later my parents told me they were deeply concerned. They thought I'd had a breakdown of some sort. They never pried, never asked me what was wrong. They let me heal in my own time and for that I have always been grateful.

I did heal emotionally, but not physically. My knee was a continual aggravation and still is. Even now, cosseted and propped up on pillows, it complains to me constantly. My left knee is having a harder time, bent under the meditation stool. My back hurts so much it feels as though the skin is stretching, as though something is pushing through between my shoulder blades. Little nubs growing out of my back. The beginnings of wings, prising open the flesh. A slow painful growth into angelhood.

My monkey mind leaps to another tree, a more familiar topic. If I did win that twenty-two million dollars I wouldn't need to meditate. I'd be free. Nothing would bother me. I'd be happy just like the teacher wants us to be. Why wouldn't I be? No worries, no concerns. I've never understood the poor little rich girl thing. If they're so unhappy and their money's not helping, they should just give it all away to the poor. Me, for instance. I wouldn't waste their money. I'd use it to be happy. I've never known anyone who's won the Lotto but I've met someone who has. She told me about a friend of hers.

'What did she do with the money?' I asked.

'She bought a house, gave some money to her family, went on a holiday with her best friends, including me, and then she bought herself a nightclub.'

'A nightclub?'

'Yeah, she wanted to party every night. Buying a nightclub was the perfect solution.'

I wouldn't buy a nightclub. My wild dance-all-night days are behind me. All they did was stuff my knee up. But I smile at the thought of this young woman and her seven-night-a-week party. The smile doesn't last. Wasn't she just trying to buy friends with her money and her nightclub? In primary school when I had no friends I would give my classmates chocolate, bought with stolen money, just so they'd talk to me. One of their mothers turned up at our house one day asking my mother why I was giving her son bars of chocolate. I couldn't tell my mother, let alone my classmate's mother, that I did it because I was lonely and left out. I wanted to be included. If that meant bribing my classmates with chocolate I didn't care. I wanted to belong. If I won that much money would I belong? Or would I never know who my true friends were? Would I always be suspicious of people's motives? Perhaps that's why those poor little rich girls are so unhappy. Surrounded by sycophants and hangers-on. If I won twenty-two million dollars, who could ever relate to me? I would suddenly be vastly richer than everyone I know. How would my friends cope with me having that much money? How would I cope? I'd feel guilty all the time. I'd have to keep giving it away just to level the playing field. Why on earth did I buy that ticket? I don't want to win that much money. It would alienate me from everyone I know. It would cause jealousy and meanness. I'm better off as I am. I have enough money to pay the mortgage and the bills, to buy things for my young niece, to have the occasional treat. Winning twenty-two million dollars would be a disaster. God, I hope the ticket in my wallet isn't a winner.

And thus my mad mind moves from craving to aversion without missing a beat.

Lunch is the high point of the day. Today plates are piled high with rice and spinach pie, vegetables and hummus. Salad is always available and many of the women fill a separate bowl with leafy greens, grated carrot mixed with orange juice and currants, and cabbage tossed with vinaigrette and mustard seeds. I remember the teacher's discourse from Day One. He smiled and said, 'By now you realise you will have no dinner. Only two small pieces of fruit. And so at lunchtime you go back for a second helping. Then because you are working so hard, you think you need your strength, so you go back for a third. Oh no.' He shook his head. 'Do not do this. Meditation is best done on a stomach that is not full. For concentration, for sensations, it is best not to eat too much. So have a small serve at lunch only.'

I don't think many of the students heard him.

I long for the deep purple of the beetroot salad we had a couple of days ago but it isn't on the table today. Yesterday there were trays of peanut cookies still warm from the oven, tempting me with their aroma. No sweet things today. If the pattern continues there will be a dessert tomorrow. Every alternate day I do battle with the sugar demon in my head. It's tough to go without my greatest source of comfort in my greatest time of need.

We have a whole hour to enjoy the biggest meal of the day and then another hour to rest, to stretch out our backs and legs. To nap. Meditating so many hours a day I'm surprised I need extra sleep. But we are woken early in the morning, the meditation is painful and exhausting, and the miles my mind runs in circles every day would be enough to undo an elite athlete.

Another highlight of the day is the teacher's discourse in the evening. Once I realised we didn't have to sit in our assigned spots, I joined the rush for the back wall at the beginning of each session. There's only so much wall space in the meditation hall and some of it is permanently claimed by the weak spineless ones. If I'm quick enough, I too can join them on a makeshift sofa of comfy cushions. I lean my tortured back against the wall and enjoy the evening's entertainment. The teacher is very amusing when he tells us stories but he also teaches a lot of theory. The Eightfold Noble Path, the Four Noble Truths, the Three Stages of Wisdom, the Four Elements, the Six Senses, the Four Aggregates of the Mind. I can't keep up with it all. Nor was I expecting this. The Introduction to the Technique states that this course has nothing to do with organised religion or sectarianism. But what we're being taught is clearly Buddhist doctrine. Fortunately the teacher told us early on it wasn't necessary to believe all the theory. We are to experience the technique for ourselves, give it a good try and see if it works for us. Then perhaps later, if we find the technique works, we will delve more into its depths. I like his attitude. It reminds me of a saying in the Twelve Step programs, 'Take what you like and leave the rest.' Perhaps it's just reverse psychology but being told I don't have to blindly accept what is being said makes me more open to it. Except when it comes to reincarnation. As soon as the teacher mentions the word all I think is 'hogwash'.

I don't believe I've been reincarnated. I feel too young, too new. Gullible and naive. I am not what you'd call an old soul. I'm happy for other people to believe in reincarnation, I'm sure it works for them. But I don't believe I or anyone else in my family has been reincarnated or ever will be.

A friend questioned me about this. 'Do you believe you existed before you were born? In the spirit form perhaps?' she asked.

'Yes, actually, I do.'

'Then you believe in past lives.'

'Well not lives, per se. But I don't think I arrived out of a vacuum.'

'And do you believe that after you die your soul or spirit will continue to exist?'

'Absolutely. But it won't be here on earth.'

'Then you believe in past and future lives.'

'True. But I still don't think I've been reincarnated.'

But maybe I have been here before. Perhaps I was starving in my last life, which is why I eat so much in this one. Like Scarlett O'Hara in *Gone with the Wind*. 'I'll never go hungry again.' But she still kept her eighteen-inch waist. Fortunately I don't have to believe in reincarnation to be a Vipassana meditator. Even the teacher says the present life is the most important. If the present is good, the future will be good. But if here in the present life we keep generating negativity, then we will keep ourselves miserable. Here and now we must break this habit and come out of misery.

The teacher often has a sparkle in his eye and when he does I know he's about to tell a story. 'Story is story,' he says. The telling of parables is a classic religious tradition for a reason. They are a great way to get a message across, to entertain, engage and teach a lesson at the same time. It's the kind of lesson I never resent, when it's taught by a storyteller a good as the teacher. He's a joy to listen to: funny, intelligent, with great timing. I am desperate for any kind of stimulation, other than my own mind going round and round, so naturally I'm going to enjoy a good story. He told one the other night about a sick man who goes to his doctor. The doctor gives him a prescription and tells him it will cure his illness. The man is so impressed he tells everyone his doctor is the best. Other people's doctors are rubbish, he says. Only his doctor is any good. The man sets up an altar in his house, gives offerings to the doctor and worships him. But he doesn't take the medicine.

A second man goes to a doctor and gets a prescription. He questions the doctor about the prescription and the doctor tells him it will eradicate the cause of the disease. Once the cause has gone the disease will disappear. The man is so impressed with the cleverness of his doctor he tells everyone his doctor is very wise, very learned, and that their doctors are rubbish. He goes home and while burning incense he takes the prescription and recites it solemnly. 'Take two pills in the morning. Two pills in the afternoon. Two pills in the evening.' But he doesn't take the medicine.

The third man – all good stories have three examples – goes to the doctor, gets a prescription, has it filled and takes the medicine.

The teacher tells us that it's only by taking the medicine he's prescribing for us, this meditation technique, that we will be cured of our disease. There is no use in worshipping the teacher or building a religion around him and insisting it is the only true and worthy religion. Do what's being taught, experience it for ourselves, and keep it if it works for us – that's what we have to do.

Unfortunately before tonight's discourse there are two more Group Sits to be endured. But these are no longer mere Group Sits, they are now known as Sittings of Strong Determination. Now we have been taught the technique of Vipassana these meditations have morphed into an hour of even more excruciating pain. If my foot falls asleep or my knee screams at me or my back throbs in agony, I'm not supposed to move. We are instructed to maintain our postures and not give in to the habit pattern of the mind, the endless reactions that govern our existence. This what the Buddha did under the bodhi tree. This is how he achieved enlightenment. He said, 'I will not move until I become enlightened.' It took him forty-nine days. What is one hour compared to forty-nine days? If we feel the urge to move or if the pain becomes unbearable, we are to remember that this urge, this pain will pass. *Anicca, anicca, anicca.* On the board outside the dining hall the word is defined as 'impermanent, ephemeral, changing'. By not giving into these urges, this pain, we will gain experiential wisdom, the only wisdom that can liberate. We have entered the field of wisdom and we must use that wisdom to cure ourselves, to create our own futures by our actions. Why are we here? To be free from our crazy minds, our reactions and resentments. How to we achieve that? By sitting in rigid and absolute pain without moving for an hour. Sittings of Strong Determination? I think of them as the Sittings of Mass Destruction. *Anicca, anicca, anicca.* This pain is impermanent. This pain will pass. Yeah, right. If I'm lucky I can half sit, half kneel comfortably sometimes for fifteen minutes. By the time thirty minutes are up I'm in pain. Forty-five minutes of not changing my posture is torture. I haven't been able to make an hour yet. Maybe if I attain the goal of sitting in one position, perfectly still for a whole hour, I will attain enlightenment. Maybe

I will be free of the tyranny of Elliot Purvis. Ever hopeful, I settle into my lopsided sitting position. Maybe today.

Sometimes I wonder what the assistant teacher sees when she looks out at the seething mass of meditators sitting in front of her. I know my face changes expression all the time, from irritation to anger to wild grimaces of pain and sometimes there must be glimpses of stillness or mirth. I wonder if she took a snapshot of us how many different expressions there would be. I can't believe everyone else meditates all the time with a perfectly still face. The photos would be like the ones taken on the thrill rides at a theme park. Horror, joy, silent screams. The hall creaks in the heat. The atmosphere settles heavily on us all, like meditating in treacle.

I feel ridiculous in my meditation posture. If only I could sit cross-legged like everybody else. Apart from my bad knee, a sports doctor once told me I had the worst flexibility he'd ever encountered in a woman. 'Your lack of flexibility is bad even for a bloke,' he said.

The cool hippy chicks stretch and show off in front of the hall between meditations while I can hardly touch my knees, let alone my toes. I see the looks on their faces. They smirk and sneer at me. I'm self-conscious about everything I do. I know they're watching. I know they're laughing at me. I know they whisper about me in the toilet block. They talk about what I eat, how I walk, the fact that I can't even sit cross-legged and my dumb clothes. Who wears Hawaiian shirts to a meditation centre, for God's sake? No one else notices but I see the secret signs. I know what they're thinking: you don't deserve to be here, you're an outcast and should never have been allowed in, you don't belong, why don't you just go away and leave Vipassana for the cool chicks like us? I'm the loser no one wants to be friends with, the left-out, left-over fat kid. No one wants to play with me, no one wants me in their gang. Why do they hate me so much? Why do they gang up on me like this?

Apart from a few words with the assistant teacher and Lisa, it's been five days since I've talked to anyone. Five days since anyone's talked to me. In that time my mind has been grasping for reasons why, and this is what it's come up with: everyone hates me. It's what the teacher calls *the old habit pattern of the mind*. I'm used to thinking the worst of people, and even though no one here has given me any reason to think that way, my old negative patterns have taken over.

The fact that we're not allowed eye contact with anyone has also fed my mad monkey mind. Rationally I know the other women are just following the guidelines but irrationally I think they're shunning me and so the old fears rise up to taunt me. Why won't anyone smile at me? Bless me when I sneeze? Why won't anyone ever look me in the eye? I must be a pariah. They want to avoid me so badly. No one will talk to me. I'm all alone. I have no friends. No one to play with. No one to talk to. I'm all alone, abandoned – and worse, ridiculed. I just want a friend. I want to belong. I'm alone as always. There's only me. I can't rely on anyone. No one loves me. No one will take care of me.

The teacher told us a story about an artist who painted a picture of an ugly demon. The artist became terrified of this painting, scared out of his wits. His friends told him to stop being stupid. It was just a painting, and one that he'd painted himself. It couldn't possibly harm him. But the painter was beyond reasoning with. He believed the painting he had created was real. The teacher told this story to illustrate how our own thoughts can send us mad.

And thus here I am with my thoughts, creating imaginary scenarios, yet reacting to them as if they are real. Crazy person. And that's why I will not leave. I need a new way of thinking. The old habit pattern of my mind is not doing me any favours. Those cool girls think I should leave and I know I don't belong but I have to stay whether they like it or not. They can hate me for it, for messing up their cool and hip Vipassana with my ugliness and lumpiness. But I'm not leaving.

It must be time for the chanting to begin. I must have made it through an hour this time surely. The assistant teacher must have fallen asleep. I can't stand the pain much longer. Only a few more minutes and it should all be over. I will have won. Victory over pain. Enlightenment will be mine. I want to check the time, to see if the hour is over. But in order to look at my watch I'll have to move. If I move I'll have given into my craving. I'll have blown it. My watch is self-winding. I have to keep moving to keep it going. I worry with all this sitting still it will run down and stop. I bought it from a watchmaker in Sydney. He had a little shop in King Street, in among Newtown's cool cafes, bars and funky boutiques. I loved it at first sight. A man's watch with the most beautiful aqua face. A tropical lagoon sitting on my wrist. A piece of paradise I could carry with me everywhere. It was second-hand, reconditioned. Purchased in Vietnam in the late sixties, he thought, and brought back by a veteran. He hadn't seen many of them. At the time seventy-five dollars was a lot of money to me. A singer/songwriter without a record label isn't exactly loaded. But this watch sang to me. Plus it told me the time, day and date, necessary information for a muso who often didn't know what day it was.

Before I bought it he gave me a warning. 'Lots of people like the self-winding watches because they don't have to wind them up or buy batteries. But you can't sit around all day reading the paper. They bring them back in complaining the watch doesn't work. You have to move around at least a bit to keep them working.'

'I play guitar every day,' I said. 'I think I'll be right.'

But that was a long time ago. Now my guitar gathers dust while I sit at a computer all day, my shoulders hunched, waiting for the inevitable from The Hideous Mr Purvis.

The assistant teacher must have misjudged the time. I decide to check my watch. I'm sure it's been over an hour. I move my wrist, turn it over so that my watch faces me. I stare at it in disbelief. I was wrong. Five minutes to go. Only five minutes. If I had resisted the urge to look at my watch, I would have successfully got through a Sitting of Mass Destruction. The disappointment hits me hard. Hot tears run down my cheeks. Everything hurts. The pain is unbearable. I shudder with the force of it and the tears flow harder. Lisa gets up and moves carefully through the meditators towards me.

'The assistant teacher says to stay with the sensations,' she whispers to me. 'Don't let your mind wander. Stay with the sensations.'

'I am staying with the sensations,' I mutter through gritted teeth. 'That's why I'm crying. It's because of the pain.'

'Okay, well, concentrate on the breath for a while then.'

I nod mutely, knowing that the chanting will begin soon and after that I'll be able to leave this hall of torture, if just for a little while. I am so close to being able to suffer through an hour without moving. I will return. But when I do it will be without my watch. A piece of paradise has no place in this hell.

The last highlight of each day is stretching out on my bed at night, after all the hours of pain and meditation. Even though I'm hungry, the knowledge that I can lie down for the next six and a half hours is enough to make me happy. The nights here in the country are alive with sound. The frogs outside my window have clearly never heard of Noble Silence. They croak and call, singing enthusiastically into the night. A dog barks from across the valley. In the distance the echo of that bark adds to the sense of space and emphasises the stillness of everything around me. A truck doing the long distance overnight haul down the Bruce Highway growls as it climbs the incline just outside of town. The old woman snuffles and readies herself to snore. I lie with my arms above my head, easing the pain in my back, as I stare into the darkness. The sounds make me lonely. Out there in the night other people belong. They belong to dogs and houses and trucks and jobs. They are going about their days and nights with family, friends and colleagues. Even the frogs have company.

I used to belong. I used to belong to my mum in Hobart before I got too old to be adorable. I used to belong in Melbourne thanks to the drugs. In Sydney I used to belong in Twelve Step programs and with my band. I used to belong in Tamworth with a little family of friends. I even used to belong in Townsville, where I moved for my second job in radio. In those precious seconds when I wasn't working, I played Scrabble with a friend or had lunch at the C Bar overlooking the Coral Sea. Here on the Sunshine Coast I used to belong in my dream job, back when it felt like family, not a war zone. And that's why I'm now in a place where I don't stand a chance of belonging. A place where I can't even smile at anyone, let alone have a friendly chat. I can't sleep, so I listen to the world around me, a world where I don't belong. Other sounds join in the music of the night. Cracks, whistles, small explosive bangs. The sound of fireworks. Happy New Year.

Day Six

I was warned. We all were. The teacher said, 'Day Six will be full of difficulties.' He told us it would be a trial and that many of us would want to leave. He wasn't joking, not this time. The first day of the New Year and I am sleep deprived and sore. Hardly the hopeful beginning I had envisaged. Once again I'm up before the sun rises, shuffling to the bathroom in the dark. My eyes close in silent meditation as the birds begin to chatter and the sky lightens into another day. By the time my rumbling stomach is welcomed by the sights and scents of breakfast, the dawn has burnt off into the rising heat of morning.

After hours of meditation and the brief respite of lunch I am ready to see the assistant teacher. I'm sick of the pain. It's Day Six and I intend to make some demands. One of those little white chairs would be just dandy. Or a spot at the back of the meditation hall where I could rest my back against the wall. The wooden bench grows harder as I sit and wait my turn. I shift forward, resting my elbows on my legs, stretching out my back and trying to keep the weight off my backside. My poor bottom. When I signed up for this meditation course I didn't realise how intimately I'd become acquainted with my own arse.

Tents have mushroomed in the spaces between the trees and the buildings. More of them every day. The male kangaroo hops into sight. His enormous erection is still in evidence as he persists in following one of the young roos. He sidles up to her, giving her a bit of a nudge from time to time. He's letting her get used to the fact that he's keen. I'm sure she's got the message by now but she doesn't seem impressed. At least he hasn't pounced on her but neither has he given her flowers or taken her out to dinner. I haven't been pounced on, or taken out, even for a coffee, for I hate to think how long. And I'm tired of it. Sure I have my freedom, but wives and girlfriends start looking at you strangely when you're the only single woman at a dinner party and there are no spare men. They place a possessive hand on their husband's arm and bare their teeth. Claire, a married friend, told me about The List. Perhaps she saw it as a form of hubby insurance or maybe she couldn't bear to hear me moan about my single state anymore. Either way, I promised her I'd follow the instructions.

First I had to write down everything I wanted in a man, from the colour of his hair to his shoe size, and all the bits in between. Then she told me to write about the kinds of things we'd do together: Sunday brunches reading the paper, Christmases spent with the family, romantic dinners at a favourite restaurant and lots of lounging around, preferably at the beach. I had to describe the relationship he'd have with my family and friends and vice versa, his hobbies, his interests, his sense of community and his concerns. I wrote pages of intense descriptions, hopes and dreams. Then she told me to hone it down to my Top Ten, the essentials any man must have in order for me to be in a relationship with him. I reported to Claire when it was done.

'Okay,' she said. 'Now sleep with The List under your pillow for a month and burn it at the next full moon.'

I gave her my best cynical look, a look that has been known to make children cry and dogs howl.

Claire didn't flinch, she stared me square in the eye. 'And buy him something.'

'Buy him something? How can I buy him something when I haven't even met him?'

'You've got to give him a reason to manifest. If you buy him something and have it in your home he'll have to come over to use it. Make it something that makes him feel welcome.'

'But he doesn't even exist yet.'

'Yes he does, he exists right now. You can't use that negative language or he'll never appear.' She looked concerned. 'You didn't use any negatives in your list, did you? Remember I told you only positive words, no *nots* or *doesn'ts* or *nos*, otherwise it won't work. Your subconscious doesn't recognise those words. If you use them you'll get what you didn't ask for.'

'Ah,' I said, having forgotten that bit.

So I wrote The List for the second time, getting rid of things like 'He doesn't smoke' and changing it to 'He's a non-smoker.'

'Not good enough,' Claire said. 'Non is still a negative. You'll end up with another smelly smoker who spends all his money on cigarettes instead of you.'

'How about, "He happily gave up smoking years ago"?'

'Good enough, as long as you don't mind an ex-smoker who'll moan if anyone lights up near him.'

'Well, I'm an ex-smoker who does more than moan if anyone lights a cigarette in the same suburb as me.'

'You'll be a perfect match then.'

List complete and full of only positive, love- and life-affirming words, I bought a lovely breakfast bowl for this man. I already had one the same: yellow with painted leaves and flowers around the rim. It had been looking lonely all on its own. It was perfect for muesli and yoghurt and the other healthy breakfasts my perfect man would eat. And of course he would have to stay over to use it. I didn't get much sleep with The List crinkling under my pillow every time I moved and I nearly burnt down the lilly pilly in the backyard during the full moon, but it was done. Anytime soon the man of my dreams, or of my List at least, would knock on my door. I twiddled my thumbs, the bowl got dusty, I avoided Claire's inquisitive looks and got on with my job. A job that I now hated.

Elliot Purvis insisted on new photos and bios for the station website. When they were published online, we all had a look at them.

James hated his photo. 'I look as though I'm doing a poo,' he said.

He was right.

My photo was okay but my bio was completely different to the one I'd submitted.

'Are your bios the same as the ones you wrote?' I asked the other announcers.

They double-checked.

'Yep.'

I read mine again. Nothing about being a finalist in the radio awards, nothing about being a music director anywhere, and nothing about being assistant program director in Townsville. Perhaps there'd been a mistake.

I rang Sally, the online producer. 'I'm just looking at my bio on the website and it's different to the one I sent you. Was there a problem? Should I email it to you again?'

'No, that's all right.' She sounded uncomfortable.

'But it's different to the one I emailed, why has it been changed?'

'Uh, well . . .'

'Did you change it?' I couldn't understand why Sally would do that. Perhaps the ABC didn't allow mention of commercial radio awards. There were a lot of editorial policies, some of which I could never fathom.

'No, I didn't.' She emphasised the *I*. She was clearly dodging the issue but I was getting the general idea. The familiar anxiety gripped at my stomach.

'Can you change it back, please?'

'Uh, I don't think I can.'

'What's going on?'

Her voice was soft and close to the phone. 'Elliot had to read through the bios before I could publish them. He said yours was too long and told me what I had to edit. I'm sorry.'

I stopped breathing. 'Did he edit any other bios?'

'Um, no, I don't think so. Actually, I'm not sure.'

She was sure. And so was I. Elliot Purvis had edited my bio. Why? James' and Colin's bios were longer than mine. I wondered then, as I often do, whether it is resentment that makes him do these things. He may have management dazzled with his sharp suits and good looks but I have more experience and knowledge in radio. Perhaps he resents my power as music director, because what I do directly affects the sound of both stations. His stations. Music was a large part of the format but he's chipped away, piece by piece, programming more talk and demanding I add his favourite songs to the playlist. And he undermines my work every chance he has.

If you're told something long enough you start to believe it. Under the guise of an air-check he tells me I'm shit. My style is crap, my story choices are abysmal. I worry about my on-air performance and go into a panic if I know he's listening. More than once, while I've been presenting my show, he's come into the producer's booth. I've seen him, through the glass, talking at my producer. I've been able to make out what he's saying. Invariably, I'm unable to concentrate, and my show has indeed turned to shit.

I'm not the only one affected. James often asks me to check the emails he writes to Elliot before he hits send. Elliot's antics make him so angry he can't be trusted to write an email that won't inflame him further. I always encourage James to err on the side of caution.

One afternoon, while I was tweaking one of James' emails, he leant back in his chair. 'I'm so pissed off.' He sat forward again, his eyes bright with anger. 'Elliot gets away with everything, all the time, and we're the ones who have to wear it.'

'Just state your case clearly and concisely,' I said. 'Keep the emotion out of it and that way he has no ammunition.'

'Yeah, you're right.' He sighed like a grumpy dog, fed up with its lot. 'I'm just sick of it.'

'We all are, but there's no point making him angry. You know what that's like.'

We've all had it with this slick young man but there's nothing we can do. Management support him. They describe him as fearless. He isn't. Fearlessness implies some sort of recognition of the stakes. Elliot Purvis doesn't take other people into consideration, ever. As his outbursts become more vicious, sometimes I think I see fear in his eyes, but I'm wrong. It's anger and defiance. We may know more about radio than he does but he has all the power. In the end that's what matters. Power.

One of the small mercies we enjoy is the fact that he's in charge of two stations. It means he spends most of his time at the bigger one, the more important one. We know where we stand in the order of things, he makes sure of it.

Lisa's face looms into my field of vision. She can't call my name or tap me on the shoulder. Along with the Noble Silence comes Noble Non-Touching. No physical contact allowed. It would be easier if we were all given a number. Then an LED display could flash our number when it was our turn, like at the Department of Transport. It would save poor Lisa from having to bob in front of me to attract my attention.

I'm ushered into the assistant teacher's presence and make as much of a fuss about sitting as I can. I need to demonstrate to her just how much trouble I'm having. After I've shuffled about, tenderly propped up my disco knee with a spare cushion and repositioned my bottom four times, I finally look at her. There's that bloody serene smile again.

'How are you today?' she says.

'Well, actually, I'm still in a bit of pain.'

A bit of pain. Bloody hell, what a weak opening gambit. If I'd softened her up with all the fluffing about I've just undone it. I should have said, *I'm tormented by devils that use my buttocks for chewing gum and my knees for satay sticks. The pain is so great that I'm wearing my teeth down to stumps and my gums are bleeding. The torture of sitting has turned the palms of my hands into bloody pulp from digging my nails into them. Help me, oh please, please, help me, I beg you.* But no, I said, 'Well, actually, I'm still in a bit of pain.' Pathetic.

'Just keep observing the breath,' she says. 'And the sensations below the nostrils and above the upper lip.'

That's it. Not, *Why don't you have a rest up against the back wall or please have one of those funny little plastic chairs with the legs cut off and help yourself to as many cushions as you want, actually why don't we just find you a hammock and you can string it up under a tree for the rest of the course and by the way I have some great books you can borrow.* Nope, just keep breathing, keep observing.

'Okay,' I say and struggle to my feet, moaning and sighing. Perhaps she'll relent, perhaps she'll offer me some painkillers at least. I limp out the door, but she sits still, smiling gently, and says nothing. I can feel Lisa wanting to yell, *Next*, as I walk out the door but instead she just finds the next student in line to bob in front of.

Mentally I'm kicking myself. Clearly other students have a way of getting what they want that I don't know about. I'm struck by an odd thought. Perhaps they ask for what they want. No, that couldn't be it, it's too simple. And besides, who actually asks for what they want? What happens if you get told no? You never ask for what you want. You just drop hints and dance around and eventually it comes your way. If it doesn't, then fuck it, you never wanted it anyway. Did anyone ever hear you say you did? No. You never asked for it, you didn't get it, no one's any the wiser. However, I have been avoiding Claire. She knows I wrote my List and put it out to the Universe and all the Universe gave me was the finger. I prefer to hide my disappointment in a block of chocolate, sometimes two, and bury myself in a book. But there's no chocolate here and no books. No funny little chair and no back wall. I guess I got what I wanted after all. I wanted to do this meditation boot camp properly, to the letter, and that's what I'm going to do. I won't see the assistant teacher again. I'll just grin and bear it. She sits there and smiles so serenely. I'll fucking well out-serene her. Stupid bitch, not giving me what I wanted. Just because I didn't actually ask for it, that's no excuse. I hate her. I stomp off down the path and nearly slam into the older sister stomping the other way. Stupid cow, what's her problem?

I start singing; softly, covertly. No singing? Fuck the lot of them. It's a song of defiance. I called it 'Nature Girl' out of irony. It's the opposite of Nat King Cole's 'Nature Boy'. I wrote it for myself, but other people wanted to hear it. I sang it with anger and madness, a band behind me, my guitar bearing the brunt. Here I whisper it, my lips tight, my feet keeping time on the gravel.

I last saw you in a taxi, disappearing in the smoke,
Like a martyr into history, you left me with a wound that spoke.
Whispers at me all the morning, chatters to me through the day,
At night it sits upon my pillow, and its talking keeps all sleep at bay.
And I've washed myself in every river, dived into every sea,
But all the water in the ocean cannot wash this stain from me.

It's said I turned my back on nature, but nature turned her back on me.
I was never thought of as a beauty, others stole the stage from me.
I clung to where I found a foothold, fingers grasping in the cracks.
And there I found a little shelter, behind their eyes, behind their backs.
And I've washed myself in every river, dived into every sea,
But all the water in the oceans cannot wash this stain from me.

And I've wished on every star in heaven, the Seven Wonders of the World,
But every God ever invented cannot take the wound out of the girl.

Now I'm standing in the darkness, water lapping round my feet.
Is this the destiny I'd hoped for, is this the fate I'd wished to meet?
The shape of darkness is no stranger, the weight of patience makes me strong.
If this is hell then I am laughing, because I chose this place and I belong.
And I'll dry up each and every river, the oceans and the seven seas.
What use is all that water, if it cannot wash this stain from me?
And I'll stab out every star in heaven, destroy the wonders of the world,
Denounce every god ever invented, for they could not take the wound out of the girl.
And I'll spit into the eye of nature, and slaughter every sacred cow,
Bring down the fury of the heavens, 'cause heaven cannot help me now.
Help me now.

At the next Group Sit the geography of the meditation hall has changed yet again. Even more students squeeze into the small amount of space left and the number of people resting their backs against the wall has increased. But the thing that really hurts is the sight of Bernadette, my sweet smiling Bernadette, settling into one of the coveted positions against the back wall. First she abandoned me to sit in one of those funny little chairs, now she's wrangled yet another comfortable spot. Traitor. I settle resentfully into my strange mangled half-kneeling position and await the ensuing agony. As I begin to breathe I notice a strong smell. Pungent but not unpleasant. After we've been asked to avoid wearing scent of any kind, I'm curious as to its source.

Not long into the meditation my breathing becomes hard and fast. I'm even hotter than usual. Is this what the teacher means by the emotional and the physical connection? Every thought and emotion causes a physical sensation. Or is it the other way round? Is it because I feel hot I get angry?

Pain, pain, pain and heat. As the hall heats up with the press of the sun on the roof and the press of bodies within, the strange scent becomes stronger. Sweat pools at the base of my spine; it prickles and itches. I'm not allowed to wipe it away, let alone move my legs to ease the searing agony. My buttocks pulse with burning heat, my knees flare with white-hot pain, even my aches ache with a will of their own. The nubs of my fledgling wings push through the flesh between my shoulder blades, breaking the skin and stretching the muscles. It is unbearable. Tears make it worse. They slip down my hot cheeks and when they dry my skin is left tight and itchy. My eyes open of their own volition. The straight-backed girl is as cool and still as ever. The assistant teacher sits lightly in her seat. Her cotton clothes drape around her slim form in folds of white and her shawl of thin muslin falls softly around her shoulders. She is a calm, smiling totem. No sweat, no frowns and certainly no tears. I want to fucking kill her. More than that, I want to dismember her. I want to slice her into pieces bit by bit – let's see how serene she is then. I close my eyes again, my cheeks tight, my teeth clenched. I paint the picture in my mind. I have a machete, sharp and strong. I rise from my sitting position. Yes, I bloody well *change my posture*. The machete is balanced and heavy in my hand. I walk through the rows of meditators, all with their eyes closed, serene little shits, and walk towards the stage. I stand in front of the assistant teacher and raise the machete above my head. I bring it down hard on her foot. Nothing. No emotion, not even a flicker.

I return to my spot and reach for the machine gun I have hidden under my meditation stool. It's loaded and ready. My finger presses against the trigger. The gun stutters into life and the assistant teacher explodes into a mess of blood and shards of bone. Her brain is mush on the back wall; it slides down the white fabric like a slug. Her guts spill like spaghetti to the floor. No doubt about it, she is dead. But still not feeling any pain. The rage tornadoes inside me and I turn the gun on my fellow students. The straight-backed girl cops it first. Serves her right for being so bloody serene and perfect. The burpers, farters and fucking swallowers are reduced to bloody pulp within seconds. Take that, you fucking shits. The meditation hall is splattered with gore. Blood drips and pools on every surface. There are no straight backs, no snorers, no fucking gulpers, sneezers or sighers. The old woman is dead meat in her little white chair. I am alone in the hall, me and my gun. What a feeling. Triumph, relief, release. Those fucking serene shits can rot in hell. Or kick themselves into their next life if they want to. I am finally free. Be happy? You betcha.

At the beginning of each of these Group Sits I am always hopeful the pain won't be as bad but by the time they're halfway through the agony is unbearable. Once again I fail in the Sitting of Strong Determination. The Sitting of Mass Destruction. I change my posture to ease my legs and bottom. I crave the sound of the teacher's voice, the strange chanting that will release me from my agony. As soon as I hear his voice I am flooded with relief, knowing my torment will soon be over. Just a few more moments and I will be free. The teacher puts me into places of great pain and then releases me from them. It is his voice that enslaves me and his voice that sets me free. His chanting fills my head, even when I'm not in the meditation hall. I catch myself humming snatches of the tune, if you can call it that. It's a strange jaunty little chant which slows down at the end and finishes with elongated vowels. It's those last few words that I crave most of all. My liberator. His voice is in my head constantly, it's the only voice I've heard for days now and I hear it constantly – *Start again, start again, from the top of the head to the tip of the toes, from the tip of the toes to the top of the head* – as I walk the crunchy gravel paths, eat my vegetarian lunch, have a shower or explore the track through the scrub. I sing along with him in my mind. The assistant teacher's few whispered words don't measure up in comparison to his flood of instructions and unmelodious chanting. It constantly buzzes in my mind. During the discourses I soak up his words and the luxury of being able to gaze at another face, even if it is only on a video screen. It's odd not to look at anyone for such a long time. I'm having face hunger. I love his stories, his jokes, his wisdom, but most of all I adore his chanting at the end of a Group Sit. He is my saviour.

Is this brainwashing? Is this how it works? I've heard brainwashers put their victims in untenable positions, physically and emotionally. Then they save them from the pain and torment, winning them over completely when they're in a vulnerable and weakened state. Thus the persecutor becomes the saviour. That's exactly what's happening here. I am in pain. I have been put into that pain by this technique taught by the teacher. Then he grants me release with his chanting. He gives me succour with his discourses. His voice is the only voice I hear, his face is the only face I'm allowed to look at. We are woken at four am to meditate on empty stomachs, compelled to sit for hours in agony, and then he, the one responsible for all of this, releases us and in the evening makes us laugh. Then, sleep deprived and aching, we stumble back to bed for a few hours before we are woken at four am to do it all again.

All the evidence is there. I am being brainwashed. And that means only one thing. This technique is evil. I must escape. I must leave. But what did Amber tell me? The panic rises in my throat. They won't let me leave. They'll try and stop me. They'll use every technique they possibly can to keep me here. This is a cult. It is evil. I am not safe here.

The fear of being consumed by evil is a familiar one to me. When I was first in Twelve Step programs I had enormous difficulty doing my Fourth Step: making a searching and fearless moral inventory of myself. A lot of people baulk at this one. It's hard to drag all the things you've done wrong into the light, knowing you'll have to reveal it all to someone else in Step Five. Fearless and thorough? More like daunting and terrifying. I tried working through the questions in the workbook but wasn't getting very far. My sponsor told me about the AA Fourth Step guide. It was one hundred and forty-four questions long.

'If you want to do your Fourth Step thoroughly,' she said, 'you really can't get much more thorough than that.'

I became determined to do the AA questions. I wanted to do everything properly, get it right, be a good girl. I got a photocopied list of the questions and set to work. I sat in my tiny peach-coloured room in the Sydney share house I was living in and began to write. Somewhere around question six I became seriously unhinged.

Were you threatened by the Boogey Man or the Devil if you misbehaved?

'The devil loves it when people don't believe in him,' my mother used to tell me. The Prince of Lies, she called him. 'He wants you not to believe in him,' she would say. 'Then he can sneak into your life, into your soul.'

As a child the devil was a very real entity. He waited for my brothers and sisters and me around every corner, willing us to stuff up, to make mistakes, so he could pounce. He wormed his evil way into our heads, whispering poisonous sweet nothings. At night I shut my eyes tight, praying that the devil wouldn't get me. Perhaps he already had. Perhaps I was possessed. Maybe that's why I stole money and lied and ate chocolate and chips until I was sick. A full-on addict from the age of eight. It was the devil, the devil made me do it. It made sense. Nothing else did.

My tiny peach-coloured bedroom in inner-city Sydney warped and twisted around me. Barely big enough for my double bed, a clothes rack and some shelves, I had it packed with things I loved. A doll dressed as a cowgirl, a Mary-Lou's Lucky Stars poster, the angel plate my mum had brought me from the antiques centre down the road when she was visiting. I love my mum. I do. I believe in the devil. I believed he was there, right there in that moment. Cold doubt pricked my skin. Was it the devil and not my mother who led me to the Twelve Steps? Was it a trap? Acting as if, not having to believe in God but just pretending – that was the devil's work. And what about my sponsor? She was in Twelve Step programs, so she too must be possessed by the devil.

I was too afraid to do anything. Frozen in my tiny bedroom. My whole world consumed by the devil.

Eventually I calmed down enough to call my sponsor. She was

kind, soothing and not at all possessed by the devil. She suggested I leave that question for the time being and move on to the next one. But I couldn't. I put the one hundred and forty-four questions aside and never touched them again.

Later, after a meeting, I confessed to a fellow member that I was having problems with my Fourth Step.

'Keep it simple,' he said, quoting one of the slogans on a banner hanging in the meeting room.

'How?' I asked.

'This is what works for me. Four questions.' He counted them off on his fingers. 'One. Who would you cross the street to avoid and why? Two. Who would cross the street to avoid you and why? Three. What do you think of your family? And four.' He paused. 'A list of your good points. It's important it finish on something positive. It's a moral inventory and that means good as well as bad.'

Four questions, not a hundred and forty-four. I could do that. And I did. But it took me a long time. What do I think of my family? That was an epic in itself.

Despite my mad mind trying to convince me to leave, I make it through to the last meditation session of the day. It's dark outside, the heat has eased and the roof of the meditation hall cracks as the metal contracts. A small breeze drifts in through the wooden louvres.

In the evening discourse the teacher speaks about *sankharas*. There is a lot of theory behind them but as best I can understand they are our reactions. We are being trained not to react, but instead to observe, be aware and be equanimous. When we react we create a new *sankhara*: a line in the water, on the sand or on the rock depending on how many times we do it. If we react so many times we create a line on the rock, then our reactions shape who we are, and determine our futures, including our future lives. Our stock of old *sankharas* kick us into our next life. If we have no more *sankharas* then we are free and don't have to return.

If we continue to be equanimous, the old *sankharas* rise to the surface to be dealt with. If we continue not to react to the pain, we have the opportunity to clear out our old stock of hurts, resentments, fears and regrets. Physically it is a lot more painful than doing a Fourth Step but emotionally it could have a similar result. But after all those Fourth Steps do I have any *sankharas* left? After Day Six the answer is clear. I've been manufacturing these little buggers constantly. My stock of *sankharas* to do with Elliot Purvis alone could sink a battleship. Hell, they could destroy a small planet. I am here to become free of these reactions, even if I am being brainwashed. I am in the middle of a deep operation. As the teacher says, I have been sliced open and the infection, pus and putridity of my thoughts have been exposed. It ain't pretty but it must be done.

Radio, my supposed salvation, turned out the same as everything else. Hurts, resentments, fears and regrets. My first two weeks on air in Tamworth were hell. One day, when I was on air, the manager stormed into the studio and mimed shooting me in the head. Never said a word, just pretended to blow my brains out and slammed the door behind him. I was left gasping like a landed fish, terrified and confused. Later, in his office, I pleaded with him to tell me what I'd done wrong. It turned out to be a petty vendetta with the local paper that I was unaware of. I had committed the cardinal sin of mentioning the paper's name on air.

Being the only woman on air made me an easy target. I'd pick up the talkback line and be told I was a bitch and worse. Those calls never went to air. I rang Lucienne at the radio school to tell her I'd made a mistake. I couldn't do the job. I wanted to quit. She told me to stop being ridiculous and get on with it.

Things did improve. The breakfast announcer discovered I barracked for the same footy team as him and became my best mate. The old windbag who did the networked country music show began treating me as a human being once I stood up to him, and the journalist finally forgave me for my many errors in timing out to the news.

One of the other announcers was programming the music but refused to keep doing it unless he was paid more money. Fat chance. Instead the program director added it to his own workload until I stuck up my hand. My aim was to program music for ABC Local Radio one day. This would be a small step in that direction.

'Okay,' said the program director. 'But as you know there's no money in it and I'll keep programming the networked weekend logs.'

'Fine,' I said. 'All I want is to be called the assistant music director.'

He laughed. 'You can call yourself the music director if you like, I don't mind.'

I set up a desk in the music library and between programming and announcing, started dealing with record companies. The music director of the FM station told me to ignore them.

'Don't return their calls,' he said. 'They're just salespeople.'

But I was used to being on the other side when I was playing in bands, knocking on doors and being refused entry. I delighted in having the record companies chase me. Such sweet revenge.

After being a finalist for best new talent in the national radio awards, the phone started ringing with offers. I turned them down. I would do any on-air shift they wanted me to do but I wouldn't move unless I could program the music. One group program director did his homework and found out what would entice me to leave Tamworth. Eighteen months after starting my first job in radio I was head-hunted for a brand-new station in Townsville. I would be the breakfast co-host and yes, the music director. Heaven. Or so I thought.

The hours were crushing, the workload impossible, and the highly paid consultants made my life a misery every time they came to town. For my troubles I was made assistant program director, which meant more meetings and more responsibility. When I finally got home every night to my small flat with a view of the Coral Sea, a view I never got to see, I would cry in the shower and eat ice cream. The only thing I read, apart from radio and music journals, was junk mail. My brain was too overwhelmed to take in anything else. Junk mail had a lot of pictures, not many words and promised happiness.

I may not have been happy but I was learning a lot. It became obvious to me, in a way that hadn't been obvious in Tamworth, why the bands I had been in were never played on commercial radio. It was a numbers game, driven by research. I had a music call every week with the music consultant, who told me which songs were rating highly on their call-out research and which songs were in danger of being burned. A song came down to a percentage, nothing more. I would take this information to my program director, who would go along with whatever the consultant said. There was little room for gut instinct, passion or falling in love with a good song. The record company reps would call, cajole and send presents. When they came to town they'd take me out to dinner. Waste of time. I'd be falling asleep in my entree by eight and having to go home to bed before my pre-dawn start the next day. Besides, their pleading would go nowhere unless the numbers looked good. Cut and dried.

The exhaustion and endless hours finally wore me down. The blokey, sexist atmosphere of the station added to the stress. The fact that I was drinking again didn't help. Slamming down a couple of quick ones to get over the nausea before pretending to have a good time. Everyone drinks in Townsville. It's an army town full of pubs, clubs and beer gardens. I may have been learning valuable radio lessons but if something didn't change I was on the way to a breakdown. One of my mentors suggested I read a book. The book's premise was that if you want the externals to change, the internals need to change first. It suggested meditation. Even though I was barely getting enough sleep, I set my alarm forty minutes earlier each morning, got out of bed and meditated. I tried a guided meditation which involved a grassy meadow and a pyramid with seven steps. The idea was to visualise stepping on to each of the levels, which then turned a different colour, depending on the step. The top of the pyramid was pure white light. It was supposed to be very relaxing. I would start off okay in the grassy meadow but as soon as I approached the pyramid it would start revolving. The harder I tried to step onto the first level the more the pyramid would spin, until it was going so fast I could only watch it in despair. It took many weeks before my mind began to slow down. A meditation that involved just staring at a candle helped. No pyramids, no steps.

I began to consider other possibilities. I had been with the station for less than two years but in those two years I had put in at least three years' worth of work. I had been a finalist for best music director in the national awards and thought I might be ready for the next challenge.

There comes a time when, no matter how much you love your music, you grow out of most music stations' demographic. People like me don't want to be foisted off onto talk radio or Classic FM or Hits and Memories. We want interesting music made for adults. But no radio station was supplying it. In my search for the next challenge I discovered the ABC was advertising for an announcer and music director. Not the music director position I was ultimately aiming for, but another one, for an ABC station I'd never heard of. I listened to it on the internet and, to my amazement, heard the radio station I always thought should exist. Up until now I hadn't known that it did. Had I willed it into existence? Or did the meditation draw it to me? However it manifested, this was my dream job. I applied with all the resources I could muster. During the interview I was astounded to be talking with like-minded souls who knew and appreciated music the way I did. I had all the skills they were looking for and they had everything I desired. Not only that, the job was on the Sunshine Coast, a place of incredible beauty: long white beaches, verdant hinterland, views that stretched to infinity and weather so perfect everyone wants to move there.

When I arrived I felt as though I'd always belonged there. The music format mirrored my own CD collection and the vibe was just like the Coast, friendly and laid-back. I liked James, the station manager and senior broadcaster, from the moment we met. He was passionate about life, events, causes and most of all surfing. There were only three of us taking care of the on-air duties and a couple of journalists in the newsroom. A small family who loved what they were doing. Later James told me I nearly didn't get the job because they were worried I would get bored. After my job in Townsville, with its responsibilities, commitments and endless meetings, they thought I'd find this tiny, relaxed radio station a yawn and move on too soon. They were wrong. I never had the chance to get bored. I'd been working there just over a year when the suits arrived.

The restructure changed everything and I moved with it. We had a sister station on the Gold Coast and I became the music director for that station as well. I assimilated the databases, supervised the loading of music into the computer system and ensured that one music log would work for both stations. I made use of the skills I'd learnt while slogging it out in Townsville. I was just what the ABC wanted, a loyal employee but with the discipline and smarts learnt in the commercial world. I worked hard and was rewarded by being told that one day the national music director's job would be mine. My Holy Grail was in reach.

Then along came Elliot Purvis. Perhaps my friend Christine was right. Concerned with my anguish and despair, she told me to beware the boiling frog syndrome.

'If you put a frog in a pot and put a fire under the pot the water will gradually heat up,' she said. 'The frog won't jump out – even though the water is getting warmer, it doesn't perceive it to be a danger.' She looked at me quizzically. 'You get where this is heading?'

'I think so.'

'So the water gets hotter but the frog gets used to the heat. It doesn't make any attempt to jump out. It's not until the water is boiling that the frog goes, *oh shit,* and tries to get out. By then it's too late, the frog is cooked. Boiled alive.'

'You're suggesting that if I keep adapting to a destructive and dangerous environment, I'll end up as dinner for a Frenchman?'

She smiled. 'I'm worried about you, that's all. You used to be so happy. You had a job you loved in a place you called paradise. You said you were blessed. Now all I see and hear is confusion and misery.'

I immediately felt guilty. I'd started thinking everything was my fault. I'd certainly been told that enough at work. 'Perhaps I should stop boring my friends with the details.'

'That's not what I meant. You need to look after yourself. You have to do something before it's too late.'

'I guess a boiled frog isn't much fun as a friend.'

'I love you, even when you're unhappy. But I'd rather see you happy again.'

But I refuse to jump. I refuse to let The Hideous Mr Purvis win. I dreamt of this job before I knew it existed. This is my destiny and I won't let him take that away.

I feel like throwing up. Sweat and tears mingle on my cheek. Long stabs of pain radiate through my thigh and lower leg. My right knee is a pulsing mass of agony.

'This will pass,' I try to convince myself. 'This will pass.'

I have been at the meditation centre for six days. I have four days left to go. I could get up and walk out the door right now. No one could stop me. But then nothing would change. And everything has to change.

Day Seven

Bang! Like an unexpected kick in the guts. I've been winded before and it feels just like this. I am in a meditation hall outside a country town in Queensland, yet here she is. Front and centre in my mind. Ruby Rowe. So real I could touch her. I thought I'd left her behind a long time ago. She has been a thread, so intimately woven into my life for over twenty years that she is impossible to unpick from the fabric. A thread? She is barbed wire. In Twelve Step programs I'd done Fourth, Fifth, right through to Ninth Steps on Ruby many times. Yet I'm rocked by the power of this resentment still inside me.

The first time I worked with a sponsor on a list of people to make amends to it was revelatory. Usually, after you've done a Fourth Step, you do the Fifth with your sponsor: admitting to God, to yourself and to another human being the exact nature of your wrongs. Step Six is being entirely ready to have God remove all these defects of character and Step Seven is humbly asking Him to remove your shortcomings. Then you work with your sponsor on your list for Step Eight: making a list of all persons you have harmed and becoming willing to make amends to them all. When it came to Ruby all I could say was, yes she was on my list, even though she had betrayed me over and over, had fucked me up royally and almost caused me to lose my sanity, the stupid bitch. My sponsor stopped me. 'I don't think you're quite ready to make amends on that one.'

'Why not?'

'We'll just put Ruby aside for a while and work on the others. Have you ever heard of the Resentment Prayer?'

'Yes.' Every sponsor I'd ever had told me to do the Resentment Prayer with Ruby Rowe as the subject. If you want to be free from resentment, they'd told me, pray for the person you resent for two weeks, even if you don't believe it. Pray for every good thing you'd like for yourself to happen to the person you resent, even if you actually don't want them to have it. And I did. Over and over again.

Were all those counselling sessions and times spent talking with my sponsors for nothing? I thought I was over this and yet here it is again to confront me. Why can't I let it go? My ability to hold on to resentment confounds me. This is the mother of all *sankharas*. This is no mere line carved into rock. This the Mount Rushmore of resentments. I must be doing something right because it has surfaced with all the pain and betrayal, confusion and love, that embodies my relationship with Ruby. The amount of work I've done to forgive and forget is useless to me now because here she is, smiling at me. I used to love that smile. There was a time when I couldn't get through a day without seeing it. When we first met she was my nemesis and she would become my nemesis again. But somewhere in the middle she was the only person I wanted to be with. And I wanted to be with her all the time.

I let go and flow with the energy. If I am to be rid of this resentment I cannot resist it, no matter how humiliated I am to find it's still inside me. Ruby is here but there would have been no Ruby without Sam.

When I returned to Hobart after my adventures with the drug dealers in Kings Cross I came back a different girl. I had left as an overweight, naive virgin and in less than twelve months I had transformed into a drug-slim pseudo-punk. Sydney had fed me more than drugs and violence; it had also fed me music. I heard bands that opened my ears to new possibilities and I wanted a part of it. Hobart is a small town and in the early eighties the amount of people playing the music I liked was minuscule. So when the word got out that a girl had returned from Sydney wearing black plastic jeans and lugging a bass guitar around, I was hot property. I turned up to a rundown share house with my newly acquired bass to meet a band who were looking for the last member to complete their line-up. A small weedy guy with bucked teeth opened the front door onto a scene that would send shudders through the core of any landlord. A drum kit, amps, guitars, and every spare space littered with overflowing ashtrays and empty bottles.

'Hi, I'm Paul,' said the weedy one. 'Welcome to our humble room of musical meanderings. This is Andy.' He nodded towards a slight dark-haired cherub behind the drum kit. 'Matt.' A wild-haired and bearded saxophonist. 'And Sam.'

Sam. Blonde, blue-eyed, broken-nosed and shining with a light I didn't understand. He smiled at me and I felt a chemical reaction within my body.

'So,' Paul said. 'We're looking for a bass player.'

A bass player? I began to panic. Sure I wanted to play bass and sure I even owned one, but neither of those things meant I could actually play it. I'd thought they might be after a singer. That I could do. I'd just brought the bass along for show.

'I don't know,' I said. 'I'm not all that good. I haven't played in a band before.'

Sam, with his dark lashes and hypnotic eyes, was surrounded by a halo of light. The energy poured from him in golden shafts. 'Let's have a look at your bass.'

I bent down, flipped the locks on the case and opened the lid. There it was, a 1973 metallic green Burns Flyte. It looked like a space age Christmas tree. It sounded like crap but I didn't know that then, all I knew was that it was a lot lighter than any of the other bass guitars I'd hung around my neck. And it stood out from the pack.

Sam's golden energy engulfed me. 'Say yes.'

'What?' He startled me with his positivity, his lack of pretence, his self-confidence, his overpowering light.

'Say yes. I say yes. I say yes you're in the band.'

Paul started spluttering, one of Matt's eyebrows arched in a question, and Andy watched warily from his drum stool.

'Are you sure?' I was dumbfounded. They hadn't even heard me play a note.

The light around Sam glowed brighter. 'Say yes and let's get started.' He jumped off the amp he'd been sitting on, flicked a switch and strummed a chord. 'Let's go.'

My bass playing was bad. At our first gig I stuffed up every song. Why they persisted with me I'll never know. But Sam loved that funny old bass guitar of mine and I loved him. He captivated me from that very first meeting. The golden glow around him etched itself into my soul. I wanted to be with him all the time. I wanted his arms around me. I wanted to be bathed in his golden light for eternity. I thought I had plenty of time. We saw each other almost every day at rehearsals. I thought I could play it cool, get to know him better, make him fall for me. I was wrong.

I'd spent my childhood going through other people's things. My brothers and sister didn't want to play with me but that didn't mean I couldn't play with their stuff when they weren't around. Sam's stuff was no different. The boys had gone for a cigarette run and I had the house to myself. I wanted to know more about him and I started with his room. It was strewn with clothes; his bed was a mattress on the floor. I picked my way through ashtrays, books, magazines and shoes. Something caught my eye, something out of place. It was pink with a feather stuck to it. I picked it up. It was a handmade card. Inside was a message in large confident letters. 'If you enjoyed having me last night you can have me any time.' It was signed with stars and kisses and the name Ruby. I was heartbroken. My beautiful golden boy was already entangled with someone else, a brazen, confident, hussy who wrote notes I would never dare to write and made her own cards, in pink, with feathers. I couldn't compete. I had played it cool and lost. Ruby had won. But I never gave up.

It took almost four years for Sam and I to become an item. During that time I watched him and Ruby living, loving, playing and fighting together. Even when they were fighting I was jealous. I wouldn't have dared fight with him. I'd be too scared he would leave me. He was perfect. Playing alongside him in the band I saw him being sullen, argumentative, petty and withdrawn, as if he were shrouded in grey mist. But I knew the golden light I had seen when I first met him would burst through and dissolve the cold damp exterior. He was all I wanted.

The band split up eventually, as bands do. I played in other bands, had other boyfriends, including Sam's own brother for a few months, but even when I was accepted at the Victorian College of the Arts and moved to Melbourne I still thought about Sam. I saw it as an omen when, in my second year at acting school, Sam's latest band moved to Melbourne. Ruby didn't come with him. His band wanted me to sing backing vocals. I was thrilled to be back in that familiar world of rehearsal rooms and the stale beer stink of pubs. Sam was a little greyer around the eyes than I remembered but still shining with that light I never understood. He surprised me by coming round to the small flat I shared with a friend in St Kilda. My flatmate wasn't home. It was just him and me. We'd never really been alone together before. I was tongue-tied, and he had never been gregarious. We just sat there, saying nothing. Week after week he kept turning up. I never knew what to say and neither, it appeared, did he. I couldn't work out why he was there but he seemed to like it because he kept coming back. It made me nervous. As far as I could figure he and Ruby still had some kind of relationship, even though instead of coming with him to Melbourne she had moved to Sydney and had started studying acting, of all things.

The lead singer of the band had a fling with some floozy, his girlfriend still being in Hobart. The rest of the guys didn't bat an eyelash. After a gig, I decided to take the plunge. Ruby had always had other lovers, even when she and Sam had been living together. Perhaps she wouldn't mind if he had just the one. I sat on Sam's lap and said, 'So when am I going to be your floozy then?'

He was startled. I thought I'd made a fool of myself and blown the only chance I'd ever have. But after that first flash of surprise he said, 'How about now?'

Afterwards, back at my flat, I rubbed his beautiful back, massaged his gorgeous shoulders, indulged myself by watching him as he slept; his long dark lashes, the broken nose, the scar on his cheek that he'd had since he was a child. His skin was smooth and almost hairless, his body lean, the muscles in his arms well defined. He was beautiful and he was with me. I had waited four years to hold him inside me, to taste his sweat and to feel his breath on my cheek, his tongue in my mouth. It was worth it. I didn't have any expectations for the future but I did have hopes.

The next few weeks were a delirium of joy. Sam and I were inseparable and all my days and nights were golden. The guys in the band told me they'd never seen him so happy. He was doing cartwheels! Morose, sullen Sam spinning through the air like a hoop and all because of me. They couldn't believe it. I could. I knew he was full of love and light. I'd known it since that first day. He told me he'd called Ruby with the news. He'd told her he was seeing someone and asked her to guess who. Without a moment's hesitation she had said my name. She knew, she had always known.

He went to Sydney to see her. This was more than a fling. He wanted to be with me. I begged him not to go but he said he had to, he owed it to Ruby, they had to say goodbye face to face. I thought he would never return but he did, earlier than expected. He told her he had chosen me and after that they had nothing more to say to each other. I asked him if he had slept with her, the fear worming its way out of my mouth. He said no, they had just talked. It was all over. Days later I began to itch. I found something small and insect-like crawling in my pubes. I had no idea what it was. Some research revealed I had crabs. I asked Sam for an explanation.

He was nonchalant. 'You just mention the word Ruby and you get crabs,' he said.

I believed him. I believed he had slept in her sheets and had caught crabs that way. I believed he hadn't had sex with her. I had to believe, the alternative would have broken my heart.

More than once I heard Sam's friends from Hobart say that he and Ruby were a perfect match, that no matter what happened they would always end up back together. Clearly Ruby felt the same way. Even when Sam and I moved in together her letters and phone calls didn't stop. One night Sam was on the phone to her for hours while I lay in bed waiting. Eventually I went into the lounge room where he was lying on the floor, the receiver cradled to his ear, a smile on his face. I lay next to him. No response. I lay over him. No response. It was as if I didn't exist. But I never blamed him. It was all Ruby's fault. If she just left us alone Sam and I would be fine.

His dad and mum came to visit. His mother was a delight, loving and welcoming from the word go. She'd even brought baby photos of Sam. His dad was hesitant and shy. Or was it coldness? Either way he didn't envelop me with warmth the way his wife did. Apart from that, it was the perfect afternoon. His mum and I had cups of tea and looked at baby photos, while Sam and his dad tinkered with Sam's old car. Later I asked Sam what his parents had thought about us being together.

'I think Dad's a bit disappointed.'

'Disappointed?'

'Yeah, he always hoped Ruby and I would stay together.'

The ice cold stab of fear and jealousy made me shudder. And

the casual way in which Sam said it. I never saw him as being cruel. I thought the universe and everyone in it was against my claim on Sam and supportive of Ruby's.

The letters from Ruby kept coming. I found them. He kept them all filed away in a briefcase. My lifetime of snooping and my obsession with him found me reading them over and over trying to piece together clues. Was he writing back to her? If so, what was he writing? Her letters read as if they were still together. The fear grew stronger. I had stolen an electric typewriter the last time I had visited my parents in Hobart. I told my mum it was Sam's and I had just picked it up from a friend's place to take back to Melbourne. Sam and I both used it. I did a pencil rub of the backing sheet to see if I could discover what he had typed to her. Every time he went out I would leaf through his briefcase, read the letters again and obsess. One day he walked in and found me. All those letters from Ruby in her big confident writing, signed with stars and love, piled up around me. I felt as though I was a child again, sprung by my parents for stealing, the bag of chocolate wrappers at their feet. Bad girl. I apologised and cried and told him how I felt about the letters. He was impassive. I had hoped for reassurance but there was none. Shortly afterwards another letter from Ruby arrived. I screamed at him, at her, at life, and tried to burn it. He grabbed it out of my hands and left the flat. According to him, my jealousy was out of control. He was doing nothing wrong and neither was Ruby. Why shouldn't they stay friends?

But it was more than that. I'd photocopied my face, it was ethereal and dreamy. I wrote some poetry on the photocopy and gave it to Sam. He did the same. It was a special thing we shared. We stuck them on our bedroom wall. In among her letters in his briefcase I found a photocopy of Ruby's face with the words she'd written on it; the colour in her life had frozen, she said, and she was asleep in the dark without him. Sam had taken our special thing and given it straight to Ruby. He had ruined it. She might have been asleep in the dark without him but I was living in a technicolour frenzy of fear, jealousy and rage. Drugs were a very attractive alternative.

I knew that Sam was using, everyone in the band did smack. Melbourne was heroin city. It was the drug of choice if you didn't want to do speed. Everyone was using something and I'd used plenty of both. But when I was first with Sam, any thoughts of using completely disappeared. I was in love. I didn't need any other drug. The first time Sam turned up at my place stoned I was shocked. How could he? Why did he need to? I didn't want to be stoned, I wanted to be present and real when I was with him. Clearly that wasn't enough for him. I wasn't enough. It hurt. I told him I wanted to be with him, not the drug, and that if he wanted to spend time with me then he'd better be clean. He left in tears. But I thought it was worth it. We were meant to be together. But that was back when I thought Ruby was out of the picture. Sam clearly wanted to keep using and after a while I did too. Love wasn't enough after all. Heroin and music held us together.

After years of being ground down by the eternal presence of Ruby I realised I was never going to beat her. I was never going to win this competition for Sam's affection. I was tired of fighting. I wanted Sam to love me. He still wanted Ruby in his life. I could feel him slipping away, more distant everyday through clouds of smoke and dope, retreating to his home studio and writing who knows how many letters to Ruby, making who knows how many phone calls. Their love was not dead, it wasn't even dying. He might have chosen me but he'd never let go of her. This was before my days in Twelve Step programs, before I discovered the Serenity Prayer. I still believed that I could change other people, that I was responsible for their emotional states. I believed that if I accepted Ruby into our lives then Sam would love me more. I believed that his happiness was my responsibility and that I had made him unhappy by not wanting him to have anything to do with Ruby. If he was happy then I would be happy. If I let him have whatever he wanted he would be more generous in his affections toward me. By this stage even a few words would have been enough, let alone kind ones. So I let her in. She, like most Tasmanians, had returned to Tassie for a while. She'd hitched up with a man in the bush, her mountain man, but had got bored with country life. She wanted to move to Melbourne. I wanted to prove to Sam and to Ruby how magnanimous I was; not only did I let her into my life and my home, I even found her a job. She stayed at our place until she could get established. I was wary but thought it was best to keep my enemy close. Every moment was agony for me. Having her there didn't make Sam happier, it didn't bring us closer together. The three of us were like stilted marionettes in a macabre puppet show, frozen smiles on suspicious faces.

Ruby was staying with us when my father died. I went to Hobart for the private cremation followed by the thanksgiving service. The service was a way of celebrating his life rather than mourning it. But I didn't feel like celebrating. I returned to Melbourne, still in the angry stage of grief. I was angry with death for taking my dad away too soon. Ruby had found somewhere to live, so at least that pressure was gone, but I found it hard to be with Sam for another reason. I felt as though I was betraying my mother. She had just lost the only man she'd ever loved and here was I living with the guy I'd fallen in love with at first sight. I couldn't bear feeling like a traitor. I wanted to support my grieving mother any way I could and, to my grief-struck, mixed-up mind, breaking up with Sam was the best way of doing it. Solidarity between single women. Until he was gone I would continue to feel guilty. I dodged and weaved for a while, like I usually do, but one evening I told him. I said I couldn't be with him anymore. I'd finished my studies at the Victorian College of the Arts, and the only acting work I'd had confirmed I'd rather play in bands than be an actor. I was moving back to Hobart. I needed to be with people who understood how it felt to have their father die. I needed to be with my mother, to prove to her I was a loyal, dutiful and loving daughter. I just wanted to go home. I felt as though no one knew what I was going through and at least in Hobart I wouldn't feel so misunderstood.

Sam was quiet for a while and then he said, 'You can leave me if you like, as long as you promise to marry me.'

I was dumbstruck. This boy I'd loved since I first met him, the one I'd waited for for years, the one I felt so insecure with because I couldn't believe he actually wanted to be with me, was now asking me to marry him. My whole world did a complete spin and ended up on 'Yes.'

My plan to move to Hobart went ahead but now Sam was coming too. I left first and was already playing in a very cool country band by the time he arrived. We found a little house right on the river and settled into life at number 736. It was a short walk through the backyard, down a narrow path to the rocky shore below. We even had our own jetty, tumbling down and rickety, but safe enough to walk on, with a little boatshed at the end. There was a tiny beach on one side, strips of sand in among the rocks.

We discovered we could walk along the shore to the local shops. It was a bit tricky, picking our way over the rocks, but not too difficult to dissuade us from doing it. The house itself was completely wrong for the climactic conditions of a wintry Hobart: a draughty Californian bungalow with an ineffectual fireplace. But we loved it. From the back door we had unbroken views of the river. There was no shower, just a big old bath and that was enough for us. In the lounge room we put fairy lights around the fireplace. All our quirky knick-knacks decorated every surface. The picture rails were home to tiny tin robots and wind-up dinosaurs. My band used the huge front room for rehearsals and Sam became our sound engineer. I was given a kitten, Sam got a puppy. Sam had his studio to make his own music. I had my band. He baked sourdough bread for the two of us and built me a bookshelf. I made fudge and sold it at the market. Bliss.

Ruby also returned to Tasmania. She was back with her mountain man, Dave, who still lived in the country and chopped wood. They'd bring it to town and sell it by the trailer load. Sam and I had a hungry fireplace. We'd buy their wood but never invite them in for a cup of tea.

One day, when Ruby and Dave were dropping off some wood, Sam said, 'Why don't we get the gang back together, now there are so many of us back in Hobart?'

Ruby's face was stony. 'Why?'

I was shocked by her rudeness. Was this the same woman who had written all those letters I had read over and over? Even when she'd stayed with us in our Melbourne flat I sensed her passion for Sam still burned.

They stood opposite each other, the coldness was palpable. What had happened between them? I couldn't ask. Sam would discard my questions and once again I would appear jealous and unhinged. Best to let the beast sleep and be grateful that Ruby didn't want to 'get the old gang back together'.

My band became popular. The lead guitarist was good looking, the country music we were playing was hip, and the sound was great. Even the cool and distant Ruby came to see what the fuss was about. I enjoyed singing the old Loretta Lynn song 'You Ain't Woman Enough to Take My Man', in her direction. I growled it out. She had made my life hell for years. I never felt secure in my relationship with Sam because of her. But Sam was my man, and this was my band. She was not woman enough to take him or anything else from me.

Despite my venomous singing she became increasingly friendly. I was hesitant and suspicious, but gradually she wormed her way into my life, even though she was still curiously cold around Sam. Ruby and I had a mutual friend in Hobart and Ruby rented a room in her apartment once living in the country became too dull again for her. I would visit them both and have cups of tea in their kitchen.

Sam began to sigh and sulk. I wondered if he missed heroin. We never spoke about it. After all, we'd just been recreational users – we never used more than twice a week. Sure we wanted it, sure we couldn't go a week without it while we were in Melbourne, but we'd seen friends go down the slippery slope of addiction and silently prided ourselves on the fact that we could handle the drug, the drug didn't handle us. Smack wasn't an option in Hobart. It was hard to get, but why bother anyway. We were living a different life now. My father's death had shifted my point of view, and smack wasn't part of it. No one I knew in Hobart used and I was too busy to lose days from my life in a drug-induced stupor. Sam, I suspected, felt differently. He became uninterested in anything except his home studio. Doing the sound for the band had become a chore. Every time he sighed a pang of guilt pierced my heart. I had dragged him back to Hobart away from a job he'd liked and a city he loved. I had to make him happy; he was here because of me. I tried to keep him entertained, well fed and interested. His happiness, as always, depended on me. I was happy, except for my continual worrying about him. I was fronting the most popular band in town, had a lot of friends and had successfully auditioned for a role with the local theatre company. As the year progressed it became clear they were going to offer me an ongoing contract. I was the breadwinner and I was happy to look after Sam, as long as he kept loving me and kept off the drugs.

After less than a year my band decided it was time to move to Sydney and make a go of it there. We'd done all we could in Hobart. Sydney was a logical step. I told them I was giving up a lot to make this move. I asked them for assurance. They promised they'd do everything to make it work. Sam was against the move. He said if I stayed in Hobart he was happy to stay, which surprised me, given his moods. If I moved back to Melbourne he would come with me, but if I moved to Sydney with the band he would not come. When I didn't respond in the way he'd hoped, he returned to Melbourne without me. The dog went to his parents, the cat came with me to Sydney. He would visit. I would visit. We were in limbo.

I gave up my job, my boyfriend and my home to move to Sydney with the band. As soon as we got there, the band fell apart. The guys found everything too hard and ran back to Hobart. I was angry and bitter. We never even played a gig. They had promised me they'd make it work, a promise they never intended to keep.

Full of resentment, I badmouthed them to anyone who'd listen. But I wasn't going to scamper back home with my tail between my legs. I was in Sydney and I was going to make things happen without them. I had cheap rent, I found a job I liked and there was a cool country scene blossoming in Sydney. I started writing songs again and hooked up with the old friend whose departure from Hobart for Sydney all those years ago had caused me to eat all those chocolate self-saucing puddings. She'd taught herself to play the piano accordion and I had an acoustic guitar. We'd have cups of tea and play music in my Paddington bedsit. Sam and I spoke on the phone and it became obvious that he was using again. The tone of his voice, more nasal than usual, the dreaminess of it. If I'd ever considered moving back to Melbourne those phone calls put an end to it. It would be a backwards step. Backwards into the drugs, backwards into the negativity. Why couldn't Sam could move here? Sydney was shiny and bright, exciting and full of possibilities. A different Sydney to the one I'd known ten years ago. I hardly ever went to Kings Cross. Everyone I'd known back then was probably dead.

Ruby moved to Sydney. She got in touch. She was lonely. Curiously her mountain man had stayed behind in Tasmania. Ruby had played the violin when she was younger and she'd liked the music I'd played in Hobart so I invited her along to my little jam sessions. Without Sam around I even enjoyed spending time with her. Ruby's and my friendship strengthened. She missed her man and I was new in town with not many friends to call on. We were there for each other as we traversed a new landscape without our men beside us. Ruby offered me friendship and affection. She had this way of fixing the beam of her positive attention on me that melted all my misgivings. She made me feel as though I was the most important person in the world. It was extraordinary and irresistible. I'd never experienced anything like it. I'd had close friends before but Ruby wanted to get closer than that. She had no barriers. She gave herself to me completely and wanted the same from me. To someone who still bore the shame of being unwanted, ignored and ridiculed as a child, it was manna from heaven. Not to mention that she was incredibly beautiful. I fell completely and totally willingly under her spell. Soon I couldn't bear to spend a day without her company. She told me she felt the same. Ecstasy was big in Sydney at the time. Ruby said it was for people who weren't in love. She echoed the way I felt about smack when Sam and I were first together. She and I understood each other.

I encouraged Ruby to write songs. She scoffed at the idea but I told her she could do it. She knew music, she could play an instrument, she was creative and had a way with words. So she bought a guitar and tentatively started writing. She played me her first efforts. I always praised them. They were little buds of songs and needed to be coaxed into bloom. After a few months Ruby's mountain man moved to Sydney and they moved into a house together. I thought that things would change between us but they didn't. Ruby wanted to be with me as much as ever. She told me that their relationship wasn't travelling too well, that he didn't seem to love her anymore. I was astounded. How could anyone not love Ruby? She was stunning, funny, talented, delicious, creative, inventive and utterly addictive. I couldn't believe she was the same person I had hated for all those years. I knew I wasn't the same person I used to be when I was around her. I felt loved, wrapped up in her magnificence.

Sam and I were technically still together, a long distance telephone call away. His words floated down the line to my ever hopeful ear. Hopeful that he would love me enough to join me in Sydney, live with me again, make sourdough bread and bookshelves. Live the idealised version of our life: no drugs, no fear, no resentment, just the golden boy I remembered from that first day in the rehearsal room. I still craved the feeling he gave me the first time we met. Love and hope, joy and lightness of being. I wanted that back. He came to visit but it was awkward and stilted. He was like a cartoon cut-out, flat and dull against Sydney's energy and pizazz. I stayed with him in Melbourne but I felt like a tourist and I suspected that there was something I was keeping Sam from, something he'd rather be doing. He was suspicious about my friendship with Ruby. He'd become increasingly taciturn and on the subject of Ruby he was especially tight-lipped. We returned to our respective corners, still professing love for each other but with no mention of future visits. He'd change his mind, though, and move to Sydney. Despite all the evidence, I was sure he'd be my golden boy again.

Ruby and her mountain man broke up for the final time. She moved in with friends but it wasn't working out. She suggested we get a place together. Perfect. Trouble was she didn't have any money for the bond. No problem. I found us a little flat not far from the sea and paid all the expenses up front. I wanted to look after her. Just as I had looked after Sam. As long as she wanted to be with me, I was willing to do anything. The week before we were due to move in, Ruby went to Melbourne. Why? I can't remember but I do remember that she was going to stay with Sam. It didn't make sense. They'd been so cold towards each other for some time now. I didn't even know they were still in touch. Sam was a topic Ruby and I avoided. I felt the familiar clench in my gut. Nothing had changed. There would always be something going on between Ruby and Sam. It was with some difficulty, and with a sense of my own hypocrisy, that I asked her to be mindful when she was staying with him.

'He hasn't slept with anyone for some time, you know.' I could hardly believe I was saying this. My throat was tight. I was going to beg her not to tempt him. Me. Who had slept with Sam when he was still her boyfriend. They'd always had an open relationship, but even so, my double standard was blatant.

She gave me a terse agreement, dismissive even, and who could blame her. She left and I worried myself into paranoia. Ruby and Sam alone in the same flat. My worst fear, through all these years of resentment and confusion, and it had come to pass. Nothing I could do about it. I was stuck in Sydney. I waited for Ruby to return with a first-hand account of Sam's wellbeing. The news she had for me wasn't what I expected or wanted.

'How is he?' I asked. 'Not too lonely? You didn't sleep with him, did you?' I was desperate to know.

'I don't think he's lonely, no.'

'What do you mean?'

'There was a girl there.'

'A girl?'

'Yeah.' Her voice was flat. Had she wanted him to herself?

'What was she doing there? A flatmate? Sam hasn't mentioned anything.'

'No, well, he wouldn't, would he. They're both using. She arrived, they shot up in his bedroom. She didn't leave.'

So, Sam was using again. Using with a strange girl he had neglected to mention to me.

'Perhaps they're just friends. Friends sleep in the same bed sometimes.' My hopeful naivety knew no bounds.

'Neither of them had clothes on. I think they're more than just friends.' There was no warmth in Ruby's voice. She was just delivering the facts.

Sam was fucking someone else. Not her. Not me. Someone else. The old love triangle had taken on an entirely different shape. Or had it? For the first time I noticed Ruby's indifference to the situation. It was as if something had shut off. She wasn't interested in Sam anymore. Perhaps she had expected that familiar spark, a good root, a laugh and a tumble like old times. But it was clear from her attitude that whatever she'd expected it had not been delivered. And as for me, the cold reality of a love betrayed snaked its way through my stomach and chest. Lied to, made a fool of, and by the man who was supposed to love me. Hadn't he asked me to marry him? Weren't we going to be together again in the future? Wasn't this a short-term situation in a long-term plan?

Ruby's face was impassive. Her shoulder was one I couldn't cry on. I was the one who'd stolen Sam from her. Instead I sought refuge with other friends. They had a spare room and I was welcome to stay. I wanted to be somewhere Sam couldn't reach me. Somewhere I could hide and cry, be fed oranges and cups of tea, and find all the sympathy a girl with a broken heart needed. I found a telephone box down the road from their place and called him. He wasn't there. The answering machine kicked in and I spoke to it instead.

'Ruby told me. You're sleeping with someone. You have someone else. You didn't tell me.'

That's all I could manage. I went back to my friends' place, crawled into their spare room, surrounded myself with cushions and sobbed myself into a mucous mess.

Later I went back to my bedsit to pack my few possessions.

Ruby and I were moving into the flat in a matter of days. The phone rang. I didn't think, just picked it up. It was Sam. His voice was distant, cold. It was clear he was angry.

'If you think Ruby's so great,' he said, 'why don't you ask her what happened between her and me at Queen Street?'

Queen Street? Where Sam and I lived together in Melbourne. But they were never alone together there. Unless. My blood turned to ice.

Ruby was back to her usual effusive self when I went to see her. She was excited about us moving in together. The force of her attention, that high beam attraction, had been addictive, irresistible, especially after living in fear and resentment of her for so long. When I'd been pulled into her loving circle of light it had been like slipping into a hot bath after a long and dangerous trek through freezing mountainous terrain. But now the cold of the mountain air was back, the sleet was biting into my skin, my arms were goose-bumped with fear. I had to ask her.

We stood in the kitchen. She bounced and effervesced with light and love. I felt like a cold sodden lump of clay. My mouth could hardly form the words.

'I spoke with Sam today.'

'I was wondering what was wrong. What did he have to say for himself?' Her concern would have touched me on any other day.

'He told me to ask you about what happened between him and you in Queen Street.'

'Oh.' The light disappeared. It was as if it had never been there. Instead an intense look of determination crossed her face.

'What happened?' I felt as though I was wading through mud, stiff, cold and heavy.

'I was missing my mountain man so dreadfully. We'd never been apart for that long. I was homesick and sad.'

She looked at me, waiting for my response. I said nothing.

'Sam and I . . . well. I needed some comfort.'

It was obvious to me now. My fears were always founded on more than suspicion. 'You slept with him.'

Her eyes were sad but I didn't trust the sadness. 'This has been like a heavy stone in my heart for so long,' she said. 'I'm glad the truth is finally out.'

No apology. Not even a sorry. Just relief that she didn't have to carry a heavy stone in her heart anymore. Instead I was lumbered with it. Our friendship had always been perverse but now it was just a lie. The intensity was back in her eyes. 'We're still going to move in together, aren't we?'

I stumbled out the door and into my car. I wasn't sure how to drive anymore, I wasn't sure of anything. She and Sam had slept together, that was bad enough. But they had done it when I was in Hobart for my father's funeral. My dad was dead, but Ruby had been sad because she hadn't seen her boyfriend for a few weeks! My world had been shattered, my mother left bereft and alone, and Ruby chose that moment to fuck Sam. And he fucked her back. And in doing so both had fucked me up.

The road shifted and bent around my car. It was if I was in a tunnel that warped and twisted in front of me; not even my headlights could shine straight. My mind slipped towards the tunnel. My body tingled and flowed. Sensations swamped my reasoning and I felt my mind slip further into an altered state. The tunnel grew and threatened to engulf me. I was doomed, being sucked into insanity.

The sensation was the same as the one I had experienced on

the tram in Melbourne: the tunnel, the bending of light, the pull from this reality to another. I recognised it for what it was and was able to resist. I drove to the side of the road and slumped over the wheel. Sam and Ruby. My father had died, I was at his funeral, and they had thought it appropriate to fuck each other. Just as they always had. Just as they always would. I was insignificant. A speck to be flicked out of the way. Disregarded.

I loved her. I loved him. They had both betrayed me. But at least I wasn't paranoid. All those times Sam had looked down on me, belittled me for my petty jealousy. But I wasn't a mad woman, ranting and raving. I wasn't insane. I had been right. My instincts were flawless. I could trust myself after all, even though I couldn't trust Sam and I certainly couldn't trust Ruby.

I sat in my car, in a suburb of Sydney I didn't recognise, not even sure how I'd got there. It was dark and I hurt. I had nowhere to go. The lease was up on my bedsit. I had paid the bond and two weeks' rent on a flat I didn't want to move into. Not anymore. Not with Ruby. But I wouldn't be able to get that money back easily, if at all. I was stuck.

We moved in together. Ruby took the big sunny bedroom and I took the small dark one. She had a big bed that had seen many partners. She'd told me previously that her bed was imbued with happy memories and great energy from all that fucking. Some of the stories she told me were shocking, but to her sex was a form of recreation. All I had was heartbreak and misery where she and Sam had left their mark. I didn't want my futon anymore, now I knew she and Sam had fucked on it. How could they?

Not surprisingly I was sullen and withdrawn. My small dark bedroom suited me. I didn't want to emerge. Ruby bounced around the place as if nothing was wrong, she decorated and sang.

I had given her one proviso. The good-looking guitarist from my old band was back in town and she had started seeing him. As far as I was concerned, Pete was another person who couldn't keep his word. Another person who had used me up and spat me out. He was not welcome in my home.

I got back to the flat one evening and heard Ruby and Pete fucking in her room. She and I were supposed to be going to a concert. We were going to be late. I called out to her that we needed to leave and she called back that she wouldn't be long. My irritation grew. She had done the one thing I had asked her not to do. Fucking Pete was in my home and she was fucking him. I stomped about sighing and clanking my car keys. There was no sign of her emerging from the bedroom. Finally in anger I burst through the door and threw her ticket on the bedside table. She was on top, naked and curled over him. She looked up in shock. Pete lay back and smiled smugly.

'There's your ticket. I'm leaving.' I slammed the door behind me.

Later I felt ashamed and petty. 'Sorry,' I whispered.

She was stony-faced. 'I'm moving out. You're too controlling. I can't live with someone who wants to control me.'

She packed her things 'Walk by the sea every day,' she said to me before she left. 'Breathe deeply, it will help you heal.'

Kind words indeed, coming from the woman who had caused the wounds.

There are some things a soul cannot bear. I did indeed walk by the sea. I walked through the Waverley cemetery everyday among those whose misery on earth was over. The freesias were in bloom, their sweet scent reminding me of the bittersweet nature of life. Still I yearned to be covered with soil, a gravestone placed above me, never to worry again about this world. Pain was all I knew and I was tired of it. Eternal sleep, eternal bliss in the sea of unfeeling death. I walked and I breathed, but I didn't heal.

I started working with two other female musicians: Pam on piano accordion, who I'd been friends with at acting school, and Cathy on fiddle. We called ourselves Mary-Lou's Lucky Stars and played the songs I'd written. Songs about walking by the ocean and wishing I was dead. Ruby began turning up at our gigs. It was an echo of our Hobart days, me playing in a band, her coming to watch, a gulf between us. My blood went cold every time I saw her. She must have sensed it. She would stay on the edge of the crowd, hide in a corner and leave early. But I had created a rod for my own back by encouraging her to write songs. She began performing county music herself. I never went to her gigs. I had no desire to.

The trio morphed into a five-piece band with a different fiddle player, still all women, which I preferred after the bitter experience of my last band. Ruby kept coming to gigs. She turned up with a new man and they danced right in front of the stage while we played. I couldn't help my curiosity, she'd always fascinated me. I spoke with her between sets and thought about being friends again. Later I discovered she had tried to steal our drummer.

'You can't trust her, Mary-Lou.' Pam said. She had known me for many years and was more than familiar with the Ruby debacle. 'You'll never be able to trust her. If you can't remember it, I'll remember it for you.' She had my back and I was grateful.

Our band went to the Tamworth Country Music Festival many times, with different line-ups but always with three blondes up front. Even in Tamworth, Ruby started sniffing around. I resented her being on my turf, although I knew it was of my own doing.

Why on earth had I encouraged her to write and sing country music? I would never be free of her.

At the end of a particularly good gig, I watched and listened as Ruby congratulated everyone in my band, complimenting them on their playing and songwriting. Finally Ruby made her way over to me. What would she say? My singing was great, better than ever? She loved my new song? My guitar playing was solid?

She cocked an eyebrow. 'It works, doesn't it,' she said.

'What?'

'The hairy magnet.'

'What?' I had no idea what she meant.

She cast an eye around the room. 'Have you noticed how many more men than women there are in the audience?'

'No.' And I hadn't. Never had.

'The hairy magnet,' she said again, smugly.

And then I realised what she meant. It hit me with a force that made me gasp. In her opinion the only talent I had was between my legs. She didn't want to compliment me on my talent or skill, the only thing she could put my popularity down to was my cunt. I felt as though she'd spat in my face. And then the truth behind her words struck me. This was nothing to do with me, it was about her. Her hairy magnet. She had used it for love, attention, feel-good endorphins, everything. Sadness and compassion crashed over me like a wave. Ruby had so little regard for herself she thought the only reason anyone ever paid her any attention was because they wanted to fuck her. That was all she had. And she had tarred me with the same brush. I wanted to hug her, to tell her that there was so much more to her than her cunt. I looked at her beautiful face, the clear skin, the intelligence in her eyes and remembered the wonderful times we'd had together. The times when, if we didn't see each other for a day, we'd miss each other like water. Then I noticed the firm set of her mouth, her lips pressed together, her chin slightly jutted forward in defiance, and I knew she would never listen, let alone hear.

Before I left Sydney for my first job in radio I did make amends to Ruby. The Resentment Prayer had finally worked. We met in a Paddington cafe. She walked in beautiful and eager, her face open with hope. It was hard not to plunge into the seductive pool of her charm. I gathered up my resolve and stuck to the script. I apologised to her for all those years I'd feared her, hated her, tried to keep her and Sam apart. I said I was sorry for stealing him away from her. I made amends for the way I'd treated her and Pete. She forgave me immediately and effusively. It became clear that she saw this meeting as an overture to the rekindling of our friendship. I said goodbye knowing that it would never happen. She was sweet poison to me. This time I would not sell myself out.

I thought I had left Ruby behind. But she followed me to my first radio job in Tamworth in the form of a CD. It turned up on my desk in the music library. Would this woman never stop haunting me? Her first recording. Would I play it on air? No, I wouldn't. But other people would. She didn't need me.

I left Tamworth for Townsville, a blissfully Ruby-free zone. But when I came to the Sunshine Coast to take up my dream job, the haunting began anew. One day I was looking through the pile of CDs that had come in the day's mail. I noticed a song by Ruby on a compilation released by a well-known independent distributor. Anger surged through me like a bolt of electricity. What the fuck were they doing championing Ruby? Why the fuck was she on this album? How the fuck did she get her song on there? I was livid. I vowed to never play another song released by that company again.

I resolved to go through the playlist and remove any artist of theirs who was already on rotation. I wanted to ring them up and blast them with hot searing bile. I shook with rage. And shock. Shock that the mere sight of her name on a CD cover could elicit such a response.

I started visiting her website, like a peeping tom, a voyeur. I felt safe in the shadows of my anonymous web browsing. I knew what she was doing, but she never knew I was watching. She sent me her CDs, sometimes with personal notes. She wanted to get on the playlist, of course. How could she know I would never, ever play her music. 'Doesn't fit the format,' was a very convenient phrase. Secretly I was impressed by her songwriting, and part of me admired the fact that she had persisted with her music. Occasionally I would think, *that should have been me*. But I knew I didn't have the drive or the determination once my last band broke up. I prayed the Resentment Prayer for Ruby, again, and let it go with a sigh. 'Get on with your own life and let her live hers.' Radio gave me a second chance and I loved it. It had been a natural fit. Until now.

The pain of Elliot Purvis has sent me here, to this meditation centre, to this meditation hall of heat and pain. But I have stayed for another reason. A reason I didn't even recognise until today. It is time, once and for all, to rid myself of this poison. To let it rise from the depths, come to the surface and be burnt away by the light. As if I have a choice. It's happening right now. I can't stop it. The top of my head is exploding, the tension so great my skull feels stretched out of shape. How did this *sankhara* fit in my body? Or perhaps my body grew to accommodate it.

Maybe I will never be free of her. Perhaps she is my nemesis. The twisted link between us has held fast for so many years. We first met in Hobart. When I was in Melbourne, she moved to Melbourne; when I moved back to Hobart, there she was. In Sydney she turned up again. And on my turf in Tamworth. When I studied acting, she studied acting. When I sang, she sang. And I can only blame myself for her invasion of my chosen field of music.

'Sometimes something wholesome can come out of an unwholesome situation,' the Teacher said in one of the evening discourses. But I doubt any good could come from this mess.

I once wrote a song about Ruby. I used to introduce it at gigs as a song of warning. I called it 'Wreckage'.

She'll talk of love and smile in your eyes,
And her talk of love will hypnotise.
She sounds like she is praying,
But everything she's saying,
Will turn to dirt and dust and lies.
'Cos it's not love, it's only greed,
And you're just a tool to get what she needs.
She'll turn friend against friend,
Until the bitter end,
And bitter it will be.
Everywhere she goes she leaves wreckage.
Every time she speaks she leaves wreckage.
And you can join the line,
Of those she's left crying,
Every time she loves,
She leaves wreckage behind.

Day Eight

I am walking through a spacious room. White gauze curtains hang from the ceiling. They blow gently in the breeze and divide the room into smaller, ever shifting spaces. It looks like the set of a New Romantic video clip from the 1980s. People move between the curtains but I am never able to see them in their entirety, only small glimpses of legs, arms, hair, gliding through the billowing white. As I walk through the room, the curtains brush my skin. Ahead of me is a huge bed with more of the white gauze draped around it. On the bed Sam is naked with a girl I have never seen before. I stop in shock. The familiar pangs of betrayal and heartbreak flood through my body. The girl sees me, wraps herself in white, and approaches.

'You think he's yours. You think he belongs to you. But he's mine now.'

It's then I notice her skin is pierced with hooks. Heavy hooks the colour of a grey sky. I look at myself and see the same hooks puckering my arms, embedded in my chest and legs. They curve through my body, their brutal barbs puncturing my limbs, impossible to dislodge. The other people wandering through the room are also disfigured by the same hooks.

The girl sneers at me. 'He never belonged to you.'

Her words hit me like a slap. And with that slap I come to my senses. Through my senses I arrive at the truth. She is right. He never belonged to me. He was never mine. He only ever belonged to himself. He was always free. And as he had never belonged to me, as he had never been mine, all the hurt and pain I have felt was a lie. It was never based on reality. Sam once said, 'I don't think you even know who I am.' And he was right. I saw him as the golden boy I'd first met. I had fixed that image in my mind and refused to change it, never acknowledging the truth of who he really was. And because I thought he belonged to me, I fought to keep what was mine. But he never was mine. And if he never belonged to me, none of what Ruby had done was of any consequence. If he was free, then he was free to do whatever he liked. It was not my job to stop him, to tell him no, to pull on the leash and get him to heel. He never belonged to me.

My body begins to vibrate with pricks of energy. He was never mine. All the hurt, betrayal, anger, jealousy and fear flow out of my body and are replaced with joy. He never belonged to me. There was no reason to go through the torture I had put myself through. He was never mine. He was always his.

The hooks fall from my body. They leave no marks and cause no pain. He never belonged to me. The hooks have gone. I am free.

I awake from the dream smiling. I am deliciously light. The teacher speaks about the delusion of self. He tells us there is no I, no me, no mine. He tells us that any attachment to the delusion of

I, me, mine only leads to misery. I have reacted badly to those words. I want there to be an *I*. I want things to be *mine*. But in this dream I experience the liberation of letting go of the illusion, the bliss of relinquishing ownership. Had Ruby known this all along? I could never understand how she could profess to love Sam and yet have sex with everybody she met. I could never understand why Sam put up with it. And yet when I asked he said he knew, through it all, that Ruby loved him and that was all he needed. I realise that I had judged them both so that I could see myself as being better than Ruby, so that my relationship with Sam would be better, more pure, than Ruby's relationship with him. Had they had known this all along? That nobody owns anybody else. Love is a choice, not a commandment. Now I know he never belonged to me I am free of my attachment to Sam and consequently free of my aversion to Ruby.

Something more than wholesome has come from an unwholesome situation. Something awe inspiring and heart expanding. No one belongs to me. I belong to no one. We are all free. I realise I have never had a real relationship. Not one where I was present. I've always been afraid, enmeshed, hooked in, jealous and obsessive. Terrified of being abandoned but also terrified of anyone getting too close. But if I don't belong to anyone and no one belongs to me, I am free. Free to be myself. I am liberated.

In the bathroom, I smile at myself in the mirror for the first time since my arrival at the meditation centre. I'm looking pretty good. My skin is clear, my eyes shine like blue water on a summer's day, my smile is genuine. But my hair is a different story. It needs a good wash. I step into the drizzle of water, warm because I'm the first to shower for the day. The droplets hit my skin and zing along the surface of my body. My responses are amplified by seven days of awareness, of fine-tuning my mind to thumb-print-sized portions of my skin. I vibrate with the water, my senses are awake on all levels. I pour shampoo into my hand and the smell of it makes me giddy. As I massage it into my scalp I almost swoon with the intensity of the sensations. I run my hands over my breasts and hips, down over the curve of my belly to wash my pubes. My hand wants to linger. My body is screaming at me to reach inside those hidden folds, to touch myself and explore the full extent of this buzzing, vibrating, pulsing experience. To feel skin on skin in this state would be incredible. To writhe next to another, to be inside each other's mouths, inside each other's bodies with this amount of awareness, with this level of feeling, would be an experience like no other. I pinch one of my nipples and almost break the Noble Silence. Imagine an orgasm while on this meditation gear. Better than any drug I've tried, including a delicious batch of speed which was more like ecstasy than any ecstasy I'd had.

The screen door slams shut as another student enters the bathroom. I freeze with one hand between my legs and the other on my breast, suds oozing between my fingers. The Third Precept. To abstain from all sexual activity. Not to mention the water restrictions. I finish washing my hair.

I know I am a free and independent woman but it would be lovely, after ten days of experiencing such intense sensation, to know I was going home to feel those other sensations with someone I loved.

The Sittings of Mass Destruction are just that, pain and agony. But in my room my meditations form a different pattern. For the first half-hour my mind wanders. Monkey mind. Wild animal mind. I regularly obsess about winning Lotto, my house burning down, my niece being harmed, The Hideous Mr Purvis, the fact that I don't have a boyfriend. The next twenty minutes I work as I am supposed to work, observing, being aware and remaining equanimous. After that I begin to get bored. I want to move, not because I'm in pain but because I'm restless. If I can still remain equanimous and not react, then the good stuff begins. Rebellion fades and I surrender. The meditation becomes easier because I stop fighting it. All the strain and pain of resisting leaves. The energy flows from my body in shafts of pinprick light. Sometimes a pulse bounds from what the teacher coyly names *the base of the trunk*. The strength of the pulse surges through my body towards the top of my head. The pressure builds. I feel as though the top of my head will blow off. Then the energy explodes through the small dent where once my skull was soft and malleable, a baby still growing into my bones. The surge rocks and shakes my body as these unnameable *sankharas*, unknowable hurts and deep-seated resentments are released. It is worth the disappointment and agony of the Group Sits in the hall. But perhaps today I will get through a whole Sitting of Mass Destruction without moving, without reacting. Perhaps if I do, all my old hurts will finally be released. Perhaps.

The old woman is still sound asleep. I don't think she's observing her sensations. At least she hasn't coughed for a while. I'm beginning to like her, or at least admire her. We've never spoken, but I think she's very brave. It must take a lot of courage and initiative to come to a place like this when you're dying of lung cancer. She shuffles on her bed. I open my eyes just a little. Slits to peep through. I wonder if she senses me thinking about her, feels the vibrations of my thoughts. She looks at her watch. She gets up and walks out the door. Maybe she needs to go to the loo. The bell rings for breakfast. Now I understand. The mystery of how she's always the first in line at mealtimes is a mystery no more. The woman has a sixth sense when it comes to food.

After breakfast I fail yet again at the Sitting of Strong Determination. The pain overcomes me and I have to ease my legs. I thought after letting go of the physical burden of Sam and Ruby I would be able to withstand it. But no matter how much I told myself the pain would change, that it would dissolve, and that my body was just particles arising and passing, arising and passing, and therefore the pain would arise and pass, it never did. The teacher has told us that if we have no gross, solidified pain we can *sweep en masse with a free flow*. I have no idea what he means. Not in the meditation hall. Back in my room propped up on my bed, as the old lady snuffles gently in her lying down meditation, I experience again the energy pouring out of my body. Waves, pulses, rushes of sensations, all travelling up, through and out. Release, release, release. But this meditation is two hours long and before the bell rings for lunch I am exhausted.

Food is a sensation all of its own. The colours, the smells, the tastes of lunch become a magical adventure. Today Lisa and the Asian girls serve us ratatouille with glistening chunks of zucchini and melting globs of eggplant, crispy baked potatoes which I dredge with salt, and a pasta salad with the tang of a vinaigrette dressing. I ignore the chocolate cake waiting at the end of the table. In front of it the sign says, *One piece only please*. The old woman can have two; hers and mine. She needs her strength.

Outside on the verandah we take our usual positions. The older sister sits right at the other end, as far away from the rest of us as she can without falling off the edge. I move a chair to the railing, prop my legs up on the wooden posts and delve into the world of food. The kangaroos graze in front of the verandah. A couple of the older joeys enjoy a meal of grass. I didn't realise, until I came here, just how much kangaroos eat. They hardly ever stop grazing. No wonder farmers hate them. One of the joeys scrambles back into his mother's pouch. I'm amazed he can fit. There's so much of him and only a small pouch to put it all in. But the pouch stretches and distends as he wrangles his way in head first and then swivels until his head sticks out the top. I wonder how much roo poo there is in that pouch. How does it ever get cleaned out? A much younger joey braves the world outside his mother's pouch on shaky legs. He tries a tentative hop, wobbles and then tries another. His confidence grows and he begins to bounce around his mother. He's still shaky but doing well until he loses control mid leap and bounces straight into his mother, rebounds and hits the ground. I'm not the only one watching and the outburst of laughter is both a delight and a shock. In among the giggles I hear a laugh that reminds me of Ruby's. Her beautiful wide open smile and the joy pouring out. I feel only love for her. The warmth flows through me like a healing balm. I did love her. She was my beacon of light. One of my friends once commented that Ruby was in love with me; she followed me around and copied everything I did. But it was not one-sided. And perhaps what I felt was obsession not love. But it is in the past now and the past has been released. Finally. The tiny roo quickly recovers and dives back into the safety of the pouch. The laughter hovers for a moment and then we too recover and go back to our silent meal.

It's been a while since I've had an interview with the assistant teacher. Once it became obvious she wasn't going to offer me a comfortable lounge chair to sit in, let alone the back wall to lean against, I didn't see the point. But something's really been worrying me and I need to talk to her about it. By the time I reach the meditation hall the benches are already full of waiting students. I sit on the grass and watch as the queue slowly shortens. Linda alternates between the male and female side, ushering the students in turn. When a space becomes available on the bench I grab it. I don't want anyone getting in front of me in the queue.

Finally I am escorted to the small alcove beside the hall. I sit on one of the cushions and put the other under my knee. My poor old knee. The assistant teacher says nothing. After a while I realise I'd better begin.

'Aren't you worried about deep vein thrombosis?' I ask. All the airlines are in a tizzy about it. Passengers are dying from blood clots and the airlines are getting sued. 'All this sitting makes us prime targets. Aren't you concerned about it?'

She smiles, of course – she always smiles. 'People in planes have to sit a lot longer than an hour to be troubled by DVT.'

'Yes, but every posture I sit in hurts, gives me immense grief, and more often than not my foot goes to sleep. Sometimes my whole leg goes to sleep. No circulation whatsoever. Surely that's more dangerous than a plane?'

'We have had no complaints as yet, and after every sit you are free to move. You can leave the hall, whereas you cannot leave a plane.'

She had no concerns about this matter, so by default, neither should I.

'When did you first hear about Vipassana?' I ask.

'When I was a lot younger. My husband introduced it to me. We travelled and meditated together.'

'Is he an assistant teacher too?'

'He was a lot older than me and died some time ago.'

'Oh, I'm sorry.'

She is still smiling. I haven't crossed any boundaries.

'Did you marry again?'

'Mary-Lou,' she says patiently, 'we are here to talk about your meditation practice and any questions you may have about the discourse.'

It's been so long since I've spoken to anyone. I see others making eye contact with each other and communicating through gestures. I resist. But still I miss talking. 'Sorry. I just felt like having a chat.'

Her smile broadens. 'I thought so. Do you have any questions about the technique?'

'Yes. You know how we're not supposed to crave anything. What about looking forward to things? I'm going down to Tasmania in February, for my sister's birthday, and I'm really looking forward to it. Is that against the rules?'

'Not at all. Vipassana meditators are not cold, unfeeling people. In fact the more you meditate, the more joyful life becomes. Of course you can look forward to things, as long as you don't become attached to outcomes. If your life plunged into despair if, for some reason, your trip to Tasmania had to be cancelled, then it would be a problem. But otherwise relax and enjoy. Life is wonderful. Be happy.'

One of the many things I was taught in Twelve Step programs was that an expectation is a premeditated resentment. It made sense. I expect something and I don't get it. Bang! Resentment. I expect something but it doesn't live up to what I thought it would be. Bang! Resentment. The assistant teacher is telling me something similar. I can look forward to something but stay in the present. Don't expect anything and I'll be all right. But the flip side to that is how I've lived my whole life. A different kind of expectation. Expecting that I will be let down. Expecting that I can't trust anyone. Expecting that I will be abandoned.

The assistant teacher is waiting.

'What's the difference between *anicca*, the philosophy of impermanence, understanding that everything will pass, and the philosophy of ignore it and it will go away?' I'm thinking of my dad and his sweep it under the rug mentality.

'Awareness instead of denial. With awareness you experience whatever is happening. Reality as it is, without craving or aversion. You are aware and you know it will pass.'

'My next question follows on from that. When I'm in pain during a meditation I often find myself thinking, *I don't care, I don't care*. I try and trick myself into thinking I don't care about the pain and hope it will go away. How is that different from equanimity?'

'*I don't care* comes from anger, from aversion. But there is no need to fight this thought. When it arises just observe it and it will soon pass. Equanimity is mental calmness. No craving, no aversion. We work towards being aware and equanimous.'

'Is equanimous even a word? I've never heard of it before.'

She smiles again. 'I believe if you look in a dictionary, you will find it.'

'Thank you,' I say. 'I'll do that when I'm allowed to read again.'

I'm giddy from all this talk, more words than I've said in over a week, and wobble slightly when I stand. I remind myself of the tiny joey bouncing into his mother's flank and suppress a giggle. The assistant teacher looks at me quizzically but I resist the urge to admit I've been indulging in the distraction of the kangaroos.

After another hour and a half of meditation in my room, I

walk the gravel path to the meditation hall. I arrive early for once. Lisa is in the hall squirting liquid from a spray bottle along the back wall. The smell is the same one I've been noticing for the past few days. It has the scent of citronella. I'm confused. *No strong scents,* the note on the board says, probably written by Lisa herself. Yet she is the one responsible for the sharp odour which assaults our nostrils. Perhaps the fact that it's stinking hot every day means we have become stinking students. Perhaps the very mats and cushions have absorbed our odour. Maybe she is masking a stronger scent of heat and pain. I leave her to her work and wait under the portico. The hippie chicks and yoga girls stretch lithely on the grass, showing off their immodest stomachs and bare arms. Lisa emerges and talks to them quietly. Clothes are pulled back over bare patches of skin and one of the slim, tanned girls walks back to the accommodation, probably to put on something more appropriate. Clearly she has not read the Code of Conduct three times a day as I have. If she had she would have known sleeveless or skimpy tops should not be worn and partial nudity is not permitted. It's all there in the Code.

I have decided that for this Sitting of Mass Destruction I will think of the swallowers, burpers and sighers as conduits to my equanimity. Instead of wanting to smack them in the throat, I will be grateful for their contribution. As the meditation progresses, every time I hear one of those odiously loud swallows I thank them. Each time a burp bubbles across the hall I think, *Be happy, burper, and thank you for aiding my equanimity.* I pass through the monkey mind stage of my meditation and enter into the stage where my body calls the shots. It dominates my mind as the pain becomes stronger. I work through my body piece by piece, part by part, from the top of my head to the tips of my toes, from the tips of my toes to the top of my head, as the teacher has instructed time and time again. I do not allow my knees, my bottom, my back, the tops of my feet or my hands, all the parts that hurt, to distract me from the practice. If I encounter gross solidified pain, which, let's face it, constitutes most of my body, I don't create another *sankhara* by avoiding it or hating it. I observe and move on. Or I wish I could. Truth is the parts that hurt call my mind back to them time and time again. But I am getting better at this. During a recent Group Sit I was surprised to find dried tears on my cheek. I couldn't remember why I had been crying. I had moved on so successfully that whatever agony caused them was insignificant. *Anicca, anicca, anicca.* All is impermanent.

I am in the zone, my body buzzing. The painful parts throb more than buzz but it is all energy, arising and passing, arising and passing, the universal law of nature. A small explosion bursts through the hall. A sneeze. The sound waves, with all the energy of the sneeze behind them, push themselves through my body. My body stretches and flows with the force of the sound. My molecules spread across the hall in the wake of the sneeze. I am no longer solid. I am, as the Buddha said, matter arising and passing. His great truth. I feel the truth of my body as my molecules dance through the hall.

The truth is our bodies are composed of tiny particles and empty space. But even the particles have no solidity, they arise and pass in the smallest fraction of time, passing into and out of existence, like a flow of vibrations. The Buddha discovered this thousands of years ago. It took the scientists a while to catch up. The pain intensifies again, my molecules regroup, and once more I am a solidified slab of human agony. When the pain gets too much to bear I concentrate on my breathing. One breath at a time. I will not move. I will not change my posture. One breath at a time. The sweat pours from me, but I do not move.

The teacher has told us every pleasant sensation we have will become an unpleasant sensation. He's got that right. I'm still waiting for the other half of the equation. Every unpleasant sensation will become a pleasant sensation. Arising and passing, the law of nature. I think I'm getting a bum deal. I grit my teeth and persevere. I'm going to do it this time. I'm going to get through the hour without moving. I will use strong determination and I will triumph. Am I attached to this outcome? Am I craving it? Have I lost the little equanimity I had? My skin itches from the combination of dried and fresh sweat. Little needles prick me all over. There is a pressure in my skull, not pain, but I feel as though my brain is being squeezed. I forget where I'm up to in the sequence of going through my body. Was I at my left arm or was I down to my toes already? Is there any part of me that doesn't hurt? Keep breathing and don't move. It must be time. That click is going to happen any second.

And then I give up. I sigh, which probably annoys the people around me, and stop craving the click of the CD player. I steady my mind, quiet my thinking, concentrate on my breathing and start again from the top of my head. Not so quickly as to miss sensations and not so slowly that I get bored. Examining the sensations from the top of my head to the tips of my toes and back again. My poor left knee. It bears the weight my right one can't in this strange lopsided kneeling position. I have to massage it after every Group Sit and talk to it gently, coax it to keep going and not collapse all together.

The teacher's voice makes me jump. The shock is so great I am literally lifted off the meditation stool by the sound of his chanting. I am ecstatic but disbelieving. Have I really made it through a Sitting of Mass Destruction? Have I really used my strong determination for good? The chanting continues. I want to struggle out from the meditation stool, clamber over to the assistant teacher and give her a high five. This is a miracle. The teacher keeps chanting. I swear his chants get longer every day. We're not supposed to move until the chanting stops. I've made it this far. But now the distraction of his voice makes the pain I'm in even more unbearable. To have come this far and then fail? I couldn't bear it. Still the chanting continues. I'm beginning to hate it, my aversion to it growing by the second. When will it stop? This is my hour of triumph and I'm not going to blow it at the last hurdle. Finally his chanting slows into the strange upward swoop that is his finale. The other students chant, *sadhu, sadhu, sadhu*, which, thanks to the noticeboard at the dining hall, I've discovered means 'well done, well said'. Yes, indeed. Jolly well done, old chap. Marvellous chanting, tootle-pip. The students bow and I bow with them. Not out of compliance to this ritual but because it's a great way of stretching my aching back.

And then we are free. Free to move and, once we are outside the hall, to stretch. I revel in the sense of accomplishment. I have conquered the Sitting of Mass Destruction. I have finally won. I'm as high as a kite. I want to whoop and punch the air. I am invincible. I have taken on pain and I have won. I feel as though I've won a grand final, got through four quarters of gruelling footy without the aid of painkilling injections and taken out the premiership. Football teams should do a Vipassana course at the end of season. Forget about those boozy trips away, which always end up with a sexual assault case or three. Send the boys to Vipassana, get their thinking right, show them what real endurance is about. I have a smile broader than a bus. I am bulletproof. I feel so good I want to keep feeling this way forever. Another hour and a half of meditation before tea break and after that another Sitting of Strong Determination. Bring it on! I'm psyched. Bring on the pain. I can take it. I have won and I will win again. I'm pumped up and aggressive. Bring it on indeed. I'll take you on, you and your mate. Come on, have a go. I'll fucking smash you to a pulp. I have beaten pain and I can beat you. My mind flips into some kind of alternative reality. Instead of wanting the pain to go away, I want more of it, because I can beat it. I've done it once and I'll do it again. This is crazy. I thought this technique was supposed to make me happy. Instead I'm delirious and drunk on power.

The teacher talks about craving and aversion. It's all about our sensations. Everything we hear, touch, see, taste, smell and perceive creates sensations in the body. It's these sensations we become addicted to. It's not the drug, it's the sensations. It's not the food, it's the sensations. I want more of the good and none of the bad. Craving and aversion. And always misery because everything changes. But there's more. We get attached to our desires, to the habit of craving. Craving itself creates a physical sensation which we become addicted to. The teacher tells a story. 'Story is story,' he says with a smile. This story is about a man who was happy with his simple life, until he had a thought that it wasn't enough. He started craving and he started buying. More and more things. Household goods, cars, houses, boats, a plane, but none of them were enough. The man wanted a spaceship to take him to the moon.

'Even the moon is not enough,' says the teacher and chuckles. 'And oh, the misery, the misery.'

We are here at the Vipassana course to stop rolling in misery.

To come out of the old habit pattern of the mind, to come out of our ignorance, to be liberated. Instead of constantly reacting we are learning to observe. Awareness and equanimity. We stop tying new knots and the old ones are automatically untied. That's the theory. My reality is vastly different. I am addicted to sensations that don't involve any substance at all. The radical shifts that happen in my body when I obsess about something dreadful happening to my niece. The chemicals that are released into my blood as I convince myself that she's been harmed in some way. The buzz that floods my system when I get myself worked up about my house burning down. The teacher tells us there is no place for imagination in Vipassana, that we must deal with reality as it is, not as we would like it to be. But here, where there is no place for imagination, mine flourishes. I catastrophise in order to feel these sensations. They may make me shake and cry but, boy oh boy, I am feeling. I am addicted to feeling bad. I'm addicted to being miserable. So much of my life has been spent being the victim but I've done it to myself. I'm addicted to these sensations running through my body, tearing my endocrine system apart, overloading my adrenal glands. Anxiety, fear, worry, paranoia. I manufacture them myself with my monkey mind in order to get a fix of sensations. I have been indulging in intoxicants every single day of this course. I have broken the Fifth Precept repeatedly. Not with alcohol or cigarettes, but with adrenalin, the anxiety drug. And now with endorphins. That can be the only reason I've gone so wild for the pain. Craving it, whereas up to this point I've been avoiding it, fearing it. My body must be flooded with endorphins right now. Is there no end to my addictive nature? Is there any hope for me at all?

The teacher says we are working at a deep level to get to the root of the problem, to overcome these problems. We have severed connection with the outside world in order to explore the world inside ourselves. The universe that exists in the depths of the mind. Once we learn to observe all sensations, good and bad, with equanimity, the addiction at the subconscious level is removed. But I am not equanimous. I am high. It feels good. I want more. And there's something else. Something more insidious. I have triumphed over a Sitting of Strong Determination. I have won. I have this Vipassana thing sussed. Therefore there is no need for me to stay. I can leave now, happy in the knowledge that I have experienced incredible pain and have experienced the overcoming of this pain. I have released a huge resentment that I didn't know I was still harbouring. I have been liberated from the myth of romantic love, of anyone ever belonging to me. These are gifts I never expected and they are enough. There is no need for me to stay for another three nights and two days. I can go home, content and free.

I watch my mind as it twists and justifies, exalts in an orgy of self-congratulation. Then I remember the sharp clack of pointy black shoes, the flash of perfect teeth in a sneering smile. The cold clutch of doubt grabs at me and slices through my confidence. I decide to stay for one more Sitting of Strong Determination. I have to make sure I have this nailed. I need to be certain that I can endure what awaits me when I return to work in three days' time.

Day Nine

The breakfast bell is full of hope. The lunch bell is smug. The dinner bell is self-righteous and the bells calling us to the Sittings of Strong Determination are sharp and cruel. But the early morning, wake-in-the-dark bell is the saddest bell. It resonates through my body and tells me that this is lonely work. From four in the morning through to nine-thirty at night, longer if sleep doesn't come. Often I'm awake in the dark with only my thoughts and they've never been good company. The teacher tells us to meditate if we can't sleep. He says with the amount of meditation we're doing we don't need as much sleep anyway. I disagree. Sleep is an escape from the pain and the loneliness. But I'm not here to escape. I am here to confront and be free. *Be happy*, as the Teacher says every night at the end of the discourse. I was not set up to *Be happy*. The childhood lessons I learnt were of a different kind.

When I was very young I couldn't understand the abandonment. In my teens and twenties I blamed my parents. In counsellors' rooms I recounted their many sins. Of course my mother bore the brunt of it. I didn't expect my eccentric, distant dad to do too much in the nurturing stakes. He went to work, he made the money, he avoided emotional connection out of habit not spite. But my mother, the poor woman, was blamed for all my faults and fears. But as I grew older a change happened. I began to see my parents as people. And I made discoveries. I learnt that my father had been abandoned by his mother, literally. She ran off with another man and left her babies behind. Scandalous. It even made the local paper. His father then married the woman he'd hired to look after his three motherless sons. But there was no love. When the boys were grown the convenience wife declared her job done and left. My father learnt, in a more brutal way than I ever had, that parents abandon you. The pain he suffered as a child shaped the man he was. He did his best in life but only in death was he free. A miraculous thing happened when he died. I felt his presence strongly around me. Loving me. When he became free from his emotional and physical pain he was free to love me. I cried, I grieved, I missed him all the time, but through it all I felt him with me, loving me.

And as for my mother, I began to appreciate what her life was like. When I was eight, and my life fell apart due to neglect, her oldest son was eighteen, her next son seventeen and my oldest sister was at that dangerous age. My mum was dealing with a house full of bloody-minded teenagers, all experimenting with alcohol, drugs and the opposite sex. And the other people's babies that I thought she loved more than me? She looked after them out of necessity, to bring in extra money to keep us fed. No wonder she didn't have time for me. I understood. But two things, more than any others, shaped a new relationship with my mother. In Twelve Step programs I was given the freedom to develop my own spirituality. The Twelve Steps are a spiritual program, they won't work without it. I was allowed to have a God of my own understanding, not my mother's. It took me a while to get the hang of it, but when I did it was liberating. The weight of Christianity lifted and the joys of a direct connection with God bloomed. I explained to my mother, on one of my visits home, why I had trouble going to church with her. Every time Jesus was mentioned I had to replace the word in my mind with God. Yes, Jesus probably had existed, and done great things, but I could not worship a man. Saying those words to my mother, I felt as though I was on a precipice. I had never dared hold my own beliefs before, let alone voice them to the woman who had lived her life as a devotee of the man I was telling her I would not worship. I expected a tirade of derision and dogma. She surprised me.

'I'm happy for you, dear, but can you understand that not all people have your faith? For many of us the leap is too great from God to man. We need an intermediary. We need Jesus to help us connect with God.'

She accepted my new belief in God. She didn't challenge the rest. She had learnt tolerance and open-mindedness, two things that were never in evidence when I was a child.

The second event, which really cemented our growing bond, was many years after my dad died. To soothe her loneliness my mother had taken to the sherry. She would never drink until after five. But she would often pour a glass as early as four and have it there, waiting. A family gathering was being planned and she and I were discussing food and drinks. She was looking forward to a glass or two of champagne.

'Oh, but of course you can't have any,' she said. 'Because you're an alcoholic.'

She said it with meanness and spite. Sitting on the couch opposite me, glass of sherry in her hand. I felt wounded beyond measure. I'd been honest with her about my work in Twelve Step programs and she threw it back at me, as an insult. I could let it slide but I knew I would resent it.

'Mum, it makes it really hard for me to tell you things that are important to me when you say things like that.'

Her face turned from a sneer into one of open surprise. I held my breath. She said nothing. The silence stretched between us. I began to panic. I had just stood up to my mother and it didn't feel good. It didn't feel safe. I wanted to suck those words right back into my mouth. I wanted to reach out and say, 'I didn't mean it, Mum.' She sat on the couch looking shocked and hurt. *Don't say anything,* I told myself. *Just sit with this. You always try and make things better, you always deny your own feelings, your own truth. You want to be loved, you want to be the good girl. Yes, you've hurt your mother but it was the truth. Don't say anything.*

The moment stretched until the tension was so great I thought both of us might snap. Finally my mother spoke. 'I'm sorry, darling. I think it's because I'm envious of you. I would like to stop drinking but I can't.'

With that one sentence the wall between us dissolved and only love was left. After a lifetime of blame and recriminations, in that moment there was only compassion and love. And I'd allowed it to happen because I allowed it to be. I hadn't jumped in and tried to make it better. I didn't react. I sat with it. And the beautiful truth rose to the surface. Seems I had known something of this Vipassana business way before I got to this course.

The love and trust I developed for my mother reached another level when I told her about the drugs. And that it was Dad's death that stopped me using. When he died everything changed and I needed to change with it. I had spent so much of my time blocking out life, keeping it at a distance with food and drugs, wishing I was dead and actively working towards it. But when he died I realised I was going to die anyway. I didn't need to do anything. It would happen. Eventually. I didn't want to be surrounded by those who denied life, whose eyes were shut-down pinpricks, who kept nodding off in their waking hours. And I didn't want to be one of them anymore either. So I told her. Before he died I thought I was immortal. But after he died I realised life was special, not to be thrown away on drinking binges and drugs. Pushing the limits of chemical endurance no longer appealed. His death brought home to me that my time on earth wasn't infinite. It was time to start living.

My mother listened. She had become very good at it. She sat quietly and let me prattle on with apologies and justifications.

Eventually she said, 'At least something good came from his death.'

Of course I didn't tell her everything. I didn't tell her that my speed addiction had been so bad at one point, I'd had to shoot up before I could get out of bed. I didn't tell her about the heroin overdose in Melbourne, before Sam and I were together: the wrecked flat, the graze on my cheek and the vomit in my bed. I didn't tell her the St Kilda CIB thought I'd been attacked and kept those stinking sheets as evidence. They also insisted I see the police hypnotherapist. I had lost all memory of what had happened and they wanted to extract it from my subconscious. I'm sure the doctor at the hospital knew I'd OD'd. And my flatmate knew. She'd been the one to find me, dispose of the needle, take me to hospital and shield me from the hypnotherapist. I didn't dare admit the truth to anyone else, not even the boy I was seeing at the time who was called in for questioning by the police. I vowed never to use again. But I did. Even after my father died I used twice more. I didn't tell my mother that either.

The second last time was in Hobart. Sam was away. I was alone, just me and the cat. One of Sam's old drug mates rang me. He had some smack from Melbourne and he wanted to come over with a couple of mates. They'd give me a free taste if I let them cut the stuff at my house. I hesitated. I had left all that behind. Sugar was my drug and I was getting fatter. Sam was my habit and I was totally addicted. I didn't have room for any other drugs. I didn't want people cutting heroin on my coffee table. I didn't want a taste. But Todd was persuasive, he always had been. He was a happy druggy and totally unapologetic about his lifestyle. I said yes. He arrived with two guys clearly eager to taste the fruits of their bounty. They cut the drugs and gave me a foil. Enough for a good taste. I didn't have a syringe. They gave me one of those too. Me and the drugs and the means to administer them, alone in the house by the river.

I didn't have time to take drugs anymore. I had fudge to make, rehearsals – hell, I even had a band interview at midnight at a radio station in town. The drugs and I stared each other down. The drugs won. As soon as they hit, that familiar taste in the back of the throat and then the explosion of warmth through the body, I regretted it. Not tomorrow but the next day I'd feel like shit and for what? One more lonely night with pinned eyes. The band came around and picked me up at about eleven. The bass player was an ex junkie who recognised the signs immediately. He didn't say anything. I already felt bad. Once the initial euphoria had gone, I just wanted to throw up. If anyone had any doubts about my state they were completely removed by the time I had to leave the radio studio halfway through the interview. Humiliated and ashamed I ran to the bathroom and vomited in the toilet.

The very last time I used was in Sydney. Old drug friends from Melbourne were living in a share house in Darlinghurst with inner-city rock stars and dealers. I was lonely. Still new in town and the band had already disintegrated. I bought a small taste, went home to my bedsit and shot up. The warm safe glow lasted but a moment before the crush of loneliness flattened me with the brutal truth. Drugs do not work. I never used again. No smack, no speed, no dope, no hash, no cocaine, no ecstasy. The echoes of my drug use remained and the craving for the total release they gave me, however fleeting, prevailed for years, but long before I made it to the rooms of Twelve Step meetings I was clean. The food addiction, however, refused to budge.

The bell rings. The cruel bell. I've begun counting down the Sittings of Mass Destruction. Today is Day Nine, tomorrow is the last day. Five more to go. The first sit of today saw me emerge triumphant again, mentally punching my fists in the air, the high of endorphins flooding my system, every cell in my body tingling. I am hoping for the same success again this afternoon. I am still full from lunch: spicy chickpea curry, couscous doughy and rich, a cabbage dish stained yellow with turmeric, and my favourite carrot salad, studded with sweet currants and drenched with orange juice. I am hoping the food in my belly will dull the pain a little. My sisters have both been on antidepressants for years. The main ingredient in those tablets is serotonin, the feel-good drug. It's a drug the body manufactures when you feed it carbohydrates. Their endless dieting had made them carb-free zones, thus the need for serotonin in tablet form. I, on the other hand, had been self-medicating for years.

I adjust my bra. I removed the underwires days ago and it doesn't sit right. It's better than the jab of wire in my ribs though, something I hadn't noticed until I spent eleven hours a day meditating and most of it in pain. I walk up the gravel path to the meditation hall. Why gravel, for God's sake? Every time a student is late or leaves the hall, all we hear is the crunch, crunch, crunch of footsteps on gravel. When someone leaves the hall during a Group Sit, the manager gets up and follows them out, then we have two sets of footsteps crunching on the gravel. That has not happened to me, yet. In Twelve Step programs they used to threaten me with the *Yets*. Don't get too smug, just because you haven't sunk as low as others doesn't mean it won't happen. It's a *Yet*. It hasn't happened, yet. Twelve Step members say they're in recovery. But they never recover. They never get to graduate. They are told to be eternally vigilant because the disease is cunning, baffling and powerful. It waits to trip up those who get too arrogant. Fear, fear, fear. It reminded me of being threatened by the devil when I was a kid.

Ironically it was a Christian woman in one of my Twelve Step groups who opened my eyes to this. She believed she would be healed. 'I don't intend to stay in program forever,' she said. 'I believe I will recover.'

It was a radical statement. At the meditation centre I'm being taught something equally radical. I am learning a new way of thinking. I am not powerless, as the very first of the Twelve Steps would have me believe. I am the master of my own salvation. I must do the work and release myself from the endless cycle of craving and aversion, of attachment and reaction. I can be free. I can recover. But first I must master my mind and that's proving to be a big ask.

I stand outside the meditation hall with the rest of the stragglers. Lisa waits patiently, as always. I psyche myself up like a coach with their team. *You can do this, you've won before, you can do it again. This time you will sit without changing your posture. You will overcome pain, you will be equanimous. Only five more to go. You can win them all.*

For the first part of the meditation my mind roams as usual; winning lotto, my niece in jeopardy, the house burning down, no boyfriend and sex. Oh yes, sex. The man who sits just across the white line of tape in the meditation hall is long limbed and tanned. He is gorgeous, with his mussed up hair and crossed legs. Lovely legs, calm, serene legs. My thoughts have often strayed in his direction.. How I wish he would wrap those legs around me. The focus on sensations during meditation makes my mind linger where it shouldn't. Sometimes I concentrate on that dark space between my legs, the hairy magnet, as a way of taking my thoughts away from the pain. Sex, sex, sex. Pornographic images flicker behind my closed eyelids while I meditate. They should have put the men behind a wall instead of just a line of white tape. I pray the assistant teacher cannot read our minds as she sits on the low stage swathed in white.

My roaming mind becomes more productive and comes up with a piece of true brilliance. Vipassana is a technique for the overcoming of craving. It teaches us to observe craving without reacting. There is a huge market for the biggest problem caused by craving. The weight-loss market is a billion dollar industry. Every magazine cover espouses a new diet. Diet books sell like the hot cakes they tell us not to eat. We're all told diets don't work. The relapse rate is huge. I'm proof of that. But if diets don't work, what about meditation? What about a meditation technique taught exclusively to help people lose weight? *Meditate to lose weight.* It's brilliant! I could start a business teaching people to meditate to overcome their cravings for blocks of chocolate, whole cheesecakes, packets of biscuits and tubs of ice cream. I could run workshops, seminars, residential retreats. I can train others to teach the technique. Hell, I could turn it into a franchise. It will need a catchy name. *Meditate to Lose Weight* is good but too long. *Medit-ate. Medit8.* Yes. And slogans:

'If you can sit on your bum and breathe you can lose weight.'

'Eat what you want, because what you want will change. Everything does.'

And a sales pitch: most nutritionists say we need to change our eating habits but we can't change our habits without mastering our minds. Change your mind, change the way you think, change the way you react. Yes, you can eat just one. Impossible? No. Not if you change the way you think about that biscuit. It won't fix you, it won't make you feel better, it won't take the pain away, it won't bring your boyfriend back. It is just a chocolate biscuit. Reality as it is, not as you would like it to be. Eat that chocolate biscuit with awareness and it will cease to have any power over you.

'But I want to eat chocolate now,' says my client. 'And I want to eat a lot of it.'

'Observe the thought, observe the feeling.' I smile serenely. I am swathed in white, sitting cross-legged on a stage. 'Where is that feeling in your body? What is that feeling? Irritation, pain, heat, itching? Observe the sensations and remain equanimous. Breath and observe. The sensations will change, arising and passing, the law of nature. You will be free of your craving, free of your weight, free of your misery.'

It's a winner. I'll appear on all the television talk shows. I can even give a demo of a Sitting of Strong Determination during the show. They could time me for an hour and have a special meditation-cam set up to make sure I don't move. The rest of the TV program will continue and I'll be sitting in one corner of the set, eyes closed, meditating. No need for Elliot Purvis and the ABC. I'll be making a motza.

The slight ache in my knee turns predictably to a throbbing pain. The wings growing out of the middle of my back scream to be released from my skin and muscle. I observe a slight itch on my cheek turn into a searing pinprick of heat. It is time to reign in my thoughts. This will pass, this will change. The pain remains. I breathe, I sweat, I hurt. *This will change*, I chant in my mind. Arising and passing everything changes. But I can't change everything. That's why I'm here.

God grant me the serenity to accept the things I cannot change, courage to change the things I can and wisdom to know the difference. Courage to change the things I can. Courage to withstand the fierceness of the pain that is bursting out of every pore. The intensity of it threatens to incinerate my body. How much am I willing to put up with? By sitting through this agony am I not buying into my victim mentality yet again? I have been bad therefore I must suffer. Bad girl. This is crazy. I must be insane. I should have stayed with Twelve Step programs, they never hurt this much. The Big Book of AA says that God wants us to be happy, joyous and free. It resonates with the words the teacher says at the end of every evening discourse. *May all beings be happy. Be happy, be happy.* Happy. Happiness. It's the prize. Is this happiness? Is this what God wants? I breathe, observe the breath, observe the sensations. I can't tell where the pain is coming from anymore. The heat and light of my body expand, divide and separate, piece by piece, into the smallest particles. My pain is not pain. It is energy. I could light up a city, a nation, a world, a universe. A sound breaks over me like a wave. It is the teacher. The chanting has begun. I have not changed my posture. I have triumphed again. I am one step closer to reversing the wheel of misery. And best of all, there are only four more Sittings of Strong Determination left.

Day Ten

Something catches my eye before I enter the dining hall. It's the noticeboard. I'm used to checking it every day, hungry for something to read. Today it is a smorgasbord for my eager eyes. The entire timetable has changed. After the first Group Sit, we are to remain in the hall. We will learn the last section of the Vipassana technique, the healing salve. It is called *metta*. After *metta* there is nothing except lunch until the next Group Sit at two-thirty. And then there are no more meditations until after teatime. There's a video in the hall at four pm, extolling the virtues of doing service to help us on the road to liberation. The timetable for tomorrow is also on the board: four-thirty am, chanting and final discourse, breakfast at six-thirty as usual and that's it. After that it's back to the real world. I feel as though a hole has opened up in front of me. The day-to-day routine is over. Everything has changed. Will I always feel this way when things change? Threatened. Afraid. Anxious.

After breakfast I arrive at the door of the meditation hall at the same time as one of the pretty, slim students. We both reach for the door handle. I step back and so does she. I step forward again and she does too. I step back again. A silent dance of frustration. She starts to step back again then makes the decision, grabs the door handle, enters the hall and leaves me floundering in her wake of disapproval. I slink into the hall feeling both small and fat. She doesn't have time for old, slow women like me who can't even make a decision or take the initiative. Her disgust clings to me like a dirty sheet. I am filthy and stupid. *Stop!* I observe those thoughts. My insane, destructive mind. I haven't even sat down and yet I am already miserable and distressed. I have painted a picture of hell and reacted to it as if it is real. Again. I breathe. Observe the breath, observe the sensations. Observe the rush of anxiety my thoughts gave me. Be aware of my body's addiction to sensations. Observe, be aware and remain equanimous. It is constant, the need to keep practising. In every situation I am challenged by the habit patterns of my mind, the way I slip into being a victim, into being miserable. I create my own torture. I can liberate myself from it too. I sit. I breathe. Soon the familiar pain begins.

Once again I am able to make it through a Sitting of Strong Determination, but at a cost. When I try to stand my legs are stiff and my knees ache through to the bone. I try to walk towards the gauzy light of the door but I have to stop and rub my kneecaps, willing them into motion. Outside the yoga girls stretch and bend. I stagger slowly to the toilet and back. I need the healing balm for my wounds. I am looking forward to learning about *metta*. On the noticeboard it's described as selfless love and good will, the qualities of a pure mind. We settle back into our positions in the hall. The assistant teacher presses the button and the teacher's voice fills the space. He gives us instructions in his lilting, strongly accented English. He takes us through a long slow process, a kind of chant in which each of his vowels and consonants is stretched out to the limit of his breath, until there is no sound left for them to make. The effect is excruciating. Not the balm I had hoped for at all.

Metta boils down to this: after meditation you make yourself comfortable, then you ask to be free of all defilements. If there are any defilements remaining you can't practise *metta*. Sorry, no balm for you, you have an evil mind. If you are free of defilements then you can share your merits with all beings. The process of *metta* ends with the phrase which he's been ending each of the discourses with. 'May all beings be happy. Be happy.' Why he has had to stretch the whole deal out for so long is beyond me. Especially as I do not feel as though my wounds are being healed at all. The heat is oppressive as always and honestly I prefer his chanting in the language I don't understand to this quasi-chant of 'may I be freeeeee, be freeeeeeee of all defilements'. Clearly I am full of defilements. No balm for me. But towards the end of the session I feel strangely relaxed. Maybe I have benefited from the other students' merits. Perhaps there is something to this *metta* after all.

As we stumble out into the light, full of selfless love and good will, we are greeted by an impressive sign. So impressive it has its own frame and is hung on a post directly in front of us. Noble Silence is over, the sign tells us. As the teacher warned us last night during the discourse, 'It is time for the Noble Chattering to begin.'

The sign asks us to refrain from talking within the immediate surrounds of the hall and to maintain the rule of no physical contact. I walk away from the door, into open space, expecting an explosion of sound, but everyone is tentative. Little fledglings leaving the nest. I have no idea what to say or who to say it to until I see Bernadette. Her eyes light up. We rush together and can hardly restrain ourselves from hugging. Without a word we cross the dry grass and kangaroo droppings to the nearest bench. In the shade of a spreading gum tree, words finally trickle between our teeth until a river of sentences begin to describe our experience of the last ten days.

'What about that pain!'

'Oh God, the pain.'

'I was so jealous of your little white chair,' I say, trying to keep the bitter tone out of my voice.

'That was a disaster.' She laughs. 'It was more uncomfortable than the floor.'

'But what about the back wall? Having that to lean on you must have been okay?'

She laughed again. 'Another disaster. Did you smell the stuff Lisa was spraying? That was for the ants.'

'Ants?'

'Yep. At first I thought it was sensations. I mean the teacher does talk about ants crawling, after all.'

We both smile.

'But I wasn't expecting the ants to bite,' she adds. 'Nasty, biting little ants. I was in enough pain without them adding to it.'

'So everyone who sat against the back wall was getting attacked by ants?' I am delighted. What beautiful irony. Serves them right.

'I had to move again. I couldn't stand it.'

'But that spray Lisa was using. We're not supposed to harm anything.'

'It was a deterrent, supposedly. It didn't work and it stank.'

How wonderful. All those people who I thought were having an easier time of it than me were suffering in other ways. The Buddha was right, life is suffering, there is no escape. Get used to it, get over it, and get happy.

Bernadette and I talk and talk. It is delicious, having a chat after so much pain and silence. We talk about the meditation technique, our troubles and triumphs. We talk about our lives and our hopes. She is a naturopath hoping to open her own practice. I am a music director who doesn't get to direct and a radio announcer who is told she is shit. She tells me they moved her out of the room she was supposed to share with me into a room with the pregnant woman. They thought Bernadette would be more helpful for a woman in her last trimester than the old dying woman whose snores I've been listening to for the past ten days. We sit under the tree, just the two of us, talking until we know each other's dreams, until we've shared secrets and visions, until the lunch bell rings.

We stock up on vegetarian lasagne, thick and rich with tomatoes and cheese. There is an apple crumble with custard that smells delicious but is not for me. Lisa and the two Asian girls do not serve us today. Today we help ourselves and the three women who looked after us so well are free to mingle and talk with us.

'I was not a popular woman,' says Lisa. 'Modesty is one of the requirements. Telling girls to cover up in this heat was a bit tricky sometimes.'

I search the babbling group for my roommate, the old woman. I find her outside, her plate already clean. Before she goes to get seconds I sit down beside her. I'm keen to find out how she went, how she coped with the pain, and if the technique has helped her in her battle to give up smoking.

'Hello, roommate. I'm Mary-Lou.'

'Yeah. I'm Dorothy.' Her face is a wreath of wrinkles. I examine it for the first time. Pale and craggy, her eyes are a dingy yellow.

'How are you feeling?' I say, with what I hope is sympathy.

'Still a bit hungry.'

Not the answer I was expecting but I press on. 'What brought you here to the Vipassana centre?' Now I will hear her sorrowful story.

'I wanted a holiday.'

'A holiday?' I blink in confusion.

'Yeah. I live in a boarding house in Brisbane. Full of noisy young people. Noisy kids, noisy suburb. I wanted a bit of peace and quiet.'

'Oh.' But her lung cancer. 'It wasn't to give up smoking?'

She cackles and starts coughing the phlegm-ridden chesty cough I have grown to know so well. 'Give up smoking! Why?'

'Your cough, I thought...'

'I love smoking.' She sits up straighter in her chair. 'In fact as soon as that last meditation was over I was out the front gate having a fag.'

'What?'

'Yeah. I found out that we're allowed to leave the centre once we're allowed to talk. Not far, mind. But I didn't have to go far. Smoking isn't allowed here but once you're out the front gate you can do what you like. I only came back for lunch.' She picks up her plate in readiness to go back for seconds.

'But you didn't smoke for ten days.' I'm not willing to give up my fantasy yet. 'And you've stayed this whole time. All those meditations...'

'Like I said. A holiday. Peace and quiet. That's all. And I must say that first fag was great.'

Oh my mad monkey mind. Nothing I had thought about her was true. More revelations follow. I catch up briefly with the older sister. Just long enough to find out she had three showers a day.

'It was so hot. I was so sweaty. I had to.' She looks at me defiantly.

I'm disappointed she could flout the requests to save water so blatantly. I leave her to seek out other companions. I'm equally shocked to discover some of the girls had talked at night in their rooms. So much for Noble Silence. Was I the only one to obey the rules? Except, of course, for breaking all the precepts.

I talk with a teacher from Melbourne. She tells me she felt nothing during the course. Nothing at all. Well, okay, a bit of pain from time to time, but apart from that no sensations, no insights, no lifting of resentments. She looked at me with dull eyes and I wondered where she had been for the last ten days. Shut tight in her little box. I also wondered why she had persevered. Ten days of nothing? I was bored some of the time but if I were her I would have been rendered senseless by it. Perhaps she had. Perhaps that was why she felt nothing.

I share a brief moment with the younger sister. In her gentle company I can admit to feeling embarrassed by the strange posture I had to adopt in order to get through the Group Sits.

'I thought you looked like a dancer,' she says with no trace of sarcasm or ridicule.

'A dancer?' My strange down-on-bended-knee position?

'Yes. It looked as though you were doing a grand jeté, frozen in mid-flight.'

I want to hug her. The kind, younger sister. I have to be content with a grateful smile.

I introduce myself to the graceful woman. She laughs when I ask if she's a model.

'Oh goodness no,' she says. 'I'm glad you thought I was graceful, though. I'm the clumsiest person alive. My arms and legs are too long and I have to concentrate really hard not to trip over all the time.'

Another misconception corrected. But what about the straight-backed girl who sat in front of me? What was her secret? How did she get through eleven hours of meditation a day without pain?

'No pain?' She is genuinely surprised. 'Are you kidding? I was in agony.'

'But your different postures, the way you sat, always with your back so straight. You looked so serene.'

'Looks are deceiving.' She laughs. 'When I sit cross-legged my back causes me incredible pain. When I kneel on the cushions my back is okay but my knees suffer. I was constantly sacrificing either my back or my knees.'

In Twelve Step programs they used to say, 'What other people think of you is none of your business.' It was a saying designed to liberate us from the eternal worry about other people's opinions. Today it is clear – what I think of other people is none of their business. Truly, what I think of them has got nothing to do with them. I have got it so wrong, every single time. I make things up in my head and believe they are true and treat people accordingly. *Madness,* as the teacher would say.

The barrier between the male and female dining rooms has been removed. Instead the noticeboards are covered with information about the centre and the technique. Books are on display on the male side of the verandah and I brave the short journey to the other side. Before long I find myself doing what I do with blokes, shooting the breeze, hanging out and talking shit. It's a legacy of playing in bands for so long and working in radio. Both, for the most part, dominated by men. You have to fit in to get along. I impress the male students with my murder fantasies in the meditation hall. They had them too but never thought a woman would have those kinds of thoughts. I feel pumped up. Male attention. I love it. I begin sussing them out, wondering if one of them would make a good boyfriend. It's not until we start talking about the sex fantasies we had during the meditations that I realise I have crossed the line. Only a few hours after the lifting of Noble Silence and I'm talking sex and violence in an attempt to impress these men. I'm boasting, showing off. At first it makes me feel good, then it makes me sick to my stomach. Have I learnt nothing? I say a quick goodbye and scurry off.

Without thinking I end up at the meditation hall. All the talking has been too much, too soon. I am overwhelmed and sad. I slip off my sandals and do what I never thought I would. I sit in the hall and meditate during a time when I'm not required to. The louvres allow a gentle breeze to skim through the empty hall, deliciously free of the hot press of bodies. The hall is mine. I am alone in the soft gloom. I arrange myself into my grand jeté and breathe.

After some time a rustling sound surprises me. I open my eyes to seek out the source. One of the long-limbed young men is meditating on the other side of the hall, across the sea of cushions. We are alone. The two of us in this hall. Full of vibrating energy. Sensitive to the slightest sensation. I close my eyes again. How wonderful it would be to have sex in this hall, on all these cushions. Him and me and the sensations, the vibrations, the arising and passing, the rising and falling, the breath, always the breath. Every atom in my body tingling, every atom in his body pulsing, every atom, every particle in this room, in this universe, vibrating with us. My body dissolves, the space between my atoms expands infinitely. I am no longer in the meditation hall. I am in the realm of creation. I am a spark among other sparks. Little stars in the velvet dark. My time has come. And I say, *yes*. I choose. My decision. My choice. A surge of energy carries me forward, looping through the blackness. I am in my parents' bedroom. But I am not a child. I am beyond human. I float above their bed. They are making love. I sense my mother's craving. She wants another child. She is desperate for another baby. 'Yes, yes, yes,' she is calling in her mind. Calling for another child as my father thrusts inside her. I sense my father's aversion. They have more than enough children, he only wanted four and there already five. Yet she is insatiable, always wanting more. He is angry with himself for submitting to her. With each thrust he holds back a little. He doesn't want another child. 'No, no, no,' he is resentful. No more children. But his body betrays him. I speed through the final space, I am a comet of light. No more darkness. I am home. Joy explodes around and through me.

My eyes snap open. I am back in the hall. Overwhelmed by the realisation. All those personal growth gurus are right. We choose our parents. I know it. I have just experienced it. Experiential wisdom, the only true wisdom, the wisdom that leads to liberation. I am not an accident. I am not a victim. I chose my parents. I chose my entire family. I was the last of six. I knew what I was getting myself into. But more than that, I chose to be here, in this world, in this life. I have spent so much of my life, the life I chose, trying to avoid it, numb it, negate it, divorce it, wishing I was cold and under the ground like those lucky corpses. Hearing about plane crashes, car crashes, senseless deaths and wishing it was me. But the truth is I chose to be here. I am home. I am safe. I belong. I was given the choice and I chose life. This life. That is power. The power of choice. And I made it in full knowledge of the facts. I am astounded. I was fully conscious at conception. No one could ever have told me this was the case. I had to experience it for myself. And I have. And that experience has given me freedom, power and joy. *Be happy.* I am transformed.

I am also reminded that no matter how bad I have felt about myself, and no matter how unbearable my work situation is at present, I have, for the most part, been free to live the life I chose: acting, music, radio, a life full of creativity and adventure. I don't have a big bank account. I have virtually no superannuation. I don't own the things most people my age do. But I have lived a life of *yes*.

A friend once asked me why all the good stuff happened to me. Why did I have such an interesting life while he was stuck in Hobart working for the public service? I told him it was because I said *yes*. I didn't hang back and worry about security, even though on reflection I sometimes wished I had. I said *yes*, and plunged into another new experience. It's as though I've lived three lifetimes already. I don't need to believe in reincarnation. I have been reincarnated many times, within the span of one life.

During the day, among the displays on the noticeboards, the books and the chat, strange faces have sat behind a desk collecting payment for the course. Many years ago the teacher discovered that to charge a set fee generated ill feeling. Students had expectations of what they should get for their money. Meditation is not a business, so a new system was developed. These days no one has to pay. The course is free. What students do instead is make a donation, so that someone else can do the course. We pay whatever we can afford to allow someone else to receive the benefits we have received from these ten days. I had thought about how much I would pay at various stages during the course. At some times I thought they should pay me for going through such trials. But I am surprised when I sit down at the table, retrieve my wallet from the big metal box and hand over three times the amount I had decided on. The gifts I have been given are beyond measure, certainly beyond money.

I eat my last supper of two pieces of fruit, get through the last Sitting of Mass Destruction, and then settle in for the last of the evening discourses. The teacher reviews what we have done over the past ten days: the precepts, *anapana* meditation to concentrate our minds by using the breath, developing our wisdom with Vipassana meditation, observing reality as it is, sensations arising and passing. He goes further to talk about *bhanga*, the experience of the dissolution of the apparent solidity of the body into subtle vibrations which are constantly arising and passing away. I wonder if that's what I experienced when my body was blown across the hall by a sneeze. He tells us, as always, to keep working seriously, to give this technique a decent go before we decide if it is for us or not. I've always appreciated this. It reminds me of the *take what you like and leave the rest* attitude of Twelve Step programs. Find out what works for you, and if it works, use it. If not, let it go.

The teacher has always told us he is what he calls a householder, not a monk, not a priest. He existed in the world of business. He was rich and successful. Amassing money was his chief purpose in life. Because of the stress he developed migraines. He tells us he considers himself fortunate that he became sick. The best doctors around the world could not help him. All he was given was morphine and a warning that eventually he would become an addict. A friend suggested Vipassana meditation. It was being taught in Burma by a government official, a family man. At first the teacher was not accepted into the course; the Burmese official said he could not do it if all he was after was a cure for his migraines. The purpose of Vipassana was not to cure disease but to liberate the mind. Our teacher decided that liberation was what he wanted and, after overcoming his religious upbringing, he began walking along the path. He fulfilled his worldly responsibilities as a family man but he kept meditating and every year did a retreat of ten days or longer. After fourteen years he took a trip to India to visit his parents. His mother had developed a nervous disease which he knew could be cured by the practice of Vipassana. But there were no teachers in India. He took his parents through a course, then more and more people wanted to learn. After his teacher died, the teacher decided to devote the rest of his life to serving others, to live the life of *dhamma*. *Dhamma* is the truth as taught by the Buddha, the ultimate reality, the Universal Law of Nature. It is the knowledge and experience of these truths; doing the right thing, at the right time, in the right way, for the right reason, to attain balance. He kept teaching Vipassana so that others would receive the seed of *dhamma* themselves. But still at every opportunity he describes himself as a householder. He has children, grandchildren, a wife. The camera pans back and to the right slightly. All this time it has just been the teacher in a tight camera shot. All we have seen are his head and shoulders. But as the camera pans back into a wider shot he says, 'Here is the monumental testament to my status as a householder.'

It is his wife. She has been sitting next to him all this time. She is indeed monumental. The shot, being wider, shows more of the teacher himself. He is not a slim man. In fact he is quite rotund. Some might even call him fat. Monumental, perhaps. Here he is, an experienced Vipassana meditator, well versed in the observing and overcoming of craving, yet it is clear both he and his wife like their tucker. Apparently Vipassana is not the answer to being slim and it is certainly not the way to make a lot of money franchising my weight-loss idea. Meditate to lose weight? Looking at the teacher and his wife, clearly not.

At the end of the discourse the teacher begins to sing. His monumental wife joins in. With a rustle of lapel mics they stand, and still chanting, walk out of the room. The camera follows them to the door but they disappear into a corridor, still singing, still chanting. As the sound of their voices fades my feelings of abandonment surface. The teacher and his wife have gone, singing, to a better place where I cannot follow. I yearn to go with them to that mystical place only they know. But I am left in this hall, longing and sad, yet happy. Melancholy can be sweet. Bittersweet.

At the end of the last meditation of the day I'm smug again. I make it through without changing my posture. I share my pride with the older sister.

'That last meditation is only forty-five minutes long. It doesn't count.'

What is with this girl? Why does she have to be so surly about everything? Perhaps a better question would be, why do I let her affect me so strongly? I was happy, now I'm miserable. The eternal yoyo. Breathe, be aware, be equanimous. Be happy.

I have succeeded. Ten days of pain, anguish, intense suffering, intense joy, relief and release are over. My solace and refuge welcomes me for the last time. My bed. The old woman is already snuffling gently. Her peaceful break from the bedlam of the boarding house has kept her fed and watered. If she needed to catch up on her sleep she's certainly achieved that. I won't miss her snoring. I roll over and stretch my back. When I get home I will not meditate sitting on the floor, that's for sure. A strong straight-backed chair with a heavy-duty cushion will do the trick. My bottom will take the brunt but at least my knees won't sing their agony song. I roll over again. My buzzing mind and body are more than just a mass of bubbles. I'm fairly effervescing with energy. Tiny points of restless power tickle through my muscles, laughing and giggling, picking up friends along the way. These points grow in number and strength until my body jumps with their giggling energy. I twitch and jitter in my sheets. I wait for it to pass. My legs are out of control but I've experienced this before. Restless legs are easy to deal with. I swivel in my bed and stretch my legs straight up against the wall. Usually after a while the muscles and nerves calm down. It doesn't work. It's more than just my legs. Every muscle, from face to feet, is alive with rampant electricity, jumping, twitching, demanding release. The tingles, tickles and tremors continue without any sign of abating. Sleep is impossible. Tossing, turning, twitching, jumping. The hours crawl by. I have never experienced anything like this before. My body is alien to me. How can it be so full of this uncontrollable power? I jump off the bed with the force of it. I want to walk, stretch, run and bound about, but I'm still aware of not disturbing the other students. It will subside soon, I tell myself, while my legs continue to flail about. The muscles twitch and contract without ever asking my permission.

This is worse than the meditation hall, worse than the sugar cravings, worse than the tedium and boredom. This is unbearable. I am not in control of my body. It's as if someone has connected electrodes to every surface and an electric charge is being pumped in. I shudder and jerk like a puppet at the mercy of a drunken puppeteer. Surely I must be able to control this, slow it down, make it manageable. I observe my breath while my body bounces around. I observe my sensations. Every inch of my skin tingles and spasms. It's overwhelming and it's not abating.

Earlier today when we paid our donations, we were offered our lives back in the form of wallets, money, identification. I left my car keys in the security box, though, thinking I wouldn't need them until tomorrow morning. Tomorrow morning when I go back into the world, leave these gates, these people, these grounds. But I need to leave now. I can't bear this. Pain was expected. Both the teacher and assistant teacher talked about the pain. Amber talked about the pain. Even a colleague's husband talked about the pain. At the work Christmas barbecue only a couple of weeks ago I discovered he'd done Vipassana a few years back. I spent most of the evening fetching him beers and picking his brain.

'I've heard that it might hurt, is that true?'

'Well, yes and no,' he said. 'The first few days are the hardest and you do a lot of wriggling around trying to get comfortable, but after that it's not too bad.'

'So you didn't have much pain?'

'God, I found the whole thing painful.'

'Really?' I felt a moment of panic. Perhaps I'd made a bad mistake, either in enrolling in the course or in talking to him about it.

'Don't listen to him.' Jane, his wife, leant over and put her hand on his leg. 'He just wants to put you off because he didn't make it all the way to the end.'

'I made it most of the way through,' he protested.

'Yeah but you left on Day Nine. Who leaves on Day Nine? One more day and you would have finished the whole thing.'

'I was bored out of my brain. I was going insane. There was nothing to do.'

'You just wanted a cigarette.' She turned to me and explained. 'He wanted to give up smoking. He'd heard that Vipassana was good for that kind of thing and thought he'd give it a go.'

He rolled his eyes. 'And I did *give it a go*. Just because it didn't work doesn't mean I didn't give it a go.'

'But you left,' she said. 'Who knows what might have happened if you'd stayed.'

'I don't think one more measly day would have made any difference.'

'Well, we'll never know, will we.' She stood up and walked away.

He watched her go and lit a cigarette.

At the time I had thought he was crazy. How could anyone get that far into a Vipassana course and leave just before the end? You might as well just stick it out. Yet here I am on the very last night, wanting nothing more than to flee. My body jerks again. And it won't let up. My arms flail about the bed. Why won't it stop? The energy builds at the base of my spine and thumps me in the sacrum, propelling me into the air. I am not in control and I hate it. Not in control of my own body. If I can't control my own body, what can I control? All those desperate years of eating, driven by compulsion and fear. I had no control, I couldn't stop it. Every time I thought I'd be able to, the same madness started again. Out of control, bingeing and crying, desperate, alone, sad and ashamed.

And my body growing fatter. The shame, the fear. Out of control. My body lurches across the bed. The old woman snores on oblivious. How can she be so serene? How can she be so unapologetic about her addiction? No intention at all to give it up. No need to. I want to stop my madness, my insane behaviour. It brings me undone every time and I'm sick of it. Sick to my heart and soul.

I have to leave. I have to get out of here. More desperate than anything I have experienced through the pain and tears of the past ten days. My body is an alien. I can't control it. I must control it. Beat it into submission. Run it out, tire it out, deplete it, exhaust it. It is exhausting me. Sleep is not an option with my limps jumping like crickets, my body writhing like a worm exposed on sandy soil. I hate this. The tears come and I hate them too. Stupid, this whole thing is a stupid mess.

Too much stimulation. Too much talking and laughing with the beautiful Bernadette. Too much showing off and flirting with the men. How could I have sat there on the male side of the dining hall and talked about the pornographic thoughts I had during meditation? Where are my boundaries? Where is my shame? I want a man so desperately I even try to impress them at the meditation centre. Talking about sex and impressing them with my coolness. Surprising them with my candour. Revealing that I was like them. That they could relate to me. That I was worthy of their attention. And perhaps, maybe, if I tried hard enough, one of them might even be attracted to me and want to pursue a relationship. With me. A boyfriend. A lover, a companion. Spend time with me. Love me, love me, love me. I roll over onto my stomach. Perhaps I should masturbate. Perhaps that would dispel this energy. The sensations are intense. Imagine having an orgasm with the intensity of this awareness. I can't do it, of course. Not here. I've taken precepts. Oh, so bloody what! I've killed, I've stolen, I've lied. What's one more broken precept? But then there's embarrassment, modesty, shame. The old woman only feet away may wake up. With these heightened sensations who knows how loud I might be. Still, if she's even half aware of my thrashing through the hours she may think I'm already engaged in the activity. But I can't do it. The morality of a Christian upbringing. Hah! I've stolen so much, taken so many drugs, lied and cheated and brought myself and others undone time and time again and here I am worried about one little wank. But I have always been repressed in that area. Well, nearly always. I did jump the lighting guy from a famous eighties band. Dragged him back to my place and forced him to fuck me. I blame the speed I'd shot up earlier that night. I highjacked an Irish boy once, too. It was my last week in Sydney and I was flat-sitting in North Bondi. The bed was nestled up against a window overlooking the entire sweep of Bondi Beach. It was too good to keep to myself. A friend was keen on this boy but I didn't care. I filched him from her and fucked him while watching the surf break. Then there was the time I interviewed an ex-football star. He was too tall for my bed and left after we'd done the deed. And there was a stunt car driver – great driving is such a turn-on. Long gone, all of them, and not one of their names remembered.

The trucks howl along the highway. Lonely. How can they keep driving those trucks all night? Lonely. One more twitch and I'll get dressed. Throw my stuff in a bag and walk to the highway. Hitch a ride. Two lonely drivers together. Am I driving my own life? Am I powerful? I don't think so. I thought I was in control of my career until the restructure. How can a workplace treat people like that? I hadn't done anything wrong. In fact I was doing everything right.

In other jobs you get rewarded for doing everything right. Instead I've been shafted, undermined and lumbered with a boss whose actions are soul-destroying. I am not in control. I am not in the driver's seat of my job. It has been made patently clear that I am a powerless pawn. That management can do what they like with me. They shove me round the chessboard any which way they like. If I get knocked off the board by a strategic piece of play that hasn't taken my future, my ambitions, my desires and needs into consideration, then so what? I'm just a chattel, a number in their budget, an annoyance on the phone, another ego to have to deal with, and they'd rather not. Oh, they'd be happier with faceless drones, with no personality and no confrontation. They say they want ideas and personality, but when it comes down to it, management hate pawns with personality. Too much trouble. Workers with opinions? They despise us questioning their plans. Consultation is a buzz-word and that's all it does, buzz around in management mouths and emails, signifying nothing. Were we consulted when the hammer came down? Were we even warned that the restructure was coming? No. We were collateral, not people. Numbers, not human beings with feelings and aspirations. And now The Hideous Mr Purvis. What of him? He has the full support of management to continue on with his destructive ways. Why am I surprised? Management protect their own. We mere minions are reminded every time our complaints are dismissed out of hand as whingeing. Every time we are belittled by those who are supposedly there to manage us. Manage? It's more like ruling. We are their subjects. We don't have a voice. We are certainly not respected. We are at the coalface doing the work while they indulge Elliot's every whim. He has no idea of what he's doing but

I suspect he knows the effect he has on people. He gloats and preens and devastates.

This whole meditation thing has been a waste of time. I hate him. I hate myself. I hate my body, lurching and twitching with an energy I have no power over. I have no power. I am powerless. Powerless over everything. The Twelve Steps. We admit that we're powerless and that's supposed to be a good thing. I am powerless over alcohol, over drugs, over food, over The Hideous Mr Purvis, over the ABC. Where does that leave me? An unmanageable life. But only if I stop at the first step. The Second Step is coming to believe that a power greater than ourselves can restore us to sanity. But the teacher has spent the last ten days telling us we are our own salvation, that the power to be happy lies within ourselves, nowhere else. We can find real peace, real joy, real happiness by observing and remaining equanimous. I am not equanimous. I am insane and powerless. I want to leave and I want to leave right now. Why on earth did I leave my car keys in the security lockup? I could be on the highway. I could be home in my own bed. Doing what? Twitching, jerking, masturbating? I am here. Accept it. Twitch. Jerk. Breathe. Accept. Twitch. Jerk. Breath. Accept.

The teacher has told us a lot of stories, most of them parables and some of them funny. But this next story he told us was true. He was the assistant teacher at a meditation retreat in India, where he lives. One of his students did a very bad thing for a living. During this course we have been taught about right thoughts, right words, right actions and also right livelihoods. For example, working in an abattoir is bad, and being a teacher is good. The student the teacher talked about during this discourse had designed intercontinental ballistic missiles. A very bad livelihood! The teacher told us that when this student was meditating his body would jump in the air.

'Two feet off the floor,' the teacher laughed. 'Jumping and leaping.'

It was all the badness from his wrong livelihood being released. All the *sankharas* he had created through his work leaving his body with such force that his body was pushed up with the power of them. The teacher chuckled. It was a very good thing.

My body twitches relentlessly. I feel as though I'm being pushed from behind, kicked in the small of my back by an elephant. My body flails through the air yet again. Are these all the bad things I've done? Are they leaving my body with such force I am being pushed around my bed like an air puck? Is this a good thing? If so I'm grateful, I really am. I know I've been a bad girl but enough already. Please, let me rest. Let me sleep.

Day Eleven

The bell rings me awake. Four am. It's my birthday. The Feast of the Epiphany. Happy birthday to me. In the final discourse the teacher tells me about the birthday present I've been given. It is the seed of *dhamma*. During these ten days it has been sown and has begun to sprout. He explains that a good gardener protects a young plant so it can survive and thrive, and in return, when it is a huge tree with a strong trunk and deep roots, the plant will give and keep giving for the rest of its life. But there will be dangers along the way before this tender shoot is able to fend for itself. Other people will criticise, they may even object to this practice of meditation. Daily meditation is essential but as householders we are pressed for time in our busy days. If we are good gardeners we will find, as our practice deepens, that we'll need less time for sleep and our ability to work will increase. When we are at work, all attention should be on the work. It too can be a form of meditation. He suggests we check our progress along the path, both in our behaviour and how we deal with other people. I immediately think of Elliot Purvis.

'When unwanted situations occur, do you remain balanced?' he asks. 'If negativity starts in the mind, how quickly are you aware of it? How quickly are you aware of the sensations that arise along with the negativity? How quickly do you start to observe the sensations? How quickly do you regain a mental balance, and start generating love and compassion? In this way examine yourself and keep progressing on the path.'

Love and compassion for The Hideous Mr Purvis. That's a radical thought.

'Whatever you have attained here, not only preserve it, but make it grow,' the teacher continues. 'Keep applying *dhamma* in your life. Enjoy all the benefits of this technique, and live a happy, peaceful, harmonious life. Good for you and good for others.'

The discourse ends with his words, 'May all beings be happy, be peaceful, be liberated.'

He begins to chant, his wife joins in, and they rise and walk away. Once again I feel the sense of yearning. They are moving on to a better place and I am left behind. Left behind with the daunting task of living a happy, peaceful, harmonious life, good for myself and good for Elliot Purvis. I stay in the meditation hall while the other students file out. The teacher's words linger. How do I start generating love and compassion for Elliot? I know that I have played a role in his antagonism towards me. I'm scared he won't give me what I want. I'm afraid he'll take away what I love. My craving and aversion cause me to react constantly, whether he's done anything or not. I'm so convinced he'll attack me that sometimes I go on the attack first. I want to hurt him. I want to humiliate him. Just as he has done to me.

I'm always defensive. Constant knee-jerk reactions. I want to win. I want him to die a horrible death. This is *dhamma*, the Law of Nature, that the teacher has so often spoken of: any action that harms others harms ourselves. I see now how I've resented every manager or boss I've ever had. I resent them for having power over me. I don't believe they deserve it. I also put expectations on them they can never hope to meet. I expect them to love me. I expect their unconditional positive regard. I expect them to be the loving parent I never had as a child. No wonder I've always had trouble with authority. I want them to love me and I resent them when they don't. No matter how hard I work, no matter what I do, I am unloved. But it is not in their job description to love me. Never has been. They have never failed in their duty of care to me. I have failed myself. I am not a child. Elliot Purvis is not my mother. This is my part in the fiasco of my working life. This is the part that I have the power to change.

A special breakfast is presented for us on the morning of our liberation from the meditation centre. It's a dish we have all heard much about. Clearly it is one of the teacher's favourite foods because not one, but two, of his many stories dealt with this dish in detail. 'Story is story,' he would say with a twinkle in his eye.

Two young boys lived in the city. They were beggars. One of them was blind from birth and the other one helped him on their rounds together, begging for food. One day the blind boy was sick, so the other went out begging for the both of them. That day the boy who went out was given a very delicious dish, an Indian milk pudding called *khir*. He'd never tasted it before and he liked it a lot. Unfortunately he had nothing to put the dish in to take it back to his friend. So he returned to the blind boy without any to share.

'I'm so sorry,' he said. 'Today I was given a wonderful dish, milk pudding, but I wasn't able to bring any back for you.'

'What is this milk pudding?' asked his blind friend.

'It is white.'

'I have been blind since birth, I don't understand. What is white?'

'It's the opposite of black.'

'What is black?'

'Oh, you don't know. Then you must try to understand white.' The boy looked around and saw a white crane. He caught it and brought it to his blind friend. 'White is like this bird.'

The blind boy reached out and touched the bird. 'Oh, now I understand. White is soft.'

'No, you have not understood, white has nothing to do with being soft. Try to understand.'

So the blind boy reached out again and touched the crane, passing his hand from the beak to the tip of the tail. 'Oh, now I understand. It is crooked. The milk pudding is crooked.'

The teacher used the story to show us how important it is to experience reality as it is. 'If you do not have the facility to experience reality as it is, it will always be crooked for you.'

The other story was about a spoilt child who refused to have the *khir* unless it was in his bowl, with his spoon, sitting in his chair. His mother kept accommodating him but still the child would not eat the pudding because he didn't like the 'little black stones' in the pudding.

'This is not a black stone,' said the mother. 'This is cardamom, try it, it's very good.'

But still the child refused to eat the pudding. I was not feeling fondly towards the child by this stage.

'All right, take the black stones out,' said the mother. 'But eat the pudding, it is still good. Maybe later you will enjoy the taste of cardamom.'

'Only a mad child would throw out a delicious pudding because of the black stones,' said the teacher. We do not have to accept all the teachings, all the theoretical aspects of *dhamma*. 'If there is something you don't agree with, take it out. If you don't want the black stones, remove them, but enjoy the rest and have it in your own plate. That's okay. There are some things that must remain – morality, mastery of the wind, and wisdom – but the rest of it can be left out until you are ready.'

I'm glad, because there has been so much theory. Every evening in the discourses I became hopelessly lost and understood very little. But I did enjoy the stories. And this morning I have decided to enjoy the milk pudding, black stones and all, in any bowl and with any spoon, but hopefully on a seat on the verandah. Once again the day is bright clear and blue. No rain, at a time of year when it should be falling in slabs from the sky. I scoop a steaming ladle full of *khir*. It smells of rice and coconut, milk and spices. I know it is sweet. The teacher has told us in his stories. For ten days I have resisted Anzac biscuits, carrot cake, peanut cookies, passionfruit slice, chocolate cake and apple crumble with custard, but today I will accept what is in my bowl. Delicious Indian milk pudding. It is my birthday and I will celebrate. For the last time I sit on the verandah. For the last time I watch the kangaroos. I chat and smile and laugh and eat. The sugar monster doesn't stir. The compulsion doesn't raise its head. I enjoy the *khir* with a mind clear of panic, guilt or remorse. Be happy. Soon I will pack my clothes, load my car and drive to work. Work, for goodness sake! I'm due to start in a few hours' time.

After final goodbyes and exchanging details with Bernadette, I sit in my car, in the driver's seat. I have no idea what to do with this machine. I turn the key and wait for instinct and habit to take over. Slowly the car and I roll down the dirt road. Even at thirty kilometres per hour the trees seem to fly by. How will I ever manage the Bruce Highway? Better to take the back road than risk the hurtling speed of a national highway. I cautiously turn right. No cars coming, thank God. Everything feels new to me; the turn of the wheel, the press of the pedal against my foot. At least I have an automatic car, otherwise I would be stuck in first gear all the way to work. The speed makes me dizzy. The sensations come at me from all directions; the blur of trees dense and verdant beside the road, the rush of the grey beneath the wheels, the sharp ping of a stone scuttling under my tyres, the fecund decay of the creeks as I pass. I long to hear music, the teacher's chanting still drones in my head, but I resist turning on the CD player. I am afraid the richness of music will overpower me. I need all my concentration to wrangle this machine that, insanely, I am in charge of.

I have another motive for taking the slow way back. My lotto ticket sits in my recently retrieved wallet. Am I a millionaire twenty-two times over? My life has changed but has it changed financially? I pull over outside a small newsagency and hand over the source of my entertainment, of my stories and fantasies, of my desire, craving and aversion of the past ten days.

With a whirr of the machine the sales assistant looks up and says, 'Nothing there, sorry.'

And with those three words the powerful scrap of paper becomes fodder for the recycling bin.

After travelling carefully at sixty kilometres an hour for some distance, I brave eighty. Finally, as I become used to the landscape rushing beyond my vision in a sweep of formless images, I merge into the one hundred and ten zone of the Bruce Highway. The increase in speed grips me in the groin. It's the feeling I have when standing on top of a cliff looking down into the void. The unknown is so near. We drive every day but never acknowledge it.

The closer I get to work, the heavier the traffic becomes. I'm happy to slow down, crawling along Aerodrome Road, wondering if the traffic lights are out or if there's been an accident. But no, it's just the bumper to bumper traffic that goes with the holiday season on the Coast. I take it easy, avoid the lane hoppers and let cars in front of me as they sidle up. I'm in no hurry. And I won't get where I'm going any faster by being impatient, tense or angry. People who suffer from road rage should be sent to the Vipassana centre for ten days. Anger management with bite.

I arrive at work and walk through the door just as James comes off air from his breakfast shift.

'Welcome back. How was it?'

'Fabulous.'

He raises an eyebrow.

'No, really. It was.' I realise I've left my shoes at the door. James isn't wearing shoes either. It's a habit of his to walk around barefoot, often wearing one of his many Hawaiian shirts.

Tony comes round the corner from the newsroom. He is like a big happy puppy. 'Did you make it? Did you do the whole ten days? Or have you been hiding out in Noosa and going to the beach?'

I smile at them both. I love these guys. 'I did it. Just got out this morning and here I am.' My whole body is buzzing. I can sense every little bit of my skin, and under the skin the blood moving, the nerves responding. Strange, to be at work and feeling all these sensations.

Laura, my producer, comes over and gives me a hug. 'Well done. I knew you could do it.'

'Was it hard?' James' eyes are like little beetles. Curious and busy.

'Yes. And painful.'

'Yeah, you not talking. That would be pretty tough.'

'The not talking was wonderful actually. It was a relief not to have to do the whole social interaction, small talk stuff and just meditate. No, it's my bottom and knees and back that suffered. But it was worth it.'

Adrian emerges from the bathroom. 'Oh look, the meditation queen returns!' His voice booms and bounces off the walls. Has he always been so loud? 'And happy birthday, darling. I'll get the gnome.'

We don't give birthday presents at work. We give the birthday gnome. Always the same gnome, although it is looking a little worse for wear. Whoever is having a birthday is presented with the gnome and they keep it until the next person has their birthday. Laura and the boys hand it over, dutifully singing an out of tune version of 'Happy Birthday'. It's still a lot better than the teacher's chanting.

A phone rings. Laura answers it. It's for James. He goes into his office, puts his feet up on the desk and settles in for a long chat. Tony and Adrian amble off and Laura and I discuss this afternoon's program. She's lined up a few things but as usual for this time of year there's not much going on. I'll play more music, which pleases me greatly. Music. I remember I need to program the music logs. I excuse myself and get to work. The computer screen is harsh and bright, the colours are too gaudy and I am slow, slow, slow. My whole body tingles and I jump every time the phone rings. Everything is so loud. I wonder if I haven't made a mistake coming back to work today. I had no idea what I was in for before I went to Vipassana. If I'd known I would have taken a few extra days off afterwards, to adjust.

I go to the toilet and forget to flush. I've been in a different world for ten days and picked up all its customs. I make an announcement to the rest of the staff. 'I'm sorry if I forget to flush the loo. I haven't been doing much of that for the past ten days.'

'Didn't they have toilets?' Laura is shocked.

'They had toilets. They didn't have much water.'

'Don't worry about it,' James says. 'We're on tank water at home. I'm used to it. If it's yellow, let it mellow.'

'If it's brown, flush it down.' I finish the rhyme I first heard in Tamworth, staying at a friend's farm with the rest of the band during the festival. How he coped with having five women in the house and hardly any water was a miracle. But he never complained. Just asked us not to flush the loo unless absolutely necessary.

When it's time to go on air I'm reminded of sitting in my car earlier this morning. The desk in front of me is a mass of faders, switches and lights. On both sides I'm surrounded by computer screens and CD players. I stare at the desk in confusion but I'm not worried. This will pass. I drove my car here successfully, I can drive the desk. And at least the desk isn't capable of killing anyone. I come out of the news, give the weather and pre-promote my first guest; a stand-up comedian doing a string of dates on the Coast. I push the right button and a song goes to air. The music is so intense I pull the volume of the studio monitors right down. Softly, softly. Laura ushers the comedian into the studio. Now I really know I've made a mistake. He bounces off the walls with energy and I can only watch, mesmerised. I attempt an interview but my mind has slowed down so much all I can say is, 'Really?' and 'That's nice.'

Laura starts taking phone calls. 'What's wrong with Mary-Lou?' Some think I'm sick, others think I'm stoned. My speech is as slow as my mind. I sit and tingle. I do feel as though I'm on drugs. I'm still not sure which button does what. The comedian bounces around a bit more and I'm bemused. He's so tightly wound, so tense. I hope some of the peace I have encountered rubs off on him. He could do with a bit of serenity. He finally bounces out of the studio and I play another song, quietly.

When I open the mic I tell the listeners that I've just returned from a ten day silent meditation retreat and apologise for not being my usual self. 'I'm all right,' I reassure them. 'In fact I'm better than ever. But I'm still adjusting to being back in the real world.'

What is the real world, I wonder, as I sit and buzz quietly within myself. All these sensations I was never aware of before? A mass of bubbles? I feel them in and on and under my skin, arising and passing. I watch the clock as I time out for the news. The second hand sweeps through its arc. So many seconds ticking by. In meditation, sitting in the sweat and pain, the seconds crawled. But timing out to the news, they fly. Will I fit in the song, the promo, the segment and the top of clock sting? My chest tightens and my stomach clenches. The sensations increase in their vibrations. I breathe. This too will pass. I hit the top of the clock exactly on time and the all-too-familiar news theme fanfares its way into the studio. I've nailed it.

When my air-shift is over, I sigh with relief. Four hours of staring at buttons, interviews with spokespeople who stay on message and never say anything real, watching the phone lines light up with concerned listeners – has exhausted me. Laura offers to take me out for a cheap and cheerful dinner at the local Thai restaurant. I decline. I just want to go home to my little place, make sure it hasn't burnt down, that the termites haven't left only a husk.

To my relief, after a slow drive, I find my home is still standing, completely unaffected by ten days of my neurotic fantasies. Not even a scorch mark. I unpack my bags, toss all my clothes in the washing machine and think about dinner. My first dinner for ten days. The fridge is empty except for some apples. The thought of going to the supermarket, or anywhere else, does not appeal. I shake my head with a smile. My first dinner at home will be the same as the dinners of the last ten days. Two apples and a herbal tea.

After dinner I have no desire to watch TV, no desire even to read after craving it so much during the course. Instead I sit on a straight-backed chair, a cushion under my bottom and in the small of my back, and meditate. Observe the breath, observe the sensations. Be aware, be equanimous, be happy. I am happy. I am home. I am safe. And after craving freedom so desperately for the last few days, I find that two apples and meditation are exactly what I wanted all along.

The next morning I weigh myself, out of curiosity more than compulsion. I wonder if not having dinner has made a difference. I stare at the dial. Three kilos. Three kilos less than I was ten days ago. How can that be possible? I ate a big breakfast every day, and a healthy sized lunch, two pieces of fruit every night. How can I be three kilos lighter? I must have been lugging around something more than physical weight. Some kind of metaphysical weight has been lifted. I have a freedom within me, now I know Sam was never mine, now I know I never had any claim on him. He was always free to do whatever he liked, as it should be with all beings. I also know that I chose this life, that I chose to be here. I am not a victim. The chains I was bound with are gone. They had a physical weight. Three kilos.

After Enlightenment

Story is story. There were two brothers. When their father died, as was tradition in India, the property was divided between them. The last things left were two rings. One was made of gold and studded with jewels, the other was a simple silver ring.

The older brother said to the younger, 'The gold ring with the jewels must be meant for me. This ring must have been passed down from generation to generation. As I am the oldest I will keep this ring safe. You will have the silver ring.'

The younger brother said, 'Okay,' and took the silver ring. Later he looked at it and thought, 'This ring must be precious, my father kept these two rings together. Clearly the gold ring with all the jewels is worth a lot of money but why did my father treasure this small silver ring just as much?'

He examined the ring closely and discovered an engraving inside the ring. The words read, *This too will change.* The younger brother smiled and slipped the ring onto his little finger. Whenever he looked at it he remembered the engraving inside the ring. *This too will change.*

Winter came and brought the ice and snow. The older brother complained and moaned: the weather was too cold, he didn't have enough coal to heat the house, the trees had lost their leaves, everything was a trial. The spring and summer came and he was happy again, joyous and singing. But then the winter returned and he plunged into depression again. Trials came and the older brother became more upset and more depressed. He took to drink and was even more miserable. He had lost the balance of his mind.

The younger brother shivered in the winter cold. 'This too will change,' he said to himself smilingly and got on with his work. The summer returned with the warmth and beauty which he enjoyed, but whenever he looked at the silver ring he was reminded: *This too will change.* And sure enough the winter returned. But he accepted it, smiled, and went about his day. 'This too will change,' he said and he retained the balance of his mind.

The silver ring was more precious than any amount of jewels and gold. The silver ring helped him maintain his balance and therefore brought much happiness.

I have a silver ring. It has been on the middle finger of my right hand for twenty-one years. It's part of my history, part of my life. When I was about twenty years old I was a member of a small acting troupe. We never had much money but we were doing what we loved and life was an adventure. We had a small office space in an arts centre by the wharf in Hobart. The centre was also home to painters, sculptors, artisans and many small shops. In one of these shops a jeweller worked and sold his work. One of our members bought a silver ring. The other three decided to follow suit. I tried to dissuade them, none of us could afford to buy rings, but they would not be stopped. I ended up not only buying a ring but a bracelet.

The jeweller must have taken pity on me. 'You can return these if you need to,' he said. 'If money gets tight I'll buy them back from you.'

I did end up returning the bracelet but the ring still sits on my finger. With much effort, a lot of soap, and eventually oil, I manage to dislodge it. I ask an engraver to mark the ring with those immortal words. When I return to pick up the ring I look at my reminder of the power and simplicity of the Vipassana course. I read the words. *This too will pass.*

'This too will pass?'

'That's what you wanted,' he says. 'Here's the piece of paper.' The evidence is pushed towards me over the counter. There it is in my own handwriting. *This too will pass.*

It's not what I wanted. My religious upbringing must have taken over at the crucial moment. My mother used to say it, her Christian friends did too. I prefer *This too will change*. It's more Buddhist, less Christian. But I guess the message is the same and now it's engraved in my ring. Nothing can change that. Or can it? Doesn't everything change?

I wonder about the kinds of changes that will manifest after such an intense experience. I'm delighted about being three kilos lighter but I've learnt that it won't last unless I maintain some kind of structure, a pattern to keep me in check. Is equanimity like losing weight and keeping it off? Do I need some kind of maintenance plan? We were given one by the teacher before we left: meditate every day, one hour in the morning, one hour in the evening, attend a Group Sit weekly if we can find one, a ten day sit every year, service whenever we can do it and also five to ten minutes in bed in the morning and at night practising the technique. I like the lying in bed bit and I can manage one hour in the morning. At the end of the meditation I practice *metta*. I include the teacher in my thoughts when I think about all beings being happy. 'Fat fees for the fat teacher,' as he requested towards the end of the ten days.

I am a lot more comfortable in my meditating posture at home than I was at the retreat. Sometimes during my evening meditation I start falling asleep. I would have found sleeping impossible there. Not like some of the blokes. I would hear their snores emanating from the male side of the hall and be incredulous. I was in an astounding amount of pain and they were slumped over and snoring. At home I sit on the wooden chair, a pillow under my bottom and another behind my back. My legs are not crossed, my knees do not complain. Meditation is a much more pleasant experience. I observe my breath. I observe my sensations. I let thoughts go and don't engage them. I remain equanimous to all sensations. But how equanimous will I be when confronted with The Hideous Mr Purvis?

At work I'm being asked to speak up for the first time in my life. Slightly deaf from playing in bands, my voice tends to be louder than it needs to be. Up until now it hasn't seemed so to me, but since Vipassana my perception has changed. My voice is loud. Everything is loud. I've turned the speakers in the studio down. The volume in my headphones is lower too. Life is so full of sensory input it's nice to be able to control some of it – well, at least the volume of it. I am getting tired of the incessant buzzing of my body, though. Sensations vibrate through me all the time. I would like some relief. A local musician I interviewed recently calls the station.

'I hear you've just done a Vipassana retreat,' he says.

'Sure have.'

'Good on you. I'm an old student. I've done a few myself.'

'Really? Well then, can you tell me when this buzzing in my body will stop? It's driving me nuts.'

He laughs. 'That's a very good sign. If you've had a good sit then that can last up to two weeks.'

'Two weeks? But I feel like I'm on drugs all the time. I don't want to feel this way.'

'I did a thirty day sit in India a few years ago. When I came out it was like I was tripping. It can be pretty wild. But don't worry. It will fade. Remember everything changes. *Anicca*.'

'Yeah. *Anicca*.'

It's good to talk again with someone who understands. He tells me he was one of the founders of the centre. The teacher came out from India years ago and taught a course there. The teacher and his wife stayed in the cottage that the assistant teacher sleeps in now. The other wooden building was the meditation hall and the kitchen was in a caravan. All the students had to camp. 'It was a lot different back then,' he says. 'The place is luxurious now.' I don't think walking in the dark along a gravel path to the bathroom is luxurious but at least I didn't have to stay in a tent.

I hang up the phone and James calls me into his office. He's received an email from Elliot Purvis. He'll be arriving later today and will be staying for a few days. I'll have the chance to use my new-found equanimity and soon.

He slides in after lunch, smoother than silk. Black suit, black shoes, black tie. Even in this heat he never breaks a sweat. He places a CD on my desk. 'I want you to add this.'

I pick up the CD. The song has been on every other radio station in the area for months and is already burned. I hesitate.

'Is there a problem?'

'Well . . .'

'We are changing the sound of this station.'

'Okay.' I turn back to my computer. I can add it and then program the song as little as possible.

He stands over me. 'There are plenty of other people out there who would love this job if you don't want to do it.' He leans closer. 'If you're not comfortable following simple instructions.'

The familiar feelings of anxiety and anger bubble in my stomach. I twist the silver ring on my middle finger and breathe. Observe respiration, observe sensations.

'Is there a problem?' he asks again, sneering. I can sense the seething anger, barely contained under his perfect skin.

I remember a story the teacher told us. A man was angry with Buddha. His family had decided to follow Buddha's teaching and were Vipassana meditators. The man was furious because his family were turning their backs on the old ways, the old religion, they were seeking their own solutions. He approached Buddha like a charging tiger. He knew that Buddha would try to change his mind, he knew he couldn't afford to let him do that. He was determined not to let Buddha speak to him. Buddha felt him coming, the anger like a wave rippling out from the old man's body.

'Good day to you, friend,' Buddha called out.

'I will not talk to you.' The old man continued towards Buddha with murder on his mind. 'I know you will ask me a question. I know that's how you work. You will distract me and then you will change my mind. I will not listen.'

'Tell me, friend,' Buddha said peacefully as he continued to sit under the bodhi tree. 'Do people come and visit you at your house?'

'What?' said the old man. 'Yes, of course, we have many visitors.'

'And tell me, do they bring presents?'

'What is this? Yes, they bring presents.'

'And if they bring you a present you don't want, what do you do with it?'

The old man stopped and stood in front of Buddha. 'I tell them I do not want their present.'

'So you don't accept their present?'

'No sir, I do not. I tell them to take it back with them.'

'Then that is what I am telling you,' Buddha said. 'You have come to my house, bearing a present of anger, and I do not accept it. It is your present, it stays with you. Take your present with you when you go. It has nothing to do with me. It does not belong to me.'

The old man was so impressed with Buddha's words he stayed to learn about Vipassana meditation and was soon united with his family.

Elliot is waiting for a response. *The problem is not mine. The problem belongs to him and he wants to give it to me. Just because I'm practising equanimity doesn't mean I'm a doormat. I will not accept this present of anger. It's not mine, I didn't bring it here. It walked in the door with him.*

'It's a matter of music balance, programming and the overall sound of the station,' I say calmly. *This is my job, this is what I do. I am a professional music director.*

His mouth is a tight hard line. 'How dare you challenge my authority?'

And here is the dilemma. If you're not Buddha and you don't accept a person's present, they don't suddenly become happy and accepting, they get angrier. I sit and say nothing. Waiting it out.

The room goes quiet. Sometimes his silence is more frightening than his outbursts. Even the phones don't dare to ring. James and Colin sit perfectly still, not wanting to draw his fire. I glance at Colin, he's suppressing a grimace, or is it a smirk? Is he happy it's not him but me in the firing line today? I watch as a vein pulses in Elliot's neck. His eyes are fixed on me. I know he is expecting me to crumble, as I have so many times before. The slump of the shoulders, the blinking of the eyes to keep the tears at bay. He must relish those moments, his victory complete. Not today. I continue to breathe. This too will pass. I remember the moment with my mother. When I'd expressed what was true for me, even though I knew she wouldn't like it. I remember how time had stretched out and how much I had feared it would snap back painfully, like an elastic band. I remember how I had held the space, the silence, felt the fear and not capitulated. I remember and I keep breathing. But how can this moment have a happy outcome? I have left Elliot nowhere to go. He's my boss, he's not my mother. I'm clear on this now. Sometimes, on days that seem surreal, he treats me as his confidant. He tells me things about himself that I don't want to know. It's as if he's confused me with his closest friend. He's like the alcoholic parent, strange and sometimes terrifying. I'm left not knowing what is real or true. Perhaps he is more like the mother of my youth than I had realised.

Elliot grabs his keys. 'I'm going out.' The back door slams behind him. The sound reverberates through the office. We shift in our seats, realising how rigidly we've been holding our bodies.

'Now you're in for it,' Colin says. This time I'm sure it's a smirk

I don't answer him. I turn back to my work. But I can't relax. I wonder where he's gone. He often disappears for hours. When people ring asking for him we can never tell them where he is because we don't know. What mood will he be in when she returns? What new misery will he have concocted for me? I observe my breath, observe the sensations buzzing through my body. It doesn't matter what he does. I am powerless over him and his actions. This fear is just a sensation, it will pass. It will pass. Everything changes.

This change is unexpected. When Elliot returns, he returns not with fury and scorn, but with a white plastic shopping bag. 'I have something for you, Mary-Lou,' he says. 'You'll love it.'

Inside the bag is a box of green chai teabags. I'm baffled. He's been to the health food store and bought me tea bags. He is often unpredictable but this complete turnaround in his behaviour is far beyond a simple mood swing. Why has he bought me tea? It's as if he's a completely different person. Or has he no memory of his behaviour? There is not a trace of anger.

'It's delicious,' he says. 'Go on, try it.'

I can hardly say no. 'Thanks, Elliot.'

'I bought a big box because I know you'll love it so much you'll want to have it again and again.'

He walks back into his office as though random acts of kindness are a normal part of his day.

I boil the kettle and steep the bag. He's right. I love it. It's spicy, aromatic, and completely out of left field. I'm amazed at how he knew I'd love it. He confounds me. Did the angry old man in the Buddha story make tea for Buddha? Or is this how people in this day and age react when you don't accept their presents? If so I may never have to buy tea again.

I make it to the end of the working week, body still buzzing. Elliot doesn't mention programming the song again and I'm happy to let sleeping dogs lie. There is a tentative sense of peace and space in the office. The calm after the storm. The CD itself gets buried in the pile of new albums that come in the mail every day. When the weekend comes I go to a dinner party. My friend Natalie entertains like nobody else I know. Everything is done properly, Adelaide style, where manners are all important. She was shocked once to discover I didn't own any pearls.

'But every girl receives pearls on her sixteenth birthday, and if not then, at least for her twenty-first.'

'They do?'

'Of course.'

I had missed out on a whole world of etiquette, not having come from Adelaide, but still she puts up with my philistine ways and invites me to parties and dinners, all exquisitely catered and themed. Parties involve games and favours, dinners have handwritten menus at each place setting, and invitations are imaginative and often rhymed. This particular dinner party is for her and her husband Allan's seventh wedding anniversary. The small dining area is arranged perfectly with little silver dolphin place-name holders and the dinner set for eight completely matched. The guests begin to arrive and we mingle and chat. Natalie likes to mix up the guests at her parties and I meet two couples I haven't met before. I fully expect to be the only single person at the party, as usual. I certainly am not expecting Ken.

He's tall and big. Big legs, big arms, big smile. And he's single. Natalie introduces us. My hackles rise. What is going on? Has she tired of my single status? Does her Adelaide etiquette involve matchmaking spinster friends? Natalie is younger than me and probably considers me an old maid at the age of forty-two. I refuse to be interested, despite Ken's intelligent eyes and beautiful hands. I move to the other side of the room. Pre-dinner drinks and canapes in the living room turn into a game of dodge ball. I steadfastly ignore him. I don't even look in his direction. I will not be hooked up with a man of Natalie's choosing. I will pick my own men to flirt with. I find the boring man from Allan's work fascinating, his wife a font of all knowledge. My suspicions are confirmed when it is time for dinner. The little dolphin place-name holders have Ken sitting directly opposite me.

Throughout the meal I angle my chair away from Ken and face Natalie, who's sitting to my right at the head of the table. Conversation between Allan's work colleague and Ken becomes heated at one point. They discuss politics and the USA, policies and our place in the world. Ken's arguments are succinct and compelling. I agree with him totally but I am not going to tell him that. He tells stories and they are fascinating but I don't laugh at the punchline or gasp at the surprises. I will not engage with this tall, interesting man. Instead I turn my attention even more fully to Natalie, effectively blocking him from my field of vision.

'How was that meditation thing you did?' Natalie asks. 'What is it called?'

'Vipassana.'

'Yes. Ten days of silence. However did you manage it?'

The energy on the other side of the table changes. Ken, who, much to my relief, has been doing a fine job of not addressing me directly so far, is fully focused on me. His eyes beam straight into mine. 'You've done Vipassana?' he asks.

Most people don't even know what Vipassana is, yet this fascinating man, with great politics and intellect, clearly does. Not only that, he's impressed by the fact that I have done it. I can ignore him no longer. I am undone, my resolve gone with that one simple question.

'Yes. Have you?'

'No, but I know people who have and I've always been interested in it.'

Eventually Natalie is the one who is left out of the conversation as Ken and I talk to each other for the first time that evening. The party ends and the couples drift into the night. I stay to help clear up and do the dishes. Ken and I are still talking. The early hours of morning arrive and I discover Ken is a house guest for the night. I have no such excuse and my motivation for lingering is suddenly very transparent. Goodbye takes a long time. This man makes me laugh; he's funny, intelligent, interesting and very tall. Boxes are ticked in a very satisfying manner.

I return to my lovely house. Everything in its place; my space, my furniture, my cutlery and crockery. And the breakfast bowl I bought for the future man in my life. Could that man be Ken? I wonder about The List. How many of the Top Ten attributes does he possess? I will never know. The List was burned a long time ago. The cinders are dust.

That night I have a dream. In this dream Ken and I meet at a dinner party. The next day he and I have a cup of tea together. Everyone assumes we have spent the night together and tut-tut under their breath. But in the dream I'm not bothered by it, Ken and I know the truth. It is a simple dream but compelling. I wake with dread and excitement. It's not often anyone gets the chance to do what I can do today. But dare I? Ken is staying with Natalie and Allan. I don't want to give Natalie the satisfaction of knowing her matchmaking has worked. I walk around in circles in my kitchen. The breakfast bowl lurks in the cupboard. I pick up the phone. What's the time? Will they have gone out? Can I take the risk that Ken might be there alone and answer the phone? He didn't give me his mobile number. Probably not the best of signs. I stop and perch on the arm of a chair in the lounge room. The phone is clammy in my hand. I'm nervous. I want to call but I don't want to call.

I call.

Natalie answers. Damn. Do I hang up?

'Hi, Natalie.'

'Hi.' She sounds inquisitive.

'Thanks for a lovely dinner last night.' I could be polite, do the Adelaide thing. It's good manners to thank your host. Then I can say goodbye and get off the hook I find myself wriggling on.

'Thank you.' She has an expectant tone to her voice. I've never rung to say thank you before and I have been to many parties at her house.

'Um . . .' It's now or never. 'I was wondering whether Ken was still there and if perhaps he'd like to have a cup of tea.' There, it's done. She can be smug if she wants to. She can be the know-it-all, told-you-so girl. She can be victorious.

'Hang on, I'll just get him.' She's more eager than smug. I'm relieved but still anxious. I am about to make a dream come true. Literally.

'Hello.' His voice is on the other end of the line.

I take a breath and step off the cliff. Will I fly? Or will I fall?

Half an hour later we're sitting at an outdoor cafe, the Sunday morning sun warming our skin. I order tea and so does he, a good sign, I think. I'm in need of a good sign. The shorts and sandals he's wearing were not what I was expecting. I can clearly see the tan marks on his feet. This is a man who wears sandals a lot. He seemed powerful and wise last night but today he's dressed like a little boy. When the tea arrives, I tuck my aversion to the tan marks away, and concentrate on his words. They are beautiful, his voice deep and soothing. Thoughts create words, words create actions. If that's true, he must glide through life. He speaks of his ageing father, living on an island in the bay. Ken left his job to help look after him when illness came to call. His father has recovered and now Ken is no longer needed in the small house owned by his father's new wife.

I sit and listen. A gentle breeze rustles the trees, cars trundle lazily by, late breakfasters chat and chew through plates of eggs and bacon. This is the soundtrack to our first date. Is it a date? Surely it's just a cup of tea. But we are going through the actions and rituals of a date. I breathe and observe the sensations. Tightness in my stomach, tension in my jaw. Is this excitement or anxiety? Am I hoping for something from this man? Are these sensations craving? Craving for him to be the one. The one who will fit. The one who will stay, or more correctly, the one I will stay with. Are these sensations aversion? Aversion to the sandal tan marks. Is this me looking for the faults, the reasons why this will never work? Already looking for an excuse to run away. Be safe, the voice of fear says to me. Better to be safe than to be happy. I observe my breath, as it goes in, as it goes out. Stay in the moment, life as it is, not as I would like it to be, or fear it to be.

'And you?' He spreads his large hands on the table and opens up the conversational space for me to begin my part of the ritual.

I look into his eyes, with hesitation at first, then with more confidence. I've already dreamt this scene. There is no reason for fear. His face is open. I feel as though I can trust this man. Me, who has never trusted anyone or anything. 'You already know I work in radio.'

He nods. Certain elements were established last night.

'I thought I was unemployable until a friend suggested I'd be good on air. Everything fell into place. Then it fell out of place. My dream job turned into a bit of a nightmare.' I laugh nervously. 'Hence the need for drastic measures.'

'Vipassana?'

'Yes.' How much can I tell this man? We've only just met after all. 'I still love my job. It's exciting, creative, full of possibilities. I wasn't ready to leave it but I didn't know how to stay. I realised I couldn't change my job, or the people around me. The only thing I could change was myself.' I glance at him, waiting for his reaction. Will he get this stuff? Will he get me?

'How's that working out for you?' he asks, without a trace of sarcasm or irony. He genuinely wants to know.

'Ten days of silent meditation has certainly helped. I have a different perspective now. I knew in my head that I couldn't change other people, places and things but now I feel as though I've really got it. In my body, in my cells. And I do feel as though I can change. That I am changing.' I laugh again. 'Everything changes. I've certainly had that drummed into my head.'

'I've worked a lot in personal growth, in the field of change.'

'Really?' Last night his stories were about being catapulted off the front of an aircraft carrier in a plane during his days in the Navy, of the reality of being away at sea for months in a leaky ship, of his transfer to the Air Force when the aircraft carrier he had lived on for half of his life was decommissioned, of adventures and war games and tracking submarines for a living, tales of mess halls, and discipline and respect. This was a man's man, a squadron leader, one of the youngest ever. And, after he left the military, stories of working in a high-powered sales team. People around him making deals worth hundreds of thousands of dollars over lunch. He had met Allan in a much more modest environment, the job he'd left to look after his father, selling advertising for a major company, but in a country town. How did his work in personal growth fit into that largeness of life?

'Really,' he says, 'through a wonderful series of events I was given a place on personal growth course. I was in need of change. I was suicidal, desperate, depressed. I used to stare at the television screen all day and the TV wasn't even on. I saw my life played out before my eyes, all the mistakes, the resentment, the fear. I always thought I was bound for better things, for glory, but everything I tried failed and left me believing what I'd been taught as a child, that I was wrong, that I was to blame, that I was bad. The teachers on the course told me later that I was more out of touch with myself than anybody they'd ever worked with. I was so far from knowing myself they didn't know whether it was possible for me to change. But I did. And I continued working with them for many years, attending courses, then becoming a facilitator.'

I shake my head in wonder and sadness. His words are an echo of my own childhood. I was wrong, I was to blame. Bad girl. There is nothing I cannot tell this man now. He will understand. The sensations in my body shift and lighten. 'I was in Twelve Step programs for years. I suppose that was my personal growth course.'

He doesn't flinch, he doesn't even ask me if I was an alcoholic or an addict. 'Definitely. I've known many people who've been helped by them.'

I decide to test the water. 'I always thought my mother owned my spirituality until I found Twelve Step programs. They gave me a sense of my own spirituality. I'll always be grateful for that.'

He smiles. 'I always thought my mother owned everything about me. I left home and joined the Navy as soon as I could, so that I could have a life of my own.' He shrugs. 'I'm not one for organised religion. It's based on fear for the most part, and cruelty. I'm a spiritual person, not a religious one.'

'Yes.' I nod. 'Yes.' And my mind, my body and, yes, my soul expand and relax. There is a level of comfort here with Ken that I haven't experienced with another man. Ever? I search my memory, sifting through the passion and pain, the drama and boredom, of my past relationships. I hadn't thought of it until now, it hadn't been necessary, but not one of those relationships had a spiritual element to them. With my friends, yes, very definitely with those to whom I felt the closest bond, but with the men in my life, never.

My tea has gone cold. He notices and calls the waitress over to order a fresh pot. I lean back in my chair. He is no hurry to leave and neither am I. The morning may unfurl as it will; we will be here, in the moment, moment by moment, with ourselves and with each other.

We talk about our experiences of living in Sydney, and as we do we realise that we were living there at the same time, never aware of each other's presence. But here we are, together now, in a small beachside town so far away from that dazzling city.

'I loved living in Sydney,' I say. 'Until I didn't. It was if one day a switch was flicked and I knew I couldn't live there anymore.

When I was at radio school they told us we'd have to move to the country for our first job. Some of the other students were dismayed. I was relieved. I was ready to leave the traffic, the smog, the noise, the exhaustion of day-to-day life in a big city behind. Why did you leave?'

Ken looks away for a moment, the first trace of doubt on his face. 'I don't usually tell people this, after knowing them for such a short time.' He pauses. I see the path. The path that I am willing to walk to get to the final destination. I am walking on it now and I know Ken is too. He begins.

'The Olympics were on the way. I saw a business opportunity. I've always loved the water. I spent most of my life on it, either waterskiing when I was young or sailing on it with the Navy, flying over it with the Navy and the Air Force. With the Olympics, I saw there would be a need for more water taxis. That glorious harbour, so much activity. My plan was to build up the business and sell it. My research showed me I would become wealthy by doing just that. I did my due diligence, raised the money, did the training, bought the boats. My big mistake was to go into the business with a partner who would let me down. Badly. There was an accident on the harbour. How no one was drowned was a miracle. But the business was ruined.'

'Oh. I'm so sorry.'

'It was my own fault. I chose him as my business partner. Something in me was not ready to succeed.'

I'm amazed. I've lived so much of my life as a victim, blaming others for everything, including Elliot Purvis. But this man sees his own part in what he has created. He takes responsibility for his actions.

Ken turns to me. His face is serious. He takes a breath. 'I feel the need to tell you this. I need to be honest with you right now, at the start.'

At the start? The suggestion is he wants this to continue. My heart leaps and then plummets. His face is tight. The news is not good. He looks down at his hands and then at me.

'I'm in debt and I'm married.'

'Okay,' I say, slowly. The debt I can handle, although a figure of hundreds of thousands of dollars flits through my mind and my stomach tightens. But married? I hadn't suspected that. Not for a moment. He's not smooth enough, not cocksure and smarmy, the way I imagine adulterous men to be. And hadn't he been living in the spare room of his father's new wife's house? Surely that doesn't speak of a married man with a loving spouse in the mix.

He senses my discomfort and rushes to explain. 'I'm still married but only because we never got round to divorcing. I'm not even sure where she is. It's been over ten years since we've seen each other.'

'Oh, right.'

'Does that worry you?'

I think about it, but not for long. 'No.' A wife he hasn't seen for ten years is more of an ex-wife.

He relaxes again. 'I am in debt, but I'm paying it off.' He turns to me. 'In fact I have a new job, a great job I'm really looking forward to. I just need to get my affairs in order and make sure my father's okay before I start.'

'That's wonderful.' The worry and tension dissolve. Everything does change, sometimes quickly, sometimes slowly.

He begins to tell me about his new job and it does sound wonderful, until I hear where he'll be living. 'The Gold Coast?' I ask.

'Yes. I'll be busy getting settled into the job and finding somewhere to live, so I won't have a chance to get up here again for a while. But I will be back.' He smiles reassuringly and I know he will. And I know there is something of substance between us that we both want to explore. But the Gold Coast? It's a two and a half hour drive away. I've done my time with long distance relationships. They didn't work for me, or Ruby, or Sam. And then I smile. I remember some of my Top Ten from The List. Ken is tall, he gave up smoking years ago and he lives, or will be living, on the Coast. I have become so used to calling the Sunshine Coast 'the Coast' that I forgot to specify which one. My friend was right. Words have power. But is this what I really want? A man who wears sandals – a lot – a man in debt, a man who spent twenty years in the military while I was playing in bands and taking drugs? This man is so different to any man I've ever shown the slightest interest in. In the past I would have relegated him to the daggy corner and ignored him. Way too uncool. He is not my type. My type is the cool musician who takes drugs, the actor who drinks, the three-quarter boy who never shows his full self but always keeps a part of himself hidden from himself and from me. Ken has, on our first date, if indeed it is a date, been more honest with me than any boy or man I've ever slept with, be it for a night or for many nights, and he has yet to as much as hold my hand. The definition of insanity comes to mind, repeating the same thing expecting a different result. Am I brave enough to try something new? Am I sane enough? At the meditation centre the insights I received about my past relationships were profound, but am I able to bring those insights into a new relationship and have it work?

There is one more story. Story is story but this one is true. It is the story of the teacher's teacher. He was a public servant in Burma. He heard about a farmer who knew a meditation technique, the technique the Buddha had taught two and a half thousand years ago. He wanted to find the farmer and learn the technique but his boss would not give him any time off. He went anyway. He was warned not to expect to have a job when he came back.

He learnt the technique and returned to find an envelope on his desk. Expecting the worst he opened it. He had not been fired. He had been promoted. He continued to practise the technique and began teaching his co-workers and staff. He was given even more responsibility. He became the boss of two major government departments and both of them worked smoothly and without corruption. A rare thing in Burma at that time. He had an enormous amount of work to do but he always managed to get it all done quickly and efficiently.

The teacher smiled at the end of the story. 'But don't expect you will get a promotion when you get back to work. Oh no. But it may happen.'

I didn't get a promotion but I never expected to. Elliot Purvis had told me that I would never get another pay rise, that I was already paid more than I was worth. I didn't get a promotion but I did have the realisation that I wasn't a victim. I had chosen this life. It was up to me how I lived it. If I reacted with anger and resentment, kept fighting fire with fire, my job would end up in ashes. Instead I kept observing, kept meditating and kept my job. And yes, it did get better. I didn't get a promotion but I went to the meditation centre to change myself, not my job, and I succeeded – but in a way that I didn't expect. I didn't get a promotion. I got married.

Acknowledgments

Writing this memoir was a journey. There were many steps along the path and many helping hands along the way.

Years ago Bill Hoffman told me I could write, even though he sounded surprised when he said it. He asked me to write a weekly column for the *Sunshine Coast Daily* which I did for four and a half years, my first professional writing gig.

My writing group; Sue Goldstiver, Jodie Miller and Petra Kelly. Wonderful women and brilliant writers all. This journey would be a lot lonelier and a lot less fun without them.

Monica McInerney was genuinely excited by an early partial. To have positive feedback from a best-selling novelist gave me hope. Clare Forster told me to get honest, really honest. Her advice terrified me so much I put the manuscript aside and wrote ten drafts of a novel instead. When I finally found the courage, I rewrote the manuscript.

A big and heartfelt thank you to Ingrid Ohlsson at Pan Macmillan for picking me out of the Manuscript Monday pile, telling me I could write and not sounding surprised. My editor Vanessa Pellat and copy editor Elizabeth Cowell guided me though the finer details of making a manuscript sing. A journey I at first found terrifying and then joyful beyond measure.

And then there's The Hubby, a man with enormous wisdom and generosity of spirit. Even through the hard times, and there have been many, he has been steadfast in his love for, and his belief in, me. He's a keeper. You can read all about our journey in the sequel to this book, *How to Stay Married*.

Now available - the truth about the happy ending.

If you enjoyed *Sex, Drugs and Meditation* you're going to love the sequel, *How to Stay Married*.

While *How to Stay Married* isn't your regular 'how-to' book, it is about creating the kind of relationship you want. It's the story of a marriage; a journey from fear, resentment and financial devastation, to a place of love, joy and trust.

Sex, Drugs and Meditation told the story of how meditation changed Mary-Lou's life, saved her job and helped her find a husband. *How to Stay Married* is the truth behind the happy ending.

How to Stay Married takes you around the world; from the glitter and glare of Las Vegas to the sub-zero temperatures of the French Alps and the tropical heat of Thailand, all with cabin luggage only.

The discoveries Mary-Lou makes regarding herself and her marriage are a modern-day parable about learning to travel light in life, love and relationships.

"*If she wrote a book a year Mary-Lou would be in my best of list every year. She is a brilliant writer and after just a few pages you are lost in her world and can't put the book down.*"

- Walter Mason, author of *Destination Saigon*

"*Mary-Lou Stephens is immensely readable, open, honest and revealing - all things I love in a writer.*"

- Toni Powell, author *The Yellow Car* and *What a Feeling!*

"*Her writing is so honest, revealing, thoughtful and very, very funny.*"

- Ikigaigirl

"*Having enjoyed Mary-Lou's first book Sex, Drugs and Meditation, I was pretty sure I would enjoy this one – and I was right. She has an easy, flowing style of writing that keeps you engrossed – so much so that I read it all in a week-end.*"

- Robin Storey, author of the *Noir Nights* series.

www.ingramcontent.com/pod-product-compliance
Lightning Source LLC
Chambersburg PA
CBHW030432010526
44118CB00011B/606